PAYNE AT PINEHURST

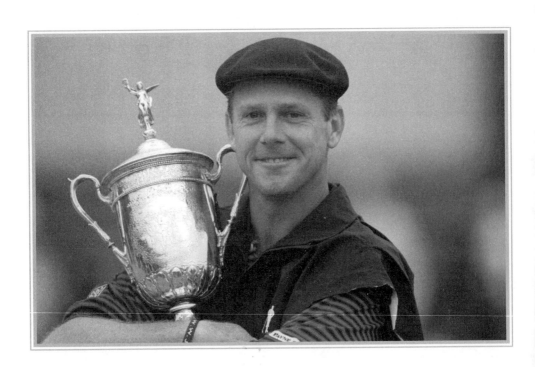

PAYNE AT PINEHURST

— ◆ —

The Greatest U.S. Open Ever

BILL CHASTAIN

Foreword by Tracey Stewart

Thomas Dunne Books
St. Martin's Press ≋ *New York*

THOMAS DUNNE BOOKS.
An imprint of St. Martin's Press.

PAYNE AT PINEHURST. Copyright © 2004 by Bill Chastain. Foreword copyright © 2004 by Tracey Stewart. All rights reserved. Printed in the United States of America. No part of this book may be used or reproduced in any manner whatsoever without permission except in the case of brief quotations embodied in critical articles or reviews. For information, address St. Martin's Press, 175 Fifth Avenue, New York, N.Y. 10010.

www.stmartins.com

ISBN 0-312-33009-X
EAN 978-0312-33009-5

First Edition: June 2004

10   9   8   7   6   5   4   3   2   1

To the memory of Payne Stewart
and that one moment in time.

CONTENTS

CONTENTS

AUTHOR'S NOTE

FRANK SCATONI AND GREG DINKIN of Venture Literary do not pull punches when asked their opinion regarding a subject's worthiness for a book. So I was pumped when Frank told me he loved the idea of a narrative about the 1999 U.S. Open; I had wanted to write a book about the tournament for some time and having my agent's approval gave me the push I needed.

During the summer of 1999, I covered the Tampa Bay Devil Rays for *The Tampa Tribune*. Major-league teams play one hundred and sixty-two-game schedules and the beat writers normally find themselves at the ballpark three-to-four hours before the game starts, which adds up to little time for playing golf much less watching it.

Nevertheless, I found myself off on Father's Day weeked in 1999, leaving me time to play the game I love and also to watch the Open. The tournament captivated me instantly.

Years of watching sporting events prevents me from recalling exactly when I met Payne Stewart behind the batting cage prior to an Atlanta Braves game. One moment I'm standing there talking to this blond-headed guy wearing a Jimmy Buffet T-shirt and blue jeans, thinking, "I know him," and the next moment several of the Braves pitchers were talking to him about golf. That's when I realized I'd been talking to Stewart. I just didn't recognize him without his famed tam and plus fours. During that brief encounter, I surmised that Stewart was a guy's guy, and despite reports to the contrary, a friendly sort.

I thought about that meeting while I watched the '99 Open unfold on TV, and felt a bond with Stewart. He was three months older than me, he had a son and a daughter like me—they were even the same ages as mine, and he was the old guy trying to win a tournament normally reserved for younger men. How could I not root for him? Other components of Stewart's life—his struggles and triumphs, life on the PGA Tour and historic Pinehurst No. 2—drew me to capturing this event in book form. I can't remember enjoying a project more than writing this account of what transpired that special weekend in the Sandhills region of North Carolina.

I would like to thank Frank and Greg for their efforts in selling the proposal for *Payne at Pinehurst*; you guys believed in me and offered encouragement when I needed a lift.

Many other thanks must be extended for making his book a reality, so I better start at the top with my wife, Patti, who keeps me well-grounded and keeps our family in working order; particularly on those days when my mind wanders. Also thanks to my kids, Carly and Kel, who amaze me every day and are so much more accomplished in everything than I was at their respective ages. And to my mother and father, who are, well, great at just being Mom and Dad.

My younger brother, Tommy, continues to be my number-one public relations man, and my older brother, Buddy, remains my best friend and sounding board.

Pete Wolverton, the associate publisher of Thomas Dunne Books, was a pleasure to work with throughout the process. He let me work with no interference, then skillfully led me toward writing a better book than I thought I could ever write. Also, thanks to John Parsley, associate editor at Thomas Dunne, who helped make sure all the details were taken care of to make this book happen.

Dave Hinshaw of the *Charlotte Observer* and Jorge Jaramillo of the *Associated Press* were terrific in helping locate the photographs for this book. And what can I say about the special people of Pinehurst Village? Beth Kocher, Paul Jett, E. Harvie Ward, Stephen Boyd, Pat Corso, and Janeen Driscoll all made my trip to No. 2 both memorable and educational while offering unbelievable hospitality.

Without Larry Grey and Frank Agliano's generosity, I would have had a hard time getting this done. Thanks guys.

Others going above and beyond to help were Joan Alexander, Bill Hofheimer, Tony Mattera, Rick Odioso, Mick Elliott, Fred Ridley, Doug Ferguson, Mike Pennetti, Dave Cook, T. R. Reinman, Rick Dreyer, John Brendle, Tim Barry, Gary Koch, Arnie Cunningham, Lee Janzen, Tommy Linbaugh, and D. J. Snell.

"Team Stewart"—Mike Hicks, Chuck Cook, and Dick Coop, were incredibly helpful providing inside information and insight about Stewart, the man to whom they showed great loyalty and love. And I also enjoyed my conversations with Bee Payne-Stewart.

Last but not least, Tracey Stewart—you are terrific! I marvel at your strength and so appreciate your kindness in helping with this book.

FOREWORD

PAYNE STEWART WAS only fifteen when his father, Bill Stewart, took him to his first United States Open sectional qualifying competition. Bill knew that his son had little chance of qualifying, but the U.S. Open held special significance for Bill Stewart and he wanted to convey that importance to Payne. "When you sign your name to enter the U.S. Open, always sign William Payne Stewart. It's our national championship, so you should sign your full name," he said. These words echoed in Payne's ears over the years and motivated him to become one of the most consistent contenders for our national championship.

Payne's desire to win the U.S. Open stemmed partly from his belief that winning majors was the standard that measured a professional golfer's career. But his passion for this event was about far more than his personal legacy. What set the U.S. Open apart from the other majors was the fact that it was the championship of his nation . . . a nation that he loved passionately. To win the U.S. Open was to represent the United States of America. As a result, the U.S. Open inspired Payne Stewart.

As you read this book, my hope is that you, too, will be inspired by this recollection of the 1999 United States Open, and that you will be stirred by the accounts of a man who inspired me daily: my husband, Payne Stewart.

—Tracey Stewart

CHAPTER ONE

GRAVEYARD
OF CHAMPIONS

June, 1998

TO BORROW THE VERNACULAR of weekend golfers: Payne Stewart had to stop the bleeding.

The approximate time wasn't clear when the smoothest swing on the PGA Tour began to hemorrhage, but Stewart clearly needed a back-nine Band-Aid if he wanted to salvage the 1998 U.S. Open.

Until the final round, Stewart's biggest worry had been matching his signature plus fours and tam; the game had been the easy part. Golf's Great Gatsby had negotiated the forested, rolling terrain of the Olympic Club's difficult Lake Course like a local muni. But Sunday afternoon at the U.S. Open magnified the evils of any golf course, adding a sinister element to the atmosphere—golf's Spanish Inquisition.

A midsummer round at the Lake Course could be bracing in the cool San Francisco air. The moisture fueling the chill restricted a shot's distance like a father tinkering with the governor of his son's go-cart. Narrow, slanted fairways, tiny landing areas, and deep rough had emasculated the Tour's would-be bombers. Fearing the punitive effects of not being able to find a safe haven in the fairway, most players played 2- and 3-irons off the tee rather than risk the driver. Further anxiety came in the form of the well-bunkered, undulating, tiered greens.

"The pressure is enormous, no question," said Gary Koch, veteran Tour professional and NBC commentator. "The conditions are always difficult, which puts you on edge to start with. When the week begins, guys often just pray for patience. To not let the elements get the best of them. It's a very tough week."

A horde of media serves up yet another distraction that makes playing well all the more difficult; stories are originated every day and the players feed the beast. Gathered together as a group, the media resembled witches creating new spells around a boiling caldron.

Matt Kuchar, a 20-year-old junior at Georgia Tech, ranked high on the list of topics for the media to pounce upon at Olympic. He had shot even-par at Augusta during the Masters and hoped to become the first amateur to win the Open since Johnny Goodman in 1933. Kuchar charmed crowds with his ever-present smile while his father, Peter, caddied for his son and turned off playing partner Justin Leonard, who did not appreciate Peter's zeal for Matt's fine play en route to a fourteenth-place finish.

Casey Martin garnished his fair share of media attention by becoming the first player to ride a cart in a major championship; he finished in a tie for twenty-third place.

Between the attention lavished on Kuchar and Martin, Stewart managed to creep into the lead like a burglar who doesn't set off the house alarm.

The 41-year-old Stewart crafted an opening-round 66 then

headed to 3Com Park for a San Francisco Giants game with his mother, Bee Payne-Stewart, compliments of his friend, Giants pitcher Orel Hershiser. Stewart's wife, Tracey, couldn't make the trip because loose ends had to be pieced together before the couple's children attended summer camps. With Tracey in Orlando, Stewart invited his mother to join him for the week at his hotel suite.

"We had a delightful time," Bee said. "Payne was always so amiable. We just had a good time together. We didn't talk much about his playing. We had other things to talk about. We had room service, watched movies, and chitchatted."

Bee went to the tournament every day and tried to keep up with her son. People in the gallery helped her find shortcuts while Hershiser and his sons brought her a bucket to stand on so she could see over the crowd.

Dr. Richard Coop, Stewart's longtime sports psychologist, thought having Bee around provided a positive for Payne, who had not won a tournament since the 1995 Houston Shell Open.

"Spending time with her got his mind off where he stood and what he was doing and how important it was," Coop said.

If anybody understood the dangers of Olympic, Bee fit the bill. She had been there with her husband and Payne's father, Bill Stewart, when he played in the 1955 U.S. Open. She told Payne how the rough had been waist high and described how poorly her husband had played; Bill followed an opening-round 83 with an 88 and failed to make the cut.

Fortunately for Payne, the son does not always imitate the father.

By the completion of Saturday's round Payne held a four-shot lead over his closest competitors, Tom Lehman and Bob Tway. And he'd been mentally tough all week, a prerequisite for any golfer hoping to win the U.S. Open, thanks in part to the work of the USGA.

The USGA runs the U.S. Open, which is different than the other tournaments on the Tour conducted by the Professional Golf Association. The USGA determines where the Open will be played, how high the rough is to be cut, the speed of the greens, and the pin placements. Why, they could padlock the Port-O-Lets should they so desire. If the USGA's fingerprints can be found anywhere on a golf course you can bet the farm playing conditions will be the toughest test of golf possible. Such creativity has earned the USGA the reputation for "tricking up" courses and for possessing a somewhat warped sense of humor; a reputation USGA officials say is unwarranted.

"The USGA never, in my opinion, tries to trick up a golf course," Tom Meeks said.

Meeks is the USGA's director of rules and competition. He wears wire-rimmed glasses, maintains an even disposition, and has a soft-spoken manner, making him appear the antithesis of a man wanting to inflict pain on PGA Tour professionals.

"Now we might do some setup procedures that differ from the PGA Tour and we certainly have a different philosophy with our setup than the PGA Tour," Meeks said. "But the word trick would never enter into this and if we ever had anything we considered tricky or unfair we would scrap it. So I think that's a misunderstanding."

Nevertheless, Stewart felt like the punch line for one of the USGA's sicker jokes: Friday's pin placement at No. 18.

The 347-yard par-4 final hole at Olympic did not have the imposing feel familiar to other Open finishing holes. The ideal sequence for playing the hole required hitting an iron off the tee to a landing area down a hill followed by a wedge to a sloped green. But once golfers found the green they felt like they were playing the hole with the fire-breathing dragon and windmill at the Fantasyland Putt-Putt. The pin sat eight yards from the left edge of the green and eighteen yards from the front, a location making it nearly impossible for any putt to stop if hit below the hole. Meeks bore the responsibility of setting the pin locations.

"When you set holes for the U.S. Open, I compare it to driving a race car at the Indy 500," Meeks said. "If you're going to win that race you're going to have to drive that car on the very edge, go all out as fast as you can, and you've got to come close to losing it several times during the race if you're going to win it. That's the way I look at setting holes for the U.S. Open. Trying to set up the four most difficult locations we can find on the putting greens and yet still be fair."

You could almost hear the laugh track when Stewart's ten-foot birdie putt eased toward the cup at 18.

He'd hit a flawless putt toward the cup where the speed of the putt said it would die. Even when the ball didn't go in, it appeared to stop. Then it quivered and slowly began to gain momentum before heading down the slope. When the brakes finally were applied, Stewart faced a twenty-five-foot par putt.

Wearing an ensemble resembling a picnic—red plaid plus fours, ivory long-sleeved pullover, ivory stockings, and red tam—Stewart stood watching with arms folded across his chest and an expression from some country and western song: he'd been done wrong.

"The guy plays two perfect shots, actually hits a good putt—I thought he'd made the putt, but it gets up there and it's just a little low and you think you've got a two-inch tap in," said Mike Hicks, Stewart's longtime caddie. "Then it just starts rolling until it ends up in a place where he needs to make a good two-putt to get home."

Stewart two-putted for bogey to shoot 71, giving him a one-shot lead after two rounds and plenty to vent about afterward.

The pin placement at No. 18 was "a little suspect in my opinion," Stewart said. "Bordering on ridiculous. I don't suppose the USGA would ever use the term 'illegal' but I don't think I was the only one who had something to say to the walking marshal with each group or an official after the round."

Though Stewart expressed his displeasure with the pin placement, a younger Stewart might have exploded.

"He obviously wasn't very happy," Coop said. "Nobody would be. But I thought he really showed some great maturity there because he didn't pout. Obviously, when they asked him about what he thought, he told them he didn't think it was a very fair pin placement. Of course, not very many other people did either. But he didn't have a temper tantrum and didn't do anything I thought was childish. I thought the maturity he showed would help him out on Sunday."

Others did not react so graciously.

Kirk Triplett's putt on 18 missed the cup and had started down a slope when he reached out with his putter to stop the ball. His misbehavior cost him a two-shot penalty.

Lehman had hit what he considered a good approach shot to 18 only to watch the ball finish fifty feet from the hole; he four-putted to make a double bogey. Lehman strayed from his born-again Christian demeanor while expressing his salty opinion about the pin placement to a PGA official. He later apologized.

The stroke average for 18 on Friday's round was 4.27, but there were at least two happy golfers in the field given the way they fared on 18.

Jack Nicklaus managed to sink a forty-foot birdie putt on 18 to make the cut, while Lee Porter's fate on the closing hole proved some higher being indeed controlled golf tournaments and that this higher being had a sense of humor to boot. Statistically, Porter ranked as the worst putter on the PGA Tour the previous year. No telling what type of display he might have put on trying to roll one in on 18.

Instead he sank a wedge shot from 112 yards away to make eagle and end any such doomsday speculation.

Fred Ridley, who has chaired the USGA executive committee since 2000, has been a member of the committee since 1993, and now is USGA President, stated the obvious: "The thing on the eighteenth hole at Olympic was a little bit embarrassing for the USGA."

Meeks found himself in the center of Friday's storm of controversy.

"I ran into Jimmy Roberts from ESPN and he said, 'Tom, you know I've got to talk about this on my show tonight,'" Meeks said. "I said, 'Jimmy, I understand that, that doesn't bother me. I just hope that you and the players realize that I did not do that intentionally. I did not want that to happen. If I had any idea that balls were going to run down that hill like they did today from that hole location I would have never used it.' And he was fine with that."

Meeks was mortified over the disaster he had created. He'd gone against one of his guiding principles by using a hole location after questioning its fairness.

"I had doubts about that one and I still went ahead and used it, so I had nobody to blame but myself; I erred," Meeks said.

He returned to his hotel room in San Francisco later that night and comforted himself by thinking he would wake to find he had experienced a bad dream. When the alarm clock rang Saturday morning nothing had changed.

"I could do one of two things after that," Meeks said. "I could throw in the towel and say, 'I can't do this job.' Or I could say, 'I made a mistake, I can learn from my mistake, and I'm going to continue with what I'm doing.'"

Meeks owned up to his mistake, telling everyone involved he knew he'd messed up and he personally apologized to Stewart and Lehman.

During the weekend rounds the USGA made certain the pin found a location where Friday's fiasco could not be repeated. Olympic's eighteenth green has since been rebuilt to where the pitch of the green is not so severe.

Despite the way Friday's round ended, Stewart had scored well during the first two rounds. He'd birdied the final three holes of Thursday's round, then began Friday's round eagle, birdie, birdie.

"So he played a stretch of holes at seven-under, six holes at seven under," Hicks said. "At one point he got it to eight under. That gave him enough of a cushion where he could afford to make some bogeys. But he was on his C game as far as his ball-striking went. He was doing it with mirrors."

Stewart shot 70 on Saturday to retain the lead. If he managed to close the deal on Sunday he would have been the first player since Tony Jacklin won the 1970 Open to win after leading from start to finish. His four-shot lead after three rounds was the largest since Jacklin's win. Only once in the history of the Open had a competitor ever blown a lead of four shots or greater in the final round, which happened to Mike Brady in 1919 when Walter Hagen caught him.

Lee Janzen trailed Stewart by five shots after three rounds and told the media the rest of the field would sleep better than Stewart would.

"How does he know how I'm going to sleep?" Stewart quipped when told about his friend's comments. "As long as my mother doesn't snore I'll be all right."

Though Stewart teased with reporters, he didn't hide his nervousness, rationalizing how something would be wrong with him if he wasn't a little nervous. Then he shifted gears to talk about how pleased he felt with the direction of his life. He loved his wife and being a father and missed being with his family. This wasn't the old Payne Stewart, rather a kinder, gentler version of the man who had a reputation of being difficult with the media; he seemed human and vulnerable.

Unfortunately for Stewart, showing his warm and fuzzy side had the negative effect of changing his routine. Like most players on Tour, Stewart hit balls after finishing his round. Doing so affirmed the swing used for a good round or purged the sins of a bad one. Due to his extended stay in the media tent he'd been unable to practice after Saturday's round. Stewart's swing coach, Chuck Cook, believed Stewart's not being able to practice had a detrimental effect. He'd been fighting a "sort of steep" swing all week and not going to the practice range allowed the flawed swing to fester. A train wreck waiting to happen.

Nevertheless, most figured Stewart would win, despite the fact he had been mired in a winning drought. First, he held a four-shot lead, so he wouldn't have to try and make something happen Sunday, he just needed to protect par. In addition, Stewart didn't carry the baggage of never having won a major, which can be an albatross for any quality golfer who hasn't won one. He knew how to compete in majors and had the hardware to prove it, having won the 1989 PGA Championship and the 1991 U.S. Open. And he did have that buttery swing that was a lyrical combination of athleticism, timing, and touch. After weighing the evidence, it wasn't a stretch to think Stewart might even be able to sleep Saturday night; hardly the easiest accomplishment for an Open leader when visited by visions of shanks, three-putts, and lost balls.

"He didn't seem nervous," Bee said of Payne's frame of mind Saturday night. "He'd been leading every day, so I was kind of complacent, because in my heart I thought it was in the bag. He'd been playing so well. But I never said anything. I knew enough about golf to know if you think you have it, that's when you get in trouble."

Coop tried to spin the situation in a fashion to help Stewart relax.

"I told Payne, 'I'd rather be ahead than behind, people are spotting you a stroke or two here, which you wouldn't want to do to any great player,'" Coop said. "We tried to take a positive out of it. I thought he was playing so well that he didn't have to play any better than how he was playing. All he had to do was maintain the way he was playing. Whereas I thought the other players had to play a little better than they had been playing to take a run at him."

All the positive spinning in the world couldn't take away the Olympic Club's history, a history that said even if Stewart led by four shots, he could not win.

The Olympic Club originated in 1860 inside the firehouse of a fledging city, San Francisco. Famous members of the athletic and social club included boxer Jim Corbett, who had been a member when he defeated John L. Sullivan for the heavyweight title; J. Scott Leary, who became the first American to swim 100 yards in 60 seconds; and William "Little Bill" Johnston, who won Wimbledon in 1923. Olympic is the oldest athletic club in the United States. Ten miles away from where the club originated sat the Lake Course, which the Olympic Club purchased in 1922. Eucalyptus, pine, and cypress were planted following the purchase and grew to become factors for golfers playing the course. The Lake Course matured into one of the top golf courses in the world and reaped the rewards by hosting Open championships in 1955, 1966, and 1987. Only four players broke par over 72 holes during those three Opens. Billy Casper and Arnold Palmer each shot two-under 278 in 1966; and Scott Simpson shot 277 and Tom Watson, 278, in 1987. Golfers of note led after three rounds in each of those Opens only to lose in hexed fashion, earning Olympic the nickname "Graveyard of Champions."

The most improbable of these finishes came in 1955 when Ben Hogan led.

Hogan was the glory of his time with sixty-three career wins and majors galore. He'd captured two PGA Championships, a British Open, two Masters, and four U.S. Opens. But down the stretch on Sunday afternoon at Olympic an unknown named Jack Fleck birdied two of the last four holes to force an eighteen-hole playoff. Fleck had been a municipal course pro in Arkansas and was in the midst of his first year on tour.

After seventeen holes of the playoff, Fleck held honors on 18 and hit a solid drive down the fairway. Accounts of what happened next vary. One of these explained Hogan inexplicably slipped, resulting in a drive that duck hooked into the belt-high rough. Another came from Fleck in later years when he said Hogan simply, "neck-pulled the shot." Hogan made double bogey on 18 and lost.

Hogan paid tribute to Fleck's extraordinary putting by removing his hat and using it to fan his competitor's hot flat stick. Fleck later said of his putting during the Open: "I was the poorest putter that ever walked a course. But that day, on the fifth hole in the second round, I got a different feeling in my hands on the putting stroke, and I didn't three-putt from then on."

Arnold Palmer handed over a seven-shot lead to Billy Casper on the back nine in 1966 then lost the next day in a playoff. And Tom Watson led after three rounds in 1987 only to get shot down by Scott Simpson, who birdied 14, 15, and 17.

Whether Stewart was familiar with Olympic's history of burying third-round leaders is unclear. Truth be known, he faced worse demons than wondering whether third-round leaders were jinxed. Rattling around somewhere in Stewart's head had to be the memory of Baltusrol, the famed club in Springfield, New Jersey, where Janzen disposed of him in the 1993 U.S. Open. Janzen had turned the trick with a prayer of a shot out of the trees and a chip-in from the rough to win by two shots. Stewart had nothing to be ashamed of since

Janzen's seventy-two-hole score of eight-under 272 tied Jack Nicklaus for the lowest total in U.S. Open history; and Stewart had shot a respectable even-par 70 on Sunday. Then again, Stewart was the guy armed with two majors. Guys with experience were supposed to carve up guys like Janzen, a 28-year-old who had missed the cut in his first three U.S. Opens and had never tasted victory in a major.

Baltusrol, 1993, cast a long shadow at Olympic, 1998, even though Stewart was paired for Sunday's round at Olympic with Lehman and not Janzen, who started the day five shots behind and playing two groups ahead of Stewart.

A precursor for the final round of the 1998 Open came when Stewart blocked his first drive of the day. Clearly he didn't have his "A" game.

Bee must have snored like Otis Campbell Saturday night.

Janzen started the final day with bogies on the second and third holes to fall behind Stewart by seven shots before he birdied 4 to right his ship. Official notification that the golf gods were in Janzen's corner came when he teed off on 5. Attempting to hit a left-to-right shot with his 4-wood, Janzen hit his ball into the heart of a large cypress tree. One fan with binoculars reported sighting the ball lodged in the tree.

Janzen had heard the story about one of the cypress trees being cut down prior to the tournament and hundreds of balls came tumbling out like candy from a piñata.

"Still, you don't expect your ball to stay up in a tree," Janzen said.

Tournament marshals searched long enough for Janzen's ball to convince Janzen he had run out of luck. His caddie had just handed him another ball and he'd started back toward the tee ready to reload when a Pacific breeze howled, freeing a ball from the tree and depositing it in the rough. Examination of the ball validated Janzen's good fortune: a Precept 2 stamped with the initials LMJ—Lee Michael Janzen.

"I remember thinking I would make double," Janzen said. "The ball didn't look like it would come out; generally they don't fall out. Then, all of a sudden the ball fell. I felt a lot of relief when I saw that ball fall from the tree. I don't know what is more odd, one staying up there or one falling out after it's been up there for a couple of minutes."

Janzen spun gold from straw. He chipped the ball back to the fairway, hit a 6-iron into the back fringe of the green, and chipped in for par.

"You can't imagine how I felt when I walked off with a par," Janzen said. "I'd been playing well all week, but everything really hadn't come together. That was really a positive for me."

Positive images of Baltusrol entered Janzen's mind following the unlikely par. He began to think, "Payne Stewart, a ball in a tree, and a chip-in." There were worse thoughts he could be thinking; he made the turn at 35.

"Seeing Payne Stewart on the leaderboard, there definitely was something there," Janzen said. "Certainly it wasn't a knock against his game. For some reason I just played better when I was up against him. I think Payne Stewart being at the top of the leaderboard had an effect on me."

Whether Janzen's feelings were a derivative of confidence or a comfort level from competing against his friend, history showed a basis for the way he felt. Janzen had worked Stewart like a pickpocket at a zoot suit convention, lifting would-be winnings from the wallet in Stewart's knickers while claiming victories at the Players Championship in 1995 and later that same year at the Kemper. And, of course, there was Baltusrol.

Standing on the tenth green, Stewart noticed for the first time Janzen creeping up Sunday's leaderboard, a sensation akin to leading the Boston Marathon at the 25-mile mark and looking over your shoulder to spot an unknown Kenyan approaching with hungry eyes and fresh legs.

"We were scoreboard watching," Hicks said. "We knew [Janzen] was shooting a good round and we were struggling. But Payne was a fighter. He was grinding."

Leading by one shot and feeling his foundation crumbling, Stewart rose to the occasion by ripping a 260-yard drive down the middle of the No. 12 fairway. His ball landed hard and rolled past the many divots filled in with sand by the ground crews. Stewart approached from the left side expecting to find his ball sitting up nicely in the middle of the fairway; instead he found his ball resting in a divot.

"I was in the first fairway I had hit in a while and sure enough, I was in a bunker," Stewart said.

He tried to remain calm, thinking, "You've got to deal with it. You've got to take the good with the bad."

"It was your classic unfair break," said *Orlando Sentinel* columnist David Whitley, who worked for the *Tampa Tribune* at the time. "But ipso facto, that's what golf is. It's how you respond to these things. And when he went up and looked at it, chewed his gum and shook his head like, 'God, I've been screwed again,' it just looked like he threw it into reverse mentally there. He just sort of came apart."

Throughout the week Stewart had looked so dashing in his plus fours with his blond hair jutting from underneath a fashionable tam, his pearly whites radiating confidence. Alas, the cruel winds of fashion. When Stewart began to struggle on the back nine he suddenly resembled a guy wearing a Hawaiian shirt and flip-flops to a black-tie affair.

Having competed in pressure-filled tournaments, Koch understood the feelings of a golfer trying to hang on in the face of adversity.

"I think the toughest thing the guy at home can't comprehend
[when watching a golf tournament], obviously because he's never
been in that situation, is how fast your mind gets racing," Koch said.
"To me, that whole scenario at twelve with the sand-filled divot was
a good example. Instead of [Stewart] just kind of assessing the situation and dealing with the situation the best he could, it appeared as
though he let the situation get the better of him. And you could tell
his mind must have been racing. You could tell by the fact he was
animated about the bad break. To me, the guys who play the best in
pressure situations are the guys who have that control of their mental capacities to not let their mind get racing. To not let it get beyond
playing the shot they're playing."

Stewart had voiced his opinion in the past that divots filled with
sand—a procedure used to help the grass grow back faster—were
"ground under repair" and should be viewed as such. Players hitting
their ball into an area or spot designated as "ground under repair"
are granted a free drop. Weekend golfers would merely "roll it over"
in the fairway. Stewart was not so fortunate. According to the rules,
playing the ball where it lies applied to his situation.

"We were just back and forth about what club to hit out of
there," Hicks said. "I think it was between a pitching wedge and a 9-
iron. I think he went ahead with a 9-iron, tried to hit a little punch
shot."

Stewart agonized about what shot to hit, then stood over the ball
undecided.

"He hit a pretty good shot, it just came out to the right," Hicks
said. "He short-sided himself and landed in the bunker."

If having to play his shot from a terrible lie wasn't bad enough
Stewart received a slow-play warning from Meeks after hitting his

shot. Though the warning had been directed toward Stewart, Lehman had played a role in their group being behind.

In USGA events players are allowed to practice putting on the course if they aren't holding up a group. Since Stewart and Lehman were playing in the final group Lehman had taken advantage of the policy.

Lehman putted "for three or four holes in a row on the front and that got us behind," Hicks said. "So I really don't think Tom would have issued that bad time if we hadn't been out of position. I think under the circumstances he would have let that slide, because that was a shot where you couldn't just grab a club and hit the shot. He had to do a little thinking about how much sand was in there. He didn't have a clue what to hit."

Still agitated from Meeks's warning, Stewart blasted from the trap to a spot twelve feet from the hole. When he missed the par putt, he fell into a tie with Janzen, losing the lead he had held since the first round.

"I could sort of feel it coming apart a little bit at that point," said Mark Lye, Tour professional and analyst for the Golf Channel. "But both of those guys were getting the most out of their games. Payne was just a fighter and so was Lee Janzen. Obviously they'd both won Opens before. The fact they had won before meant you couldn't count them out. If they've gone down the last bunch of holes to win the Open before and they're in the battle again, you're just saying, 'Which guy is going to win it?'"

Janzen made birdies on 11 and 13 and began to carry the look of a champion.

"I always felt like U.S. Open champions have a rhythm about them, the way they're walking, playing, swinging," said Associated Press golf writer Doug Ferguson. "I saw that with Janzen on the back nine. He just had a beautiful rhythm from the way he stuck his tee in the ground to the way he went through his pre-shot routine. The swing, the drive, the gait, he knew he was going to play well."

Janzen walked onto the fifteenth green and heard a rumble. When he glanced over at the scoreboard he noticed Stewart had bogeyed 12 and knew he shared the lead.

Stewart stepped to the thirteenth tee thirty minutes after Janzen had passed through and fired a 5-iron at the pin 186 yards away.

"The ball hit the green hard," Hicks said. "It was right at the pin, but it flew probably three or four yards too far. It went over the green into a horrendous lie. That was a bad break."

From a lie in matted rough, Stewart chipped the ball to within twelve feet, but missed the par putt and dropped from the lead. Meeks then stepped in to deliver another warning.

"I'll be damned if Lehman on his tee shot on 13, he gets a bad time," Meeks said. "So now I have to walk up to Lehman after the two of them walked off the tee and I say, 'Tom, I'm sorry, but I've got a bad time on your tee shot. One more bad time and there will be a penalty.' "

Another warning for either golfer would result in a one-shot penalty.

Stewart called to Meeks.

"Come here and tell me what all this means," Stewart said.

Players are issued a memo prior to the tournament addressing the penalty for slow play.

"But they don't read it," Meeks said.

Meeks summarized the situation for Stewart then told Lehman and him, "Just do me a favor, get in position with the group in front of you and I'll leave you alone."

Stewart pulled into a tie with Janzen when he birdied 14 then gave it back when he bogeyed the par-5 sixteenth hole.

Though Janzen appeared to be galloping down the homestretch, he needed to cross a major hurdle at 17. He'd played the 468-yard par 4 in five over par the previous three days. Not to worry, when you're hot you're hot. Janzen reached the green in two and two-putted for par then did the same at 18. He did not bogey a hole on the back nine en route to a 68, making him the only golfer in the field to shoot a sub-par round on the final day.

"From the fifth hole on I basically hit every shot exactly where I wanted it," Janzen said. "I missed no fairways and one green by a foot. Under those conditions and U.S. Open stress, that's about as close to perfect as I can get."

Koch covered 16 from an NBC tower high above the hole.

Number 16 "was a good example of Payne not playing a hole well," Koch said. "It was a par-5 that nobody was reaching in two; it was very long and tight. After he hit a poor drive he seemed to try and get more out of his second shot than he needed to out of the rough and was left with a lengthy third shot that he hit rather poorly and ended up in the bunker. He didn't get up and down and made a bogey."

Stewart trailed by one shot, leaving his fate to be determined on 18, the hole that had flogged him in the second round.

He barely escaped a repeat of 12 when his tee shot missed a divot by approximately six inches, leaving him a 105-yard shot to the flag. Stewart needed to land his second shot close enough to the pin to have a decent chance at sinking a birdie putt. Facing a tricky uphill shot into the wind, Stewart judged the shot too long to hit a sand wedge.

"Wouldn't this be something if I holed this shot for two?" Stewart told Hicks.

He choked down on a pitching wedge and hit his approach twenty feet from the hole.

Unlike the other three "major" tournaments—the Masters, the

British Open and the PGA Championship—the U.S. Open has an 18-hole playoff in the event of a tie rather than a sudden death playoff, or a three-hole playoff like the British Open. To play on Monday Stewart had to somehow navigate his putt over the slick green to make 3.

"I had finished playing, signed my card and became a nervous wreck when I went to the clubhouse to watch the rest of the tournament on TV with my wife," Janzen said. "My fate was in Payne's hands. Whatever he did would determine the outcome of the U.S. Open. . . . I got interviewed while I waited; seemed like it took a long time. I don't know why I was so nervous. It was stupid, really. If he makes the putt, we play the next day. If he doesn't, I win. I'd already done everything I could do that day."

Stewart put a solid stroke on the downhill, big-breaking putt that rolled toward the cup like it wanted to obey his deepest desire. Draining a twenty footer to send the ninety-eighth U.S. Open into a playoff would have erased all of Stewart's final-round transgressions. Two feet short of the hole, the putt appeared ready to split the middle of the cup. Then the ball ran out of gas and turned left, missing by several inches to give Stewart a four-over-par 74 and a score of 281 for the tournament.

"There were two things [the putt] needed," Stewart said. "It either needed to be higher or it needed to be harder. But I felt that the line I chose was the proper line. Obviously, I didn't have the proper speed, and those are the key elements in putting, you have to have the proper speed with the proper line."

Hicks laughed when asked how tough Stewart's putt had been on 18.

"He couldn't have made that putt if he'd have putted it a hundred times," Hicks said. "Nobody could have."

A tap-in par didn't cut it. Lee Janzen had just won the 1998 U.S. Open. And once again he'd accomplished the feat at Payne Stewart's expense.

"When Payne missed I felt a lot of different emotions," Janzen said. "The camera was on me, so you don't want to celebrate even though you're happy about winning. I felt really bad for Payne. He was a friend. And at his age, I thought maybe that was the last stage of his career. I felt bad about what he was probably feeling. There were a lot of emotions I went through that Sunday night."

Stewart walked from the course to the scorer's area, signed his card, then made his way to the media tent for the unenviable task of answering questions about how he had let a four-shot U.S. Open lead slip away.

Time to take one's medicine.

Years earlier, a brasher version of Stewart would have stomped away and whined about the fickle fate of golf. Instead, Stewart threw the media a curveball.

"The Payne Stewart I wanted to show up didn't show up," Stewart said. "I've matured and understand what this job is about, what playing golf for a living is about . . . Yeah, I'm disappointed, but I'm going to hold my head up. I never gave up. . . . I'll sleep well tonight because I know I went out there and did the best I could. I didn't quit."

In the aftermath of his devastating loss the new Payne Stewart distinguished himself with grace, casting him in a light in which the golf media had never seen him. He even mustered up a sense of humor when he quipped: "I guess I bring out the best in Lee Janzen."

Stewart hung around afterward, continuing to talk to the media, kibitzing with fans and signing autographs.

Bee felt proud of her son.

"He was gracious I thought about the whole thing," Bee said. "I didn't see any kind of animosity. Obviously it was a big disappointment, but we didn't talk about it."

After the tournament Stewart boarded a private plane with Bee, Justin Leonard, and D. A. Weibring and took off to play in a benefit Weibring backed in Quincy, Illinois.

"We got in the plane and Payne seemed like he'd already put [the loss] behind him," Bee said. "Payne kept teasing [Leonard] about something. They had plenty of beer on the plane and they were all having a good time. The mood was very, very light. I don't drink. I was just listening to them and watching. I think they were pleased he was still going to the benefit."

Following Monday's benefit Stewart joined Tracey, daughter Chelsea, and son Aaron to spend some quality time with his family before the kids went to summer camp. Ironically—and not exactly by accident—Stewart was paired with Janzen and Frank Nobilo for the first two rounds of the Tour's next stop at the Western Open.

To Stewart's way of thinking the ninety-eighth U.S. Open was past history.

"It won't take me long to get over it at all," Stewart said. "I'm still Payne Stewart when I walk out the door."

Tracey Stewart said she felt terrible for her husband.

"But I was so proud of the way that he handled himself after going through that," Tracey said, her Australian accent punctuating her words. "I felt like he got every bad break that was possible out there. And everything was going against him. It was like it just wasn't meant to be. But I was very proud of the way he was able to face the media the way he did. That showed how he had matured. He dealt with a situation like that. There wasn't anything else he could do. He felt like Lee played a great round of golf and felt it just wasn't his time."

To the media he became Payne Stewart, the gracious loser; or

Payne Stewart, the guy who blew the U.S. Open. Some praised him for the way he handled defeat. Wrote Bud Geracie of the *St. Louis Post-Dispatch*:

> *Some will call Payne Stewart a loser today. I will call him a winner. He is not the 1998 U.S. Open champion. That title belongs to Lee Janzen, who took home the trophy for the second time Sunday with an extraordinary comeback from 7 strokes down.*
>
> *But Stewart is a winner. For the way he handled defeat, and for the way he battled against it, he is a champion in his own right. There was a time, not too many years ago, when losing made Stewart a monster. He blew off his media obligations after losing at Pebble Beach one year. Another time, after a galling playoff defeat in Texas, he jumped out of a courtesy car to scream obscenities at the sky. Perhaps Stewart already had done that when he came to the interview tent Sunday after losing the national championship by a shot. Or, perhaps, he had himself a good cry somewhere, because he arrived with red-rimmed eyes.*

Others in the media weren't so willing to overlook the fact Stewart had lost a four-shot lead on the final day of the U.S. Open. Andy Baggot of the *Wisconsin State Journal* wrote:

> *It was hard not to appreciate the class and dignity shown by Payne Stewart in defeat Sunday. But, you know, had Greg Norman done what Stewart did in the final round of the U.S. Open—lose to Lee Janzen after leading by 7 shots with 15 holes to play—the critics would be turning the Shark into aquarium food for choking again under pressure.*

David Whitley's column read:

> *His 74 was not quite the Shark in Knickers, a flashback to Greg Norman's horrific collapse in the 1996 Masters. But it confirmed a perception so ingrained it's listed in Stewart's official PGA biography:*
>
> *"Became known on tour for wearing the plus-2s and a habit of choking in the closing stages of a tournament."*
>
> *The knickers were actually plus-4s, but the rest of the statement is all too accurate. For all his style, Stewart's reputation does not wear nearly as well as his clothes.*

"Maybe I brought too much of an outsider's perspective," Whitley said of his column, alluding to the fact he was a columnist and not a golf beat writer. "To me, I was looking at it like I was covering any sporting event. If a team has a three-touchdown lead going into the fourth quarter and they lose, there's a certain element that suggests they gagged. . . . You give credit to the opponent, but the opponent in this case went out and just played U.S. Open kind of golf, which is not spectacular, just make your putts, get your pars, then just count on whoever is up front to have a car wreck. And basically that's what happened. When you sit down to write, you try to spin it another way, where a guy came up and beat him, stole it from him. But it was more like he stole it from himself."

Given Whitley's aforementioned columnist position, he began to solicit opinions about Stewart from other writers inside the media tent to help shape his opinion.

"I started hearing, 'Payne Stewart, incredible talent, maybe the sweetest swing on Tour and the kind of guy you would have expected, after coming on early to win a couple of majors, to have won maybe five or six by then,'" Whitley said. "Factor that in with the fact he'd been in a position so many times and didn't win. If it happens once, OK, if it happens twice, OK, but this was an undeniable habit."

Whitley couldn't believe the choking statement had appeared in an official guide.

"That's like seeing the NFL putting out a media guide and next to the Buffalo Bills it says, 'Franchise has a habit of gagging,'" Whitley said. "I wondered if somebody got called on the carpet later. Whatever, it got past the proofreaders."

Generally a writer opens a media guide to gain information and facts, not character judgments.

"Normally everything has a happy spin," Whitley said. "It's like you might be the worst golfer in the world, but they'll find something nice to say about you. There were plenty of nice things to write about Payne, he had an impressive enough resume compared to most golfers out there. But has 'a habit of choking'? How could I argue with that?"

After his column, Whitley said he received the largest collection of adverse mail he ever received during his six years with the *Tampa Tribune*.

"Golf is a different breed with the public," Whitley said. "You can call a football player or basketball player a choker. If they had five interceptions, you can say, 'He played really crappy, he'll be lucky to stay in the league.' Even the fans of that team will say that. But golf, since it isn't a team sport, I think the players establish more of an identity. In a way it was like I was shooting Bambi. I took no joy in it. But Bambi choked."

The memory of the 1998 U.S. Open did not quickly go away and helped to perpetuate the image of Payne Stewart as the flashy guy who wore plus fours, chewed gum, and didn't get all he could from the swing so envied.

The cliché says time heals all wounds, and time surely would help Stewart deal with losing a major that looked to be his. But losing in the fashion Stewart had lost brought about the view Payne Stewart would never again be a serious contender at a major.

"You had to believe he'd never be back," Whitley said. "Like Scott Norwood missing that kick in the Super Bowl, or a Bill Buckner–type thing, well, maybe not to that level. But it was so emotionally devastating. Golf is ninety-nine percent mental anyway, and when you start moving around the toys in a guy's attic like that, especially a guy with a history, it just reinforced every doubt he ever had about himself."

Even Coop recognized how losing the Open in the fashion Stewart had could have been detrimental to his future.

"I knew it could be a big turning point," Coop said. "He needed to use that experience as a springboard to keep improving. Take finishing second with the mind-set that everybody else in the tournament, except Janzen, would have been happy to have finished in his position. He played well, he handled himself well. We took it as a positive, tried to get him to see the positive things in it. Obviously, the thing I was afraid of was it could have been a turning point in the other direction.

"That was where I think he made some tough decisions and chose to treat it as a positive. Actually from that time on, I saw a lot of maturity I had not seen before."

Coop remembered how Stewart handled a devastating defeat earlier in his career when he'd finished second to Nick Faldo in the 1990 British Open at St. Andrews.

"I don't think I'd ever seen him that down," Coop said. "But as we were walking back to the car with his clubs, and I was carrying his clubs for him, Scottish people walked by and said, 'Nice playing Laddie, way to go, you had one bad break.' You could just see his chin raising up a little bit. He was looking people in the eyes a little bit more as we walked around."

Coop believes the British Open experience laid the foundation for him winning the U.S. Open in 1991. After St. Andrews, Stewart made a resolution to win another major as quickly as he could.

"That really made him work harder," Coop said. "I saw the same thing in '98 after the U.S. Open. That's one thing about him. If you talked to him and he listened, he would eventually get that resolve to turn something that had been a negative into a positive."

Coop still had his work cut out for him in the aftermath of the '98 Open. Like Stewart having to deal with "choke" being used in the same sentence as his name.

"There are a lot of things you talk about in that situation," Coop said. "You try to get him to see who is using the word. Everybody has choked. Even Tiger has admitted he's choked. The only people who haven't choked are people who have never been there. You have to work very hard and be very good to get into a position where you can choke. We went through that whole bit. But Payne did most of the work. He had that kind of resolve in his eyes that I had seen in 1990 after the British Open. So I was hoping it would be that same kind of corollary. One would lead to the other."

Hicks had no worries about what was going on inside Stewart's head.

"That week [at the '98 Open], all it did was prove to him that he could do it again, that he could get into contention at a major and do it," Hicks said. "He knew he'd been there and he'd only had his C game as far as his swing goes. He was excited about the direction he was going. I know he was disappointed about losing at Olympic, but I don't think [the loss] affected him in a negative way at all."

Tracey Stewart believed the same as Hicks.

"Confidence-wise, I don't think [the loss] hurt him at all," Tracey said. "I think he felt like he had a lot of years ahead of him where he'd have opportunities to win more majors."

Stewart, Tracey, and Hicks might have felt he was heading in the right direction; Stewart just needed to prove it to the golf world. Everything hinged on the assumption to which few outside the Stewart camp would have ever agreed: Stewart had the game to fight back and win majors.

CHAPTER TWO

PAYNE STEWART'S JOURNEY

PAYNE STEWART'S PASSION was golf.

Growing up in Springfield, Missouri, Stewart's athleticism and competitiveness enabled him to play quarterback and point guard on Greenwood High's football and basketball teams. Though he enjoyed playing team sports and showed some talent, neither sport could hold a candle to golf, the sport he'd played since age three. Hitting the little white ball fueled his being and chasing the dream of playing professional golf motivated him. Upon graduating from Greenwood, he accepted a golf scholarship to Southern Methodist University.

Partying became Stewart's first priority at SMU, where academics and even golf took a backseat to cigarettes, alcohol, and raucous behavior. Despite his *Animal House* years, Stewart managed to get his act together on the golf course and in the classroom. By his senior year his teammates voted him captain of the Mustangs' golf team and he played well enough to win honors as the cochampion of the Southwest Conference. In May of 1979, he graduated with a business degree that may as well have been in physics, poetry, or crossword puzzles because he wasn't going to use it. Professional golf beckoned. He would attend PGA Qualifying School in the fall of 1979 and that would be that.

"Q School" is the test served up to golfers hoping to play on the PGA Tour. Those passing earn their Tour cards, allowing them to compete for prize money with the other select few professional golfers on Tour.

Stewart played in amateur tournaments during the summer of 1979 and won the Missouri state amateur title. Adding to the Stewart family's achievements that summer, Bill Stewart won the Missouri senior amateur title. The momentum Payne gained from winning the state amateur title did not carry over to Payne's showing at Q School, where the top twenty-five finishers were awarded their cards and Payne wasn't one of them.

"That was an eye-opener," a humbled Stewart said. "It definitely made me realize I was not going to walk out there and the other guys were going to fall down."

Not earning a spot on the Tour led Stewart to the Asian Tour, where he won for the first time as a professional at the 1981 Malaysian Open and gained valuable golf experience. Stewart also met Australian Tracey Ferguson. Their chance encounter came in Kuala Lumpur, Malaysia, at the Royal Selangor Golf Course, site of the 1980 Malaysian Open.

"The first time I ever saw Payne Stewart was across the room at a cocktail party at the Malaysian Open in 1980," Tracey said. "He was the most beautiful-looking man I'd ever seen. It was love at first sight. He always told me that it was the same for him and that we were destined to be together. I truly believe that, too."

Stewart and Ferguson were married on November 10, 1981.

In advance of their nuptials, Stewart earned his PGA Tour card in June of 1981 when he shot 69 at a Q School held at one of the Disney World courses in Orlando. He earned his first check on Tour at the Canon Greater Hartford Open in Connecticut, a whopping $715.50. At the time he was just another anonymous flat belly trying to make a name for himself on Tour. A fashion makeover would change all of that, transforming Stewart from just another pair of bell-bottoms into someone whose clothes made him stand out.

Furman Bisher, the *Atlanta Journal-Constitution*'s longtime columnist, would take inventory of Stewart's choice of fashion and characterize him as a fellow "whose mother must have dressed him."

Au contraire.

Stewart's fashion sense came from his father, who sold box springs throughout the Midwest, employing an outrageous wardrobe to make his sales calls. Bill Stewart believed if you made a living selling it was a good idea to stand out. His method for standing out was to wear sport coats that would rival legendary sportscaster Lindsey Nelson's; canary yellow, pastels, and plaids were the rule, basic blue—taboo.

"My husband was a salesman and always wore a jacket and tie," Bee Payne-Stewart said. "Sometimes the kids would tease him that the tie didn't match the jacket or the shirt. He had very loud clothes. They were good-looking, but they would catch your attention."

Though Payne had ridiculed his father's clothes while growing up, he obviously learned his lesson. Fashion-wise, the late seventies and early eighties were ugly years on the Tour. Tight-fitting double-knits had not yet surrendered to common sense, which meant the standard uniform on Tour would be: bright green, yellow, red—even pink—Sansabelt slacks, white belts, and white shoes. Stewart took a look around and noticed the rainbow collection he wore had the anonymity of making a sales call in a blue blazer.

"I wanted to set myself apart from all the players wearing Izod clothing," Stewart told *People* magazine in 1989. "My father always told me, 'The easiest way to be recognized in a crowd is with loud clothes,' which he always used to wear. It used to be a little embarrassing. I'd say, 'Dad, you're not going out looking like that, are you?' and he'd say, 'Oh, yeah, these checks and polka dots go really well together. They're both blue.'"

A switch flipped on inside Payne's head. He remembered seeing Stewart Ginn playing on the Asian Tour dressed in knickers and figured a change to knickers was in order.

Ironically, Bill Stewart wasn't crazy about his son's choice of fashion.

"Bill didn't want him to wear knickers at first," Bee said of her husband. "Payne's father just pooh-poohed it and said, 'Oh, he's just a showoff.'"

Tracey laughed recalling her reaction toward the knickers and how they looked on her six-foot-one, one-hundred-and-eighty-pound husband.

"They didn't do much for me," Tracey said. "But he liked them and he looked good in them. He had the right body to wear knickers. A lot of people can't pull it off. He'd say, 'I need to have game, because nobody is going to watch a guy in knickers shoot 80.' He knew that he had to have something to back it up."

Just like that, Stewart decided wearing knickers would be the PGA Tour's equivalent of Bill Stewart making a sales call in a canary yellow jacket.

Stewart met Tim Barry of the T. Barry Knicker Company at the Greater Milwaukee Open later that summer. Barry, who had played professional golf, opened his business in 1981 and had Bob Hope as an early client. Barry met with several players in Milwaukee and agreed to begin making knickers for them.

Fashion-wise, "Everybody on Tour had that Johnny Miller thing, the blond-hair, blue-eyed look," Barry said. "Wearing knickers was going to break through that barrier and Payne fit right in there."

Stewart and Barry signed a contract on January 18, 1982. Since both were fledgling entities in their respective lines of work and neither could determine in which direction the other's fortunes would be heading, they structured their simple agreement accordingly. Stewart received a 15 percent discount from wholesale prices on up to four pairs of plus fours, twelve pairs of argyle socks, and six pairs of T. Barry classic caps. Any additional items purchased beyond those amounts had to be purchased at wholesale prices.

"The first pair I made for him was a pair of gray-and-white shepherd check," Barry said. "Then I made lavender and all sorts of colors for him. Within a short period of time it was obvious to me Payne was going to wear these and carry on. That satisfied me as far as his interest. So whatever he wanted from then on, regardless of what our agreement said, I just made up for him and didn't charge him."

Stewart first wore knickers in a Tour event at the 1982 Georgia Pacific Atlanta Classic, where the gallery approved of his knickers and the complementing tam o'shanter; Lee Trevino, whom Stewart was paired with, did not.

Trevino skewered him for two days, peppering him with a barrage of sarcastic one-liners. While standing on one tee Trevino told the gallery, "I'll bet you thought you were going to a golf tournament, not a kindergarten fashion show."

Stewart finished in a tie for sixteenth place and a legend was born. His outfits were throwbacks to another era of golf. He called his fashion statement his own little contribution to preserving the history of the game.

Six months after signing players to wear his knickers at the Milwaukee Open, Barry ran into Clarence Rose at a tournament at Oakmont. Rose was one of the players he'd signed to a contract, but he had given up on the fashion.

"I asked him why he wasn't wearing the knickers and he said every time he turned around somebody was saying, 'Hey Payne, hey Payne,'" Barry said.

Clearly the look had become Stewart's. Even his father warmed to the knickers.

"When he won a tournament or two wearing them, his dad thought that was the trinket," Bee said.

In several Pro-Am tournaments Stewart added a tie to complete the look of what players wore in the early twentieth century. The fashion didn't hurt Stewart's wallet, either. He wore Barry's knickers until 1986 when he received an offer to wear another company's.

"Payne called me up and said, 'Tim, I just got a contract, or an offer, from Head Sportswear and they're going to get into the golfing business,'" Barry said. Stewart told Barry he had been offered $50,000 per year plus 5 percent of the gross sales. "And so he said, 'I called you up because I wanted to see what you could do.' I said, 'Well, that's a lot of knickers, I guess I'll have to wish you good luck.'"

The idea of giving up 5 percent of the gross sales "just stuck a fork in me," Barry said. "Looking back on my decision now, I probably would have sold the farm to scratch the money together. You can bet I would have figured out a way to do something."

Stewart's pants, though in the knicker family, were actually "plus fours," a name derived from the four inches of fabric draping over the knee.

Wearing his plus fours, Stewart laughed all the way to the bank. NFL Properties paid him $750,000 a year to wear his trademark ensemble with the color scheme of the closest NFL franchise.

"The NFL made sure he wore Bears colors in Bears country and so forth," said Barry, who actually made the knickers for NFL Properties. "And it was a marvelous marketing thought. I mean it crossed barriers by bringing football into golf."

At times Stewart used his color schemes to toy with the gallery.

"Payne liked to stir the pot," Mike Hicks said. "Like when we went to Dallas. He'd wear Redskins' colors, then the Eagles', then the Giants.' Finally, on Sunday he'd wear the Cowboys' colors. But leading up to that point he'd wear everybody else's colors in the Cowboys' conference. You'd hear someone in the gallery tease with him, 'What are you doing with those Giants' colors on? How come you're not wearing Cowboys'?' "

NFL Properties and Stewart parted ways after six years when the contract ran its course in 1995. Stewart eventually developed his own line of clothing.

"It got to the point where he was sick of [wearing the NFL team colors]," Hicks said. "The NFL wasn't going to renew [the contract], but he wanted out anyway. He'd gotten sick of it. I know I had. It was fun for a while, but it got old after about two years."

Regardless of whose plus fours he wore, Stewart had become universally recognized for his signature look.

When Stewart put up a For Sale sign at his elaborate Orlando mansion, pop icon Michael Jackson stopped by to consider purchasing the house. While looking at the house, Jackson was told the house belonged to Payne Stewart.

"Payne Stewart meant nothing to him," David Whitley said. "Then they told him he was the guy who wore the knickers and even Michael Jackson, the weirdest guy on Earth, knew who he was. You just liked a guy in knickers. Payne had that image."

Golf galleries loved Stewart's image, though the vocal ones might not have expressed that sentiment.

"You can't believe the comments I used to hear out there on the golf course," Tracey said. "Ninety-nine percent of the time I never said anything, but occasionally people would say things that would just chill my blood."

"Mostly when people yell at you they call you a fag," Stewart said in a 1987 *Sports Illustrated* story. "But I think guys who downgrade the way I dress are jealous. They don't have the nerve to wear [knickers]. They're afraid they'd catch too much heat from their buddies. But if you can't stand the heat . . ."

Hicks believed the plus fours benefited Stewart in other areas.

"I think he had a sense of self-confidence wearing those knickers," Hicks said. "He'd put them on and he was Payne Stewart. It gave him a sense of identity. He liked to look different and he liked to look good. Most of the outfits he wore looked good."

Stewart exuded confidence on the Tour.

"You have to have confidence in your game to play on the PGA Tour," Gary Koch said. "I just think some guys exhibit it in different ways. Some guys', it's just a little more inward. Payne's tended to be a little more outward at times, just the way he carried himself dressing the way he did." Koch allowed himself a chuckle. "A lot of guys wouldn't have been able to pull that off."

Professionally, he played well but he struggled to finish off tournaments. Like at the 1984 Colonial where Stewart needed a par on the seventy-second hole to win. Instead he bogeyed and lost in a playoff. At the 1985 Byron Nelson Classic all he needed was a bogey on the tournament's final hole to win. He put up a double then lost in the playoff when he needed only a bogey to win but made double and went on to lose. He missed a pair of short putts to lose the 1985 British Open and made a bogey on the final hole of the 1985 U.S. Open to end his chances of winning. Stewart led the 1986 U.S.

Open until he missed a short par putt on 13 before giving way to veteran Raymond Floyd and finishing in a tie for sixth.

Stewart's near misses earned him a nice living. He set a record for earning the most money on Tour without winning a tournament when he earned $288,795 in 1986.

If one wants to know what's happening on Tour, head to the caddie barn and ye shall hear the truth. The truth was Stewart had made an art of finishing second evidenced by his thirteen second-place finishes and five playoff losses in five playoffs during his first nine years on Tour. Thus, the caddies dubbed Stewart "Avis," a play off the Avis advertising slogan about being second to Hertz but trying harder.

"I think there was a time there that he kind of got into a mode where he was just happy to be in the top ten," Tracey said. "One time we were riding home and he was all excited about another top ten finish, like, 'Oh, I made a big check.' I felt like he could do better than that, so I kind of lost it. I told him, 'You're just happy to make the top ten, you should be winning.'

"It wasn't so much the money, but it just wasn't what he should have been striving for. I told him, 'You're not setting your goals high enough.'"

Shortly after Tracey's stance against complacency, Stewart shot 69, 67, 63, 65 to win the 1987 Hertz Bay Hill Classic in Orlando, a victory that prompted the *Orlando Sentinel* to run a headline that read "Avis wins Hertz." Accompanying the story in many papers nationwide was a picture of Stewart kissing his daughter, Chelsea, then 16 months old, through the fence that separated the house where Stewart lived from the twelfth hole at the Bay Hill Club.

Stewart's first order of business shortly after winning the tournament was to remember his father, who had contracted an incurable form of bone cancer, and died in 1985. Stewart donated the $108,000 first-place check to Florida Hospital in Orlando to create a house on hospital property for the relatives of cancer patients "in memory of my father and honoring my mother."

"He said to me 'I want to donate the check to the hospital,'" Tracey said. "And I said, 'The whole check?'" Tracey laughed at the memory. "I'm thinking, 'Holy cow, the whole thing? Can't you just give some of it?'"

Stewart's image as the Tour's fashion maven often overshadowed his talent. But people in the game were in awe of his game.

"The man's game has no weakness," Trevino said. "He's the next great player."

E. Harvie Ward took on Stewart as a pupil in the mid-1980s and understood sentiments like those expressed by Trevino after looking at Stewart's swing. Ward had been a golfing legend in his own right. The former University of North Carolina golfer won the 1949 NCAA individual championship and played in thirteen Masters, finishing as high as fourth in 1957. Ward stood tied for the lead with Tommy Bolt in the 1955 U.S. Open before finishing sixth. All the while he maintained his amateur status. Ward had played against golfing legends like Ben Hogan and Ken Venturi and had seen the swings of virtually every big-name player in the twentieth century, yet Stewart's swing left him in awe.

"When I first saw his swing, I just said, 'Man this is like driving a Rolls Royce, all I got to do is be sure that all the parts are well oiled and I keep the oil and gas in it so it will run,'" Ward said. "It was the kind of swing you don't fool with.

"Payne was as good an all-around player as I've ever seen tee to green. He had an excellent short game. Bunker player. He was a lot like Tiger [Woods]. He had a good imagination around the green. Hit a lot of real good shots. If he had an Achilles' heel, it would have probably been with the putter. He had his ups and downs with the putter."

Ward lived in Orlando when Tracey Stewart asked one of Ward's assistants if Ward might consider instructing Stewart.

"Payne had just lost his father a year or two before and he was kind of wandering," Ward said. "He was kind of looking for something and somebody and Tracey thought I'd be good for him."

Working with someone Ward called "one of the great feel players I've seen" meant staying away from the mechanics of his swing.

"The main thing we talked about was not overswinging, trying to shorten his swing," Ward said. "But on balance, I talked to him about rhythm and pace of swing as much as anything because generally when they get to a tournament, they're not looking for somebody to change their golf swing. They'll want to talk about rhythm and pace of the swing. Because that's about all they have to think about when they're on the golf course. You can't think mechanics when you're on the golf course trying to hit the ball."

Hicks credited Ward for being good for Stewart during the period when he helped him.

"I think Harvie really was a big part of Payne's tempo on his swing," Hicks said. "That's really all they worked on. Harvie knew the golf swing, but Harvie was old school and Payne was an old-school player. They worked more on tempo issues, ball position, alignment."

Throughout his life Stewart had struggled with his ability to concentrate. Recognizing his problem prompted him to search for solutions. One time he even tried acupuncture. Needles were placed in his ears to help him relax and concentrate better.

Ward knew about Stewart's problem and urged him to begin working with Dr. Richard Coop. Coop lived in Chapel Hill, North Carolina, and worked as a professor of education at the University of North Carolina, where he acted as a consultant to all the athletic teams in the area of mental skills training and performance enhancement. He'd coauthored a book in 1978 titled *The New Golf Mind*, which described the mental side of golf and how it directly affects every player.

"Harvie got Payne on a plane in Orlando and brought him up here," Coop said. "We hit it off pretty well from the start. We sat down and talked frankly from the start. I told him the things I thought we needed to work on to change. He thought about it and said, 'Let's get to work.'

"One thing about Payne, he might argue with you for a while, but he would always think about things. If he was wrong he'd come back and say, 'I was wrong.' That was one of the great characteristics he had."

Coop began working with Stewart in 1988 and diagnosed he had ADD [attention deficit disorder].

"I think God gave Payne a lot of physical skills," Coop said. "Tempo and rhythm and all those things you saw in his swing. But he had to work really hard on his concentration."

Working with Coop helped him learn how to make a concentrated effort to focus when the time came to focus, then he could relax between shots. Having ADD explained why he became easily distracted; he began to take medication.

"We worked with him playing his game and letting other people play their game so he didn't get too caught up in the people around him," Coop said. "Payne outwardly appeared cocky, but underneath he wasn't all that confident. So he had to work a lot at building his confidence. Many times, people like him are very outgoing, very chatty, but they don't really have as much confidence underneath that as they appear to have."

Chuck Cook followed Ward's tenure as Stewart's teacher.

"Chuck got a little more detailed with his plane and different physical aspects of the swing," Hicks said. "He just touched more where the club was at the top, where it came through the ball. And Harvie never really did any of that, no film or any of that."

Cook found Stewart to be unique, prompting him to employ unconventional teaching methods to accommodate Stewart's style of play and lack of concentration.

"Payne had a beautifully graceful swing, but it wasn't what you called textbook," Cook said. "It wasn't what you'd call a modern golf swing. It was a throwback swing. When we originally talked, Payne told me his father had told him to never change his swing. And so he and I made an agreement never to make any changes in his swing."

Before Bill Stewart died, he wrote out on a white legal pad four or five principles of Payne's swing. Tracey had the paper framed and hung it in Stewart's study.

"Every time you went into his study there was this thing hanging there, it was starting to fade a bit, but he and I would go back and look at that periodically to make sure we weren't getting away from that," Cook said. "So his dad was with him in many ways.

"Payne's dad knew his swing better than anybody. Payne had a pretty idiosyncratic swing. That little loop in there, most swing teachers would have taken that away from him early, or would have tried to."

On the yellow piece of paper, Bill Stewart's instructions read:

Watch Payne's feet on putting. Keep left foot back, right foot up.

Keep Payne with a good tempo. Slow backswing. Take it back high and finish high, keep blade open with 7, 8, 9, pw & sw at finish. Finish high.

Keep from pressing; just a good solid swing, good firm left arm.

Keep left shoulder up in air, keep head behind ball. Hold head still.

Cook's job became recognizing what Stewart had done when he performed well. If Stewart played poorly, Cook tried to decide what the difference had been between the poor golf swing and his good golf swing.

"He was way on the feel side of things," Cook said.

Cook shot video of Stewart when they worked, but he never let Stewart view the tapes.

"His eyes would glaze over if you ever got into the mechanics or analysis of his swing," Cook said.

Cook also worked with Tom Kite, who wanted to have all the analytical information available.

"It's just that was Payne's style to do things by feel as opposed to analysis," Cook said. "Payne couldn't keep his mind on anything very long. You had to have a lot more imagination to get him to do things and you had to teach him differently than somebody who didn't have that disorder."

Cook invented games to get Stewart to practice.

"I'd go to work with him in Orlando and he'd say, 'Yeah, we're really going to work hard on my game today' and he'd get up, cook breakfast, take the kids to school," Cook said. "He'd do everything he could to dodge practicing. Then we'd go out there and he'd hit balls for about thirty minutes and then he'd say, 'Let's go eat and go play.' That's what he thought practice was. So I had to develop some games and things to do."

These games would take all shapes and forms. For example, Cook might create an imaginative drill for chipping or putting.

"I'd make up tests for him that he needed to pass before he could go have lunch or go play golf," Cook said. "If his swing had gotten too long, I'd ask him to hit a bunch of shots. I'd say, 'Let me see you knock the ball down,' that type of thing, in order to tighten his swing up. So that's how I taught him. It was totally different than Tom Kite, where I'd spend eight hours a day looking at video and every other swing. It was a totally different relationship. With Payne you had to get him from point A to point B without necessarily explaining why. And it had to work quickly or he wasn't going to do it long."

Stewart had enjoyed above-average success on Tour despite the well-documented setbacks in tournaments he should have won. Prior to the 1999 season he had won nine PGA Tour titles, won three consecutive Skins Games from 1991 to 1993, played on five Ryder Cup teams, and he had enjoyed above-average success at majors with victories in the 1989 PGA Championship and the 1991 U.S. Open.

Stewart entered the final day of the 1989 PGA Championship at Kemper Lakes in Hawthorn Woods, Illinois, trailing the leader, Mike Reid, by five shots. Dressed in Chicago Bears' colors and playing three groups ahead of Reid, Stewart scorched the back nine, making birdies on four of the final five holes for a 31. Stewart placed an exclamation point on the performance by draining a twelve-footer on 18. The final birdie took him to twelve-under, putting him two shots behind Reid, who had three holes to play.

Stewart went to the scorer's tent and waited.

An old golf adage states: "Every shot makes someone happy."

Unfortunately for Reid, his shots were making the wrong person happy.

Reid pushed his drive into the water on 16 and bogeyed. He followed by botching a chip shot on 17 before three-putting for a double bogey. Finally his seven-foot birdie putt to tie on 18 missed and Stewart had his first major.

Eyes brimming with tears, Reid asked the media, "Where can you go around here for a good cry?"

In stark contrast, Stewart failed to sound gracious when asked about the tournament's ending: "I said a prayer in the tent. How about some good stuff for Payne Stewart one time?"

Stewart experienced physical problems in the months leading up to the 1991 U.S. Open. Pain in his lower back had bothered him for many years, but when he began to feel pain in his neck and lost strength in his left triceps in February of 1991, he knew he had to do something. Doctors discovered a disk problem and fitted Stewart with a neck brace that he wore twenty-four hours a day. The injury had zapped his strength to the point he had trouble hoisting a two-pound weight. Initially all he could do was sit at the house with his family and wait for the day when he could begin his rehab program. Though Stewart worked hard to recover, one of his doctors told his agent, Robert Fraley, he had doubts Stewart could ever play golf to the high level he'd played in the past.

By the end of March Stewart had begun to hit golf balls. The swing looked the same, but he still lacked strength in his left arm, which he discovered when he tried to play in the Masters in April before withdrawing. Fortunately, Stewart continued to exercise patience and allowed himself to heal. Finishing in a tie for fourth at the Heritage Classic in Hilton Head in late April offered Stewart encouragement. He believed he could make a full recovery.

The healing looked complete at Hazeltine in Chaska, Minnesota when he finished an 18-hole playoff with Scott Simpson with birdie-par-par to win the 1991 U.S. Open. Simpson had struggled, which made some suggest Stewart had won in similar fashion to his other major. Stewart would have none of that afterward.

"The first major was sweet, but a lot of people say I backed into that one," he said. "I don't feel like I backed into this one."

Hicks pointed out the differences between the two victories.

"In '89 we were seven shots behind with nine holes to play," Hicks said. "So you're not really thinking about winning. Then shooting 31 on the back side and Mike Reid made the boo-boos coming in. I'm not going to say we fell into that one, because we did shoot 31 on the back and posted a number. Anytime you post a score and lead the championship and you're finished, you have a good opportunity to win it, because once those guys see a score that's in the house, that just adds to the pressure. So I'm not going to say we backed into it, because we did post a number. But that one was more or less coming from behind. You're not really expecting to win when you're that far behind with only nine holes to play. In '91, Payne was right there the whole week. Basically he was in the hunt from day one."

Stewart had notched two majors and had come up short in his fair share of others, establishing the fact that he often could be found in contention on the leaderboard at majors.

"With Payne, looking back, I think it was easier for him to play in the major championships than it was the Milwaukee Open," Coop said. "The point being, it's not too surprising when you looked back. The majors really got his motor running. He got up for a major and got a high level of arousal, stimulation. He was able to focus."

Cook's help with the preparation for the majors proved invaluable. Prior to the Open at Hazeltine Cook did his homework on past Opens and discovered approximately 90 percent of the players winning during the modern era had faded the ball. Since Stewart hit a draw, Cook worked with him to develop a fade.

"I just got him so close to the ball that he couldn't hook it," Cook said. "I didn't tell him anything. If I did, he wouldn't have tried to play a fade, he would have said, 'Aw, I can win this tournament drawing the ball.' That type of thing. So I just told him, 'You're standing too far away, you're standing too far away.'"

Following the win at Hazeltine, chaos worked its way into Stewart's life.

"His expectations went up," Coop said. "He thought he should never miss a shot because he was U.S. Open champion."

Tracey also observed a difference in Payne.

"I remember Payne feeling like he was the U.S. Open champion so he had to act like the U.S. Open champion," Tracey said. "He put a lot of pressure on himself."

Stewart later described how winning his first U.S. Open had affected him.

"It changed my perspective on my golf career. I guess I always felt that I was good enough to win one, and then to do it," Stewart said. "I don't know that I realized that I was at the top of my game at that stage, and so I tried to become better, because I was United States Open champion. I felt that there was a pressure that I put on myself, because every time you were introduced whenever you played, 'the 1991 U.S. Open champion, Payne Stewart.' I put this added pressure on myself that I had to perform differently and better than I performed at the U.S. Open, and I didn't realize that I was already there."

Though Stewart didn't win in 1992, he'd played well enough to have eleven second-place finishes. Critical to his success was his continued use of Wilson equipment and a Titleist ball. But along came John Daly, who won the 1991 PGA Championship, capturing America's imagination while doing so. Seizing Daly's immense popularity, Wilson made Daly their No. 1 guy.

"Payne felt like he had a better record and he should have been their number-one guy," Cook said. "And so he went to Spalding to get the same deal Daly got from Wilson."

Stewart's new deal afforded him the financial wherewithal to pay for a huge new house and extended him financial security. But in the long run, the move proved costly.

"Changing equipment and the balls he used really hurt him," Coop said. "Everybody told him not to take that equipment contract. And it's a lot easier to see in retrospect. In his defense, it was a huge amount of money. It allowed him to pay the house off and have no debt.

"The clubs were the worst possible fit for him. If you drew up clubs for him, [the clubs he signed a contract to endorse and use] were the ones that fit his swing the worst. And the ball was also the worst possible ball as well."

Stewart hit one of the highest balls on Tour and had a high launch angle. To help keep the ball down he had used a Titleist ball with a low trajectory and it worked well for him.

The Spalding ball would get into the air quickly causing Stewart to hit a lot of shots that floated in balloon fashion.

"He kept moving the ball back in his stance to get the ball down and he lost his swing," Coop said.

"He played clubs that not only were offset, but they were square grooves, this is when square grooves came out," Hicks said. "And he was playing with a ball that all of a sudden was spinning 8,500 rpms as opposed to a Titleist spinning 3,500 rpms. When a ball spins that much, with a square groove and an offset, that helps the ball get into the air. His ball flight went from a nice trajectory to really high."

Stewart's emphasis on winning majors compounded the problems created by the new equipment.

"He liked winning those majors and wanted to win more," Coop said. "So what did he do? He asked everybody how to win more majors and, of course, the answer was to be more consistent."

Seeking to find a higher level of consistency, Stewart got under the hood and began to tinker with the engine hoping to find a swing that could "hold up" under pressure.

"We all talked about it and everybody agreed Payne had a little loop in his swing," Coop said. "The thinking was if he took the loop out he'd be more consistent. But unfortunately, that loop was what he played off of. That was where he got his feel and his touch. So once he took the loop out, his swing was technically better, if you drew it up on a video, but he had lost all sense of where his club head was. He couldn't cut the ball, draw the ball, hit the kind of shots he'd been able to hit before."

Consequently, Stewart had a hard time scoring and began to press trying to force the ball to go lower. Confidence is hard enough to come by on the PGA Tour when a golfer is playing well and damn near impossible when he can't even hit the ball well during practice rounds.

"He had developed a swing that couldn't hold up under pressure and one that wouldn't hold up under nonpressure," Coop said.

By the close of the 1994 season Stewart ranked a hundred and twenty-third on the money list at $145,687 in twenty-three events, a phenomenon akin to Barry Bonds finishing last in the league in home runs. Jetting around the world meant less time at home with Tracey and their children and he had the reputation of someone who could not pass up a party. Stewart also had the reputation of being brash and cocky with occasional outbursts on the golf course where he might kick the ground in frustration or put a cussing on a bad shot. *Sports Illustrated* wrote that Stewart had considered autograph seekers and members of the media "as lower life forms." While Stewart's reputation seems to have been magnified by his success and his visibility wearing knickers, there was a basis for his reputation.

"I would say there probably were a large number of players who felt like he was probably a little too cocky, a little too arrogant, and not that easy to approach, not that easy to be around," Koch said.

Ward called Stewart "kind of a brat."

"He had a bratty way about him," Ward said. "He was a little brash and all of this . . . The times that I was with him, when he was having a good time, we had dinners together at his house, my house, or we went out together. We did a lot of things socially. Payne was a lot of fun. I saw a little of [the bratty side] on the golf course, a little, but I wasn't around him that much when he was playing, unless I was with him at an Open or whatever. So I didn't see that side. Most of the stuff that I heard about him, the way he was, came from the people who were around him a lot."

Ward recalled the episode that prompted Stewart to replace him.

"I think where we got a little crossways was when he started saying he liked to play the golf course," Ward said. "Meaning that when he had to hit a draw, he hit a draw, and when he needed to hit a fade, he hit a fade."

Ward believed Stewart needed to work on one shot that when the time came in a pressure situation he would know he could depend on that one shot.

"You've got to be able to come up with that one single swing where you're going to hit it like you want to," Ward said. "And I think that kind of got him, because I just said, 'I don't think you can play golf on your level that way to where you're curving the ball one way and curving it the other. Sure, you know how to do it. You know how to fade it. You know how to hook it; how to do all these things. But day in and day out, you want to be more consistent with one swing and the ball to have one pattern.' After that I never did hear from him."

Stewart never notified Ward of the change.

"I read about it in *Sports Illustrated*," Ward said.

Cook had a falling out with Stewart prior to the 1995 U.S. Open at Shinnecock.

Because Cook worked with Kite and Corey Pavin in addition to Stewart, he told the trio he would give them each a day where they would have his undivided attention the week of the Open. Stewart selected first and chose Monday.

"Payne never showed on Monday, and Tuesday I was committed to Kite, and Wednesday, Corey," Cook said.

When Stewart did show, Cook told him he would try and watch him practice when he could, but he was committed to the other two for their respective days.

"He got mad and said, 'I'm going to do it myself,'" Cook said. "And he had been frustrated up to that point anyway because of the equipment. It limited him so much that he had a really, really hard time playing with it. So we had a falling out there for about a year and a half where we didn't work together. Then he decided he couldn't do it anymore by himself and we got back together after that."

Pavin won the 1995 U.S. Open, leading Stewart to question whether or not he would have contended had he made his scheduled appointment with Cook. Stewart's only wins after changing equipment were the 1992 and 1993 Hassan II Trophy in Morocco and the 1995 Shell Houston Open.

Stewart's problems with his game did nothing to change his ongoing love-hate relationship with the media.

Throughout his career he had been prickly with the media, which often stemmed from his feelings that certain things he had said had been misrepresented in stories written about him.

"As for how he treated the media, I do know that when some of the fellas interviewed him and misquoted him, he'd be mad about it and he'd let them know how he felt," Bee said. "He never hid any of his feelings."

Tracey attributed Payne's problems with the media to him "just trying to be funny."

"I'd tell him, 'The media does not have a sense of humor, stop trying to make them laugh because it's just going to come back to haunt you,'" Tracey said. "I think Payne really just saw the good in people and didn't feel like a person would hurt him for no reason. Like a person in the media. They're out there to get a story or make headlines the next day. He felt you were a friend unless you had a problem for some reason. So he trusted that you would treat him right and that kind of backfired at times. Because he would be so honest and open with people that it would sometimes turn around and bite him."

When Shoal Creek hosted the PGA Championship, Stewart made remarks that the press interpreted differently than he intended. Since Stewart was known for being candid, he'd been asked about his position on the tournament being held at the all-white club in Alabama and felt his words had been twisted by the media to portray him as a racist, which he vehemently denied being.

"Many times he'd call me and say, 'I've done it again,'" Coop said. "I'd ask him what he'd done and he'd say, 'Put my foot in my mouth with the press.'"

To better understand Stewart, Coop said one must remember Stewart was impulsive and tended to talk first and think second, a problem stemming from a lack of impulse control. He would say what he was thinking instead of censoring it and saying the appropriate thing.

"In some ways that made him really interesting to be around, but many times the way he said it and the way it appeared in print were two different things, too," Coop said. "He had inflections or he would say something in a teasing manner. But the way it was written you couldn't tell in print whether he was joking, teasing, or whatever.

He would come across much harsher than he intended. He always softened up what he said with his facial expression, inflection and all. He had a great heart. There was a very good person underneath."

To know Payne Stewart meant knowing a person different than the person seen on the golf course.

"I used to always be amazed, I'd think to myself what a good person he was, he was such a good person the way he treated people," Tracey said. "In the media they made him out to be the total opposite of what he really was. I remember a lot of people would say to us after they'd gotten to know Payne that he was totally different than what they thought he was.

"I guess they thought he was cocky because he wore knickers and was different. They thought he was real arrogant. And that wasn't him at all. There wasn't a better person out there. He made everybody feel like they were special. Whether it be the mailman, whoever, he didn't care what you did, he treated you with respect."

Stewart's actions at times contradicted the person people close to him knew. His behavior attending the NBA Orlando Magic's games typified the bratty outbursts that were his trademark. He had courtside seats to the Magic's games and became known for making Magic coach Matt Guokas's life a living hell with his abusive rants.

"It was embarrassing to be sitting around him and listening to the things he was saying," said Larry Guest, a columnist for the *Orlando Sentinel.* "And particularly when you consider that he was a golfer who expects total silence when he's at work. Payne was brutal, just brutal. He wasn't even clever . . . It was bordering on being obscene."

Stewart's close friend, John Brendle, dismissed Stewart's behavior at Magic games to Stewart being a born heckler, which he said stemmed from Bill Stewart being a heckler. Brendle smiled when noting the Magic relocated Stewart's seats. "You can bet Matty Guokas had something to do with that."

Stewart didn't limit his boisterous cheering to Magic games. According to his friend, Chris Millsaps, he cheered so intently at Chelsea's volleyball games that he was made a line official for the games.

"They did that really to keep him quiet," Millsaps told *New Man* magazine. "We talked about setting up a ten-by-ten soundproof box where we could get in it and just yell and scream and nobody could hear us."

In hindsight, negative portrayals of Stewart appear to be the combination of misunderstandings with a healthy dose of immaturity and behavior he regretted. Undeniable is the fun, caring person Stewart was to those who knew him best. Ready smiles typify the first expressions coming to their faces when asked about Stewart.

"He was the fun person in our family," Tracey said. "I'd be the one who got the kids to do this and do that, but 'Dad's coming home Sunday night and then we'll have fun until it's back to the grind when he's gone.' He was just a fun person to be around."

Cook laughed when asked if Stewart and he had hit it off immediately. "Oh yeah, we were both derelicts."

Cook explained, "Payne loved people. He wanted to make sure whoever was with him was having a great time. It was always fun to be around him."

Like what occurred at the Pebble Beach Lodge after media day for the 1992 U.S. Open at Pebble Beach. Stewart had to return the trophy since he was the reigning champion and asked Cook to accompany him on the trip. The trip had been a fun one. Stewart had been relaxed, he'd fulfilled his media obligations and they had played golf. Most memorable had been their trip to the bar after a round when a patron of the bar did not believe Stewart was Stewart, prompting Stewart to make a bet. If he brought back the trophy the man would have to fill the trophy with whatever they wanted to drink for the rest of the night. The man agreed and Stewart returned with the trophy. Cook and Stewart drank expensive Cristal Champagne until late in the evening. Having imbibed for a lengthy period, Stewart and Cook eventually migrated outside, taking the trophy and more champagne to Pebble Beach's eighteenth green. Sitting on a retaining wall thirty feet above the Pacific Ocean, Stewart and Cook nearly allowed the trophy to fall into the world's largest body of water. The ocean spray and the wind kicking sand all over the place worked on the trophy like a building getting sandblasted, which didn't go unnoticed by Tom Kite after he won the Open at Pebble Beach.

"A little bit later on I asked [Kite] what he thought about the trophy," Cook said. "Tom said, 'I was surprised how scratched up it was.'"

Brendle, who is now a PGA Tour official, was a club pro at Disney when he met Stewart in the early 1980s. Later he became Stewart's next-door neighbor in Orlando, which added to many good times and their friendship.

Brendle remembers setting out with Stewart in Brendle's pontoon boat on an adventure to retrieve firewood. Fellow Tour pro Scott Hoch was building a swimming pool and had cleared a lot of trees so Brendle and Stewart made the trip across the lake to Hoch's backyard.

"Payne and I loaded up my pontoon boat because mine was a little junkier than his," Brendle said. "We had Chelsea, Aaron, and Payne's dog, Taffy, with us. Scott wasn't home but his mother and father were there. We loaded up the wood and emptied all the beer out of Scott's icebox, then started back across the lake."

On the return trip the boat experienced problems.

"Payne and I were never known to be too mechanically inclined," Brendle said with a smile. "We overheated the boat on the way back and we're out in the middle of the lake. Since it was November or December we weren't about to get in the water. We had one paddle, so we started paddling."

Despite enjoying themselves, they didn't hesitate to signal for help when a boat approached.

"Payne waved them down," Brendle said. "And you could hear voices across the lake. We could hear, 'Oh gosh.' They had just opened some champagne. It was four guys. Payne's like, 'Hey guys, any chance you could drag us home through the next canal straight across? They're like, 'sure,' but they were bummed out about it totally. Payne said, 'Thanks, just take us to that canal over there. When we get in the canal the house you see straight across is mine.'"

The towing process went slowly.

"They couldn't drag us very fast because our boat was almost sinking," Brendle said. "Logs were stacked all over the place. We're standing on the logs drinking beer; the kids and the dog are doing fine."

When they reached the canal and Stewart's mansion stared them in the face, Brendle and Stewart heard the group talking.

"One of them says, 'I think that's Payne Stewart,'" Brendle said. "Another one of them says, 'Which one?' And they pointed at me."

When they reached shore Stewart displayed his typical hospitality.

"He sends Aaron into the house to get them hats, signs all the stuff, invites them in for a beer," Brendle said. "He's got beer on draft and he's got a big Texas barbecue pit. He invited them to stay for something to eat. They didn't stay. Turned out one of the guys was the general manager of the Marriott World here in Orlando. And three of the other guys were international GMs that were in visiting. And Payne was sponsored by Marriott. So it was like the greatest day they'd ever had. They got to meet and be with Payne. And they hit it off after that."

Nick Price was among the many Tour professionals to live in Orlando at one time and got to know Stewart. After Price won the 1994 British Open, Price and the Claret Jug hosted a party with plenty of expensive champagne. Price got a twinkle in his eye recalling what Stewart did.

"Payne rinsed out the Claret Jug with a bottle of the champagne," Price said, now smiling. "I said, 'What are you doing?' And he says, 'You can afford it.' "

Stewart enjoyed being a cutup, which made becoming a member of the band, Jake Trout and the Flounders, a natural thing for him to do and provided further evidence of how Stewart sought and attracted fun.

For years at PGA events, Stewart, along with professional golfers Peter Jacobsen and Mark Lye, had performed parodies of rock 'n' roll hits—converting them to golf-themed songs. Among these were Joe Walsh's "Life's Been Good," which was "Flounderized" into "It'd Be Good To Just Make Par" and Alice Cooper's "Eighteen" became "I'm on 18."

"Jake Trout and the Flounders started as a gag and it's still a gag," Lye said. "We did the one cassette in the late '80s and another in '98. They're still selling. It was what it was, it wasn't a chart buster, but we had a lot of fun doing it. The intention was never to make a lot of money or do anything. It was just to get out there.

"Peter Jacobsen was the singer, I was the guitar player, and Payne was a very average harmonica player; Payne's personality went a long way."

Lye laughed and respectfully declined to answer when asked to reveal behind-the-scenes stories of Jake Trout and the Flounders, who performed at the Hard Rock Café in Las Vegas, La Costa, and

Fort Myers, Florida's Centennial Park with Jimmy Buffet and Glenn Frey.

Tracey understood how Payne enjoyed being the life of the party.

"He loved being around people," she said. "He was a people person. And I'm not a big people person. I prefer small groups. He liked big parties and being the center of attention."

Asked if it was hard being married to the life of the party, Tracey smiled.

"No, I liked it because I knew I was the one who got to go home with him," she said.

Stewart's needling skills were on even par with his golfing skills. Stewart elevated the art of needling to new heights.

"He could give the needle, but he could take it, too," Hicks said. "And I'll tell you what, he didn't care who you were, right down to Arnold [Palmer] and Jack [Nicklaus], he'd stick it in. Sometimes he'd stick it too deep. He crossed the line quite often, especially with his friends. He'd needle Zinger so bad Zinger was ready to kill him."

"Zinger" was fellow Tour professional Paul Azinger, who was Stewart's close friend. Azinger might have been on the receiving end of Stewart's famed needle many times, but he gave it back to his friend on at least one memorable occasion.

Bass fishing had become a new passion for Stewart, prompting him to purchase a bass boat with all the bells and whistles. He kept the boat in his garage and would intermittently visit the garage to dote over his new toy. One day he couldn't resist temptation and cranked the engine without understanding the intricacies of an outboard engine. In order for an outboard engine to operate properly it needs to have water running through it. The engine purred for all of five minutes before exploding.

"I could see Payne doing that, too, because he wasn't the most mechanically inclined person," Hicks said. "And if he went fishing, he would fish but basically went out there to drink beer and have a good time."

Stewart made the mistake of spilling the beans about the incident to Azinger, who relayed the tale to anybody who cared to listen. Azinger later decorated his friend's locker at a tournament so when Stewart opened it he found an ad for an outboard motor with a note written by Azinger that read: "Just add water."

Stewart's charisma, charm, and a magnetic personality allowed him to easily collect friends.

The year after Stewart won his first U.S. Open, Coop remembered Stewart taking a group that included Hicks, Cook, and Coop for a golfing vacation overseas. Stewart attended a formal soiree in Monte Carlo where he met Princess Stephanie, who said of him, "That Payne Stewart is quite the cat's meow, you know."

"Payne loved that story," Cook said.

On the same trip Stewart's entourage found themselves eating at a restaurant in Glasgow where they encountered a group of American college students who were studying there.

"We're in this restaurant and about thirty college kids came inside," Cook said. "It became pretty clear they were from the United States, so Payne brought them over to our table. As always, he included everybody. They were attracted to him and knew they recognized him, but they couldn't tell who he was without his knickers. Finally they figured it out. When we got up to leave, Hicks, Coop, and I were standing across the street watching Payne on the other side of the street. And about thirty or forty college kids were following him along this little, tiny street in Glasgow. He was like the Pied Piper. It was a moving show."

Stewart showed how much he could care for others when he was introduced to Joel Broering, a seventeen-year-old boy from Ohio who had been diagnosed with leukemia. Broering let it be known he was a big fan of Stewart's and asked to meet him. Thanks to A Special Wish Foundation, the meeting was arranged when Stewart played in the 1993 Skins Game tournament in Palm Desert. Giving the meeting his full attention, Stewart arranged for Broering to be clothed in knickers, shirt, and tam that matched what Payne wore during the tournament that included Couples, Palmer, and Azinger. When Stewart won his third Skins Game victory in three tries, he presented Broering with the trophy. Broering died shortly thereafter, which coincided with the timing of Azinger being diagnosed with lymphoma cancer in his right shoulder blade. Suddenly life took on a somber tint for Stewart. Broering's death and the memories of his father's fight against cancer moved him to have grave concerns about Azinger.

A devout Christian, Azinger turned his fight to regain his health into a positive. Stewart observed and marveled how Azinger's faith helped him deal with his disease and grew closer to his friend during this period. While his friend endured the chemotherapy treatments, Stewart listened to him call his ordeal a "great experience." Azinger even took time to lift Stewart's spirits early in the 1994 season when Stewart had been struggling with his game to such a degree that he took a month off. The two friends were out fishing when Azinger told him, "You better get your butt back out there or I'm going to spot you seven months and still beat your butt on the money list."

Six months after being diagnosed with cancer Azinger was cured and the experience led him to believe God had revealed a plan for him to encourage and inspire other cancer patients. Stewart began to probe deeper into his own faith, revealing to himself a desire to become more spiritual.

Azinger's experience "put a different perspective on my life," Stewart said. "I know it definitely put a different perspective on his life. And that's one thing Paul taught me. You know, that golf isn't everything. And when you—all of a sudden you have to look at life as, you know, God's going to call us home sometime, and Paul thought he was going to be called home early, and it didn't work out like that, which thank God for that. God decided that Paul needed to spend a little more time down here with us, he's got some better things to do. But, hey, you know, I'm going to a special place when I die, but I want to make sure my life's special while I'm here, and when I'm done here, then my time is done."

Tracey and the kids enhanced Payne's desire to be more spiritual.

When Chelsea and Aaron began to attend school at First Academy, a Christian school in Orlando, they told their father they wanted him to go to church with them. He did. And when Aaron at age ten asked his father to wear a W.W.J.D. (What Would Jesus Do?) bracelet, Stewart strapped it on and wore it everywhere he went to show he was not ashamed of his faith. Embracing Christianity soothed Stewart, who displayed a softer side of his former self.

Players on the Tour began to notice the change in Stewart, who went so far as to publicly apologize to golf fans in 1995 for his rude behavior in the past. Tour players were close enough to the situation to admire him for what he had done for himself, prompting many of them to look inward at how they were treating the public and the press and tournament officials.

Lye said Stewart's intensified faith made Stewart "an all-world person to everyone."

"During those struggling years he didn't take it like he should have," Lye said. "He was a little bit moody and abrasive. But [after he reexamined his faith] he was never that way with anybody.

"That was a private thing for him. He said in several interviews that he didn't want to be a Bible thumper. There are a lot of people out there who are like, 'Praise the Lord and help me make a five-footer.' Payne didn't believe in that kind of thing."

Added Tracey: "He would pray to God to give him strength and concentration to get through the day, but not 'help me make putts.'"

Stewart's change didn't come overnight.

"I can't really put a finger on when he changed," Coop said. "It wasn't like he woke up one day and said, 'I've got it.' But he just got better and better."

Tracey characterized Payne as a person who had always been a Christian.

"He always had strong beliefs," she said. "He did begin to explore it more in his latter years."

Stewart longed to spend more time with his wife and kids, to be the good husband and father he thought a Christian-living man should be. Accordingly he moved his life in that direction. Meanwhile, his golf game remained in a slump. He was the first to admit his priorities had changed. A passion for his family had replaced golf and it showed. When he played an event the look on his face said he'd rather be anywhere else than playing on the Tour, which prompted Tracey to have a heart-to-heart talk with her husband. She told him he needed to either improve his outlook or quit and do something else.

"He didn't want to be out there [on Tour]," she said. "He was moping around. After a while that gets old. I support him for so long." Tracey paused to laugh. "Then it's time to get a grip."

Cook believes Tracey's talk and his revitalized faith had a distinct impact on Payne.

"You could just tell a big difference," Cook said. "He didn't act like he used to. He was more kind to people, more gracious. He'd always been fun around his buddies and that didn't change, he just got a little more tolerant of others, wasn't quite as harsh with his teasing. He'd changed. You could tell a big difference."

Mick Elliott of the *Tampa Tribune* said he first noticed a softer

Stewart at the Disney Classic in October of 1996. Tiger Woods won the tournament when Stewart's ten-foot birdie putt at 18 missed. Afterward, Stewart said, "I wasn't intimidated by [Woods]."

"The remark struck me as kind of odd since [Stewart] was a sixteen-year Tour pro with ten wins and Woods had just joined the Tour," Elliott said. "I asked him, 'Isn't that kind of strange for you, a Tour veteran to make that comment?'"

Stewart answered Elliott's question by saying, "He can do things I can't do. This was the first time I played with him and he's a wonderful player."

"He took the question in the right vein and answered it without taking off my head," Elliott said. "On another day, that might not have been the case."

Addressing his game and prolonged slump, Stewart finally gave up on the clubs Spalding wanted him to play and began using an old set of Spalding blades with new shafts and Spalding's Strata ball so he could be true to his equipment contract until it ran out after 1998.

"He had some good things happen in 1997," Coop said. "It wasn't as evident by the results [other than the second-place at the 1998 Open]. He was hitting the ball better. He got equipment that was much better suited for him. He was working hard on his game. Remember, this followed a period there where he didn't really want to work because he wasn't getting anywhere. It was hard to blame him. He was just going out there and screwing himself into the ground, so to speak, because he wasn't making any progress."

Stewart began making progress with his game in 1997, his practice habits improved and he became more systematic in his approach.

"That was something that was always hard with Payne, getting him to do anything in a systematic way," Coop said. "Anything planned or ordered, that just wasn't his deal. He was more the type to fly by the seat of his pants. Don't get me wrong, his spontaneity was wonderful. It just didn't help a lot for preparing for a golf tournament. He began to see that he needed that organization, though, around '97 and '98."

Stewart finished fortieth on the money list in 1997, earning $538,289 in twenty-three events before finishing nineteenth in 1998 at $1,193,996 in nineteen events, but he had not won a tournament since the 1995 Shell Houston Open.

"We talked in December of '98 about working hard to get off to a good start in '99," Cook said. "So he came to Austin and I got the video out and I had his old swings, you know his best swings, then I showed him his current swings and how his tendency was to be steep. That's the only time I showed him a video. We stood out there for three or four days on the range trying to hit big old high hooks to get him where he was not coming into the ball so steeply, where he was coming in on more of a shallow angle. We had a drill where I put my shaft over the top of the ball and I'd tee the ball under the shaft and he'd have to hit it. And before he'd been so steep he would have hit the shaft before he hit the ball. He really worked hard and got his swing back, really in good shape."

Cook also hooked up Stewart with a fitness expert who put him on a program that helped him physically.

"His back had bothered him in the past and that helped his back," Cook said. "He had a lot more strength and speed. Payne was very diligent [following the fitness program]. He had a lot of things going for him [heading into the 1999 season]. His mind was straight, his body was straight, his equipment was straight, and his swing was straight."

Stewart no longer had an equipment contract so he actually went to a discount golf store prior to the 1999 season and bought a black bag with no logos on the side. He also adopted what Cook called a "bastard set of golf clubs" that included a Titleist driver, Orlimar fairway woods, and a set of Mizuno irons that had returned to him in an unlikely fashion.

After telling a friend he wanted to find a set of irons that weren't offset and had a thin blade the friend told him he'd simply give back the Mizuno irons Stewart had given him years earlier. Stewart jumped on the offer. Once he had the irons in his possession he had the clubs gripped the way he liked them and the loft on each iron calibrated to the desired degree of loft.

Rounding out the clubs in Stewart's bag were a Cleveland sand wedge and a Ping lob wedge. Stewart piddled around with his wedges until he customized them the way he wanted them.

"Payne did all the grinding and stuff on his wedges," Hicks said. "He liked them a certain way. Some guys like a lot of bounce; other guys don't like bounce. He would shape his wedge where he might round the toe off. He'd actually grind it down."

In normal conditions Hicks said Stewart hit his pitching wedge 130 yards and his other clubs ten additional yards in descending numerical order. He hit his sand wedge approximately 110 yards and his 60-degree wedge right at eighty yards; his driver ranged from 260 to 280 yards.

Stewart liked to "work the ball."

"Payne was working it mostly right to left, but if he needed to cut it he cut it," Hicks said.

Stewart used a Titleist 90-compression professional ball, a ball that facilitated a golfer who wanted to work it. Such a ball is now prehistoric compared to those used on today's Tour.

"The ball has changed so much since '99," Hicks said. "The ball just doesn't curve anymore. The older guys, who are from thirty-five to fifty, have had a hard time adjusting to that. For the younger guys it's kind of all they know.

"All the balls now are harder, the dimple configuration is different. They don't spin as much. Spin is what makes a ball curve. To hit a draw you have to put the right spin on it. To hit a fade you have to put the right spin on it. And today's balls, they just don't spin enough to work them."

Stewart felt invigorated and excited about the 1999 season when Tracey and he examined the Tour schedule and mulled over where he should play based on past performance.

"I remember we sat down at the kitchen table and we were talking about the schedule and decided we were going to take family vacations every opportunity that we could," Tracey said. "And Aaron made the comment, 'Dad you don't have to play so much, just play better.'"

Tracey laughed at the memory. "Payne went, 'Okay, makes sense to me.'"

Upon reviewing the schedule they saw two events scheduled for San Diego during the early part of the season along with the AT&T Pebble Beach Pro-Am.

"He'd always played so well at Pebble Beach," Tracey said. "He had years where he played well at San Diego, too, but he never really had the opportunities to win there like he did at Pebble Beach."

Stewart had twice been the runner-up at Pebble Beach so they passed on the San Diego events and penciled in the AT&T on his calendar for February.

Additional positive karma came in the form of a Brass Blade SeeMore putter.

Arnie Cunningham, a longtime golf equipment rep, saw Hicks on the practice tee the Wednesday prior to the start of the AT&T and showed him the SeeMore putter.

"I had just started with SeeMore, but I'd been working for thirteen years as a rep, so I knew most of the guys [on Tour]," Cunningham said. "I showed it to Mike and he thought it was kind of a neat concept, so I then approached Payne with it and showed it to him."

The SeeMore putting system has a unique way of lining up the putter with the target through the use of two white lines and a red dot on the blade. Stewart had been struggling with his putting after ranking fortieth on Tour in average putts per hole the previous year. He liked the way the SeeMore putter felt.

"I kind of knew Payne's putting style pretty well," Cunningham said. "I'd started messing with the product in the fall and really believed in the product, it was a way to really change your putting. I believed in it so I wasn't real apprehensive about showing it to Payne. I told him I thought it could help his putting. Obviously he was a great putter at times, but maybe not as consistent as he wanted to be."

Cunningham had tweaked Stewart's curiosity.

"I'll meet you on the green when I'm done hitting balls," Stewart said.

After Stewart finished at the driving range he joined Cunningham and Hicks on the practice green where they remained for two hours.

"I measured his alignment, really showed him how the putter works and how it could improve his putting," Cunningham said. "I think he could feel right away how he was aiming better and his stroke was better and he had a reference point for consistency. He set up the red dot cover, got his hands in the right position, got his ball in the right position, head in the right position, aimed properly, then putted and putted and putted."

Stewart remained stoic on the outside. He didn't say much to Cunningham other than to ask a few questions. Then he left the practice green for a meeting before returning to work with the new putter for another hour.

"You could tell he was intrigued," Cunningham said. "I don't know if excited was the right word at that point, but he was pretty intrigued. He was starting to buy into it."

Tracey remembered Payne being more than intrigued.

"I remember he called me the Wednesday night before the AT&T and was real excited because he'd found this new putter and he was draining everything," Tracey said, smiling. "I'm like, 'That's great, you're the one who has to make the putts.'"

Stewart decided to use the SeeMore putter in the AT&T.

"Here he is, he's never putted with the thing in a competitive round and he lights it up on Thursday morning," Hicks said. "There aren't a lot of players on the PGA Tour brave enough to play a tournament using a putter they'd never played a round with. Payne did."

Cunningham said it was unusual for a Tour professional to make such a drastic change on the eve of a tournament.

"Particularly when you're not just talking about a product," Cunningham said. "You're talking about a form of usage. He formerly was kind of aiming left. He had his hands forward, pushing the putter blade out.

"It was a radical change. The SeeMore is an entire putting system. It's a way to putt. He changed to a total shoulder stroke. But I think it felt so right to him that he could tell it was correct. If it didn't work that week he probably thought it would work in the long run. But as it worked out, he didn't have to wait for results. Him being a great player, he went to the forefront that week."

Cunningham thought Stewart's maturity had led him to be more receptive to the idea of a major equipment change.

"It was strange, but I think Payne had come to terms with some things in his life," Cunningham said. "He was a lot more humble and more open to listening. I think he trusted me, he'd known me for a while out there. We're all trying to get better at golf. It might have been a waste of time or he might have caught on to the thing and really improved his putting."

Stewart could do no wrong at the AT&T. His eight-under-par 64 in the second round earned him a three-shot lead over Vijay Singh and Frank Lickliter.

The third round turned into a battle of man against nature on the Monterey Peninsula. Playing Spyglass, Stewart birdied the last hole for a one-over 73, which gave him a fifty-four-hole total of ten-under 206 and was good enough for a one-shot lead over Lickliter.

Rain pelted the Monterey Peninsula throughout Saturday night, making a washout of the final round inevitable. But at 8 A.M. Sunday, players were sent out to start the final round. Twenty minutes prior to the leaders teeing off, just before 10 A.M., play was suspended because the soaked greens made play impossible. After a four-and-a-half-hour rain delay officials declared Stewart the AT&T winner. Just like that, he had his tenth career PGA title, $504,000 for winning, and his win drought had run its course.

Actor Clint Eastwood presented Stewart with the tournament trophy. He seemed pleased to be declared the winner but recognized he had work to do.

"I'm going to take this and run," Stewart said after being declared the winner. "It's not a tainted victory by any means. [But] I still have to prove to myself that I can win a 72-hole tournament. That is still a void that I have to fill this year."

Coop remembered Stewart feeling unfulfilled by the victory.

"He called me and said he didn't get as much out of that win as he would have if it had been seventy-two holes," Coop said. "He was still quite uncertain about himself. He wasn't quite that confident as if he had won it in seventy-two holes. He told me he wasn't sure if he would have held on."

On a positive note Stewart had won, he'd found a new putter, and he had the determination to have his game in top form by June at the U.S. Open, where he'd try to write a new Payne Stewart chapter in the grand old tournament's history and erase the memory of Olympic.

CHAPTER THREE

THE U.S. OPEN

BILL STEWART TOOK PAYNE to his first U.S. Open sectional qualifier when he was 15. In line with Bill's insistence that Payne follow golf etiquette and protocol, Bill instructed his son to sign his full name on the entry form because the U.S. Open was the national championship, which demanded a formal name. Thus, Payne signed the form "William Payne Stewart" and a lasting love affair with the U.S. Open began.

But love for an Open usually is strictly a one-sided affair. Few golfers receive love in return from the tournament with which they are so enamored. Stewart learned the hard way that it takes a special player to win a U.S. Open when he found himself in contention in 1985 and again in 1986. He missed a final-round par putt at Oakland Hills' eighteenth hole in '85 that killed his chances to win, then led during the final round of the 1986 Open at Shinnecock Hills Golf Club before the cup spit out his birdie chip on 13 like a bass spitting out a hook. Stewart then missed the short par putt that followed and veteran Ray Floyd, his playing partner, turned the youngster into roadkill en route to becoming the oldest U.S. Open champion at 43.

"The pressure [at a U.S. Open] is something you have to learn to deal with," Stewart said. "And I think that that comes just over time spent [at U.S. Opens] putting yourself in that situation. I think you learn how to deal with it. . . . At Shinnecock, when Raymond won, I didn't understand I wasn't prepared [to win]."

Stewart overcame the baggage from Floyd's lesson and earned a reputation for being a player equipped to always be in the hunt at the U.S. Open. A well-earned reputation given the fact that heading into the 1999 season he'd entered the final day of a U.S. Open five times trailing by five shots or less and he'd led after three rounds twice; a fact he attributed to the mind-set that par is a good score.

"And however I go about making par, whether it's two beautiful golf shots and two putts or two ugly golf shots, a chip, and a nice holed putt, whatever it is, I accept it and take it, I take my par and go," Stewart said. "Because you're never losing to anybody, you're not losing to the field on any hole if you're making par."

Mark Lye characterized Stewart as being a "U.S. Open-type golfer" as compared to others on Tour who constantly played attack golf.

"Greg Norman is a good example," Lye said. "He could never really hang on by making pars. He just had to attack. That's probably why he never won a U.S. Open. He probably threw away more U.S. Opens because he couldn't make pars. You have to know bad holes are out there. I don't think Payne Stewart made a lot of 'others' on the scorecard. He was one of those guys who could really scramble. He was such a good chipper and sand player. Greg Norman was, too, but he would shoot his wad, he'd make X on a hole and be out of a tournament. Payne would just kind of hang in there. That's why Payne was such a good Open player, he just hung in there. And everyone knows it's the back nine on Sunday. That's when it all happens."

"Par is a good score" is a sound philosophy at a U.S. Open due to the fact no harder test of golf exists.

Each year in mid-June, one of the nation's most challenging golf courses—made even more challenging by the USGA, hosts the U.S. Open. Since 1965, the four-day tournament has ended on Father's Day. The Open is unique for the difficulty presented to golfers and the fact it is an Open that truly is open, not only to professional golfers, but to amateurs as well. Skill is the determining factor as to whether a golfer can qualify. Professional golfers who haven't earned a place in the Open and amateurs alike must survive the nationwide qualifying process. Hoping to become the proverbial "Cinderella Kid" who comes from nowhere to win the most prestigious tournament in the United States, almost seven thousand golfers take to these qualifying tournaments each year to try and shoot their way into the Open. A sectional qualifier is played in early June in which thirty-six holes are played to determine who gets the final few spots in the Open. In golf circles, this day is known as the most difficult day in golf. By the time all the qualifying has taken place and the opening round of the U.S. Open is played, just one hundred and fifty-six golfers are in the field. Of that final field, it has often been written and said that 75 percent of the players could be eliminated due to the physical and mental demands of the Open.

The Open has a history dating back over one hundred years.

The Amateur Golf Association of the United States was formed on December 22, 1894. Charter members of the organization included the Newport Golf Club, Shinnecock Hills Golf Club, the Country Club (Brookline, Mass.), St. Andrew's Golf Club (Yonkers,

N.Y.) and Chicago Golf Club. Evolving from this organization would be the United States Golf Association, which has served as the national governing body of golf since.

The first U.S. Open was played in 1895 at Rhode Island's Newport Golf and Country Club. A litmus test gauging the prestige of that first Open would be the fact it played second fiddle to the U.S. Amateur Open, which also was played in Newport that week. Horace Rawlins, a 21-year-old assistant pro at the host club, defeated a field of eleven golfers to win the first-place prize of $150 from a total purse of $335. Obviously, the event grew.

In 1898 the U.S. Open began to gain an identity of its own by being staged at a course other than the one hosting the U.S. Amateur.

Going low wasn't a prerequisite for winning early Opens.

Willie Anderson and Alex Smith finished the 1901 Open tied at a record-high 331. Anderson then won the tournament by shooting 85 in the playoff. Anderson shot an Open-record 72 in the final round of the 1904 Open to win his second consecutive Open and third in four years with a 303 total, then won his third consecutive Open in 1905.

Alex Smith, who had finished second three times, became the first to break 300 for the seventy-two-hole Open when he won the 1906 Open.

British golfers dominated the Open's early years until 1911 when Johnny McDermott became the first American to win the tournament. McDermott's victory proved to be a harbinger for a shift from British dominance to a sport dominated by Americans. Two years after McDermott's victory Francis Ouimet won the Open, which is remembered as the Open that captured America's attention.

Today, the Open is recognized as the national championship for the United States. Personified in the tournament's open qualifying process are the beliefs of a country that has always believed anybody with gumption, talent, and hard work had a shot to accomplish anything. Ouimet's story helped to establish this theme.

Ouimet had a blue-collar upbringing. He began caddying at the Country Club in Brookline at age nine for twenty-five cents a round and learned to play the game on a modified pasture behind his house, which stood across Clyde Street from the Country Club. In the early morning hours Ouimet could occasionally be found sneaking in a few holes on the prestigious course.

By age twenty, Ouimet earned a spot in the 1913 Open played on his turf, the Country Club in Brookline. The former caddie's greatest golf accomplishment to that point had been winning the Massachusetts state amateur tournament earlier in the summer of 1913. He almost passed on playing in the Open in September because he'd used up all of his allotted vacation time at the sporting goods store where he worked. Fortunately for golf history, Ouimet's boss learned his employee had qualified for the Open and gave him time off to play for the national championship on a course with which he had grown so familiar.

Seasoned British professionals Harry Vardon and Ted Ray finished their final rounds of the tournament ahead of Ouimet tied for the lead at 304 and content that they would battle among themselves the following day in a playoff to decide the Open. It's safe to say the amateur Ouimet hardly registered as a threat to join the pair. With two holes remaining, Ouimet needed to birdie one of the holes to reach the playoff. On 17 he hit his approach to within fifteen feet to set off a celebration that did not cease when he stood over his putt. The crowd noise did nothing to distract the youngster, who sank the winding, downhill putt for a birdie. When Ouimet made par on 18 to qualify for the playoff the fans carried him from the green on their shoulders. Nobody expected him to have any chance in a play-off against the golfing heavyweights; no amateur had ever won the Open.

Ray won the previous year's British Open at Muirfield and Vardon had won five British Opens and the 1900 U.S. Open. Even today Vardon is recognized as one of the purest ball strikers in the history of the game and easily one of the game's greatest players. He popularized the overlapping grip where the pinky finger of the right hand overlaps the index finger of the left hand. Appropriately the grip came to be known as the "Vardon grip."

Approximately five thousand spectators followed the trio during the playoff on a soggy day. The atmosphere felt like a modern football game given the raucous cheers for Ouimet, who cruised to victory defeating Vardon by five strokes and Ray by six.

News of Ouimet's victory was celebrated coast to coast. The working-class kid's victory changed the perception of golf being a wealthy man's sport dominated by British golfers. Ouimet also sparked a great interest in golf in the United States. In 1913 an estimated 350,000 people played golf in the United States; ten years later the legions had expanded to over two million.

The format of the Open changed over the years. Initially the tournament was nine holes in 1895, but by 1898 the USGA expanded to seventy-two holes for the championship with golfers playing thirty-six holes on two days. The format changed again in 1926 to eighteen holes on two days followed by thirty-six on the final day. In 1965 the Open moved to its present format of four days with eighteen holes each day.

Prior to the 1999 U.S. Open, only nineteen players had won the tournament more than once. The list of multiyear winners reads like a who's who of golf including Ben Hogan, Bobby Jones, and Jack Nicklaus, each of whom won four times. Hale Irwin won the Open three times, while Walter Hagen, Gene Sarazen, Cary Middlecoff, Julius Boros, Billy Casper, and Lee Trevino all won twice. In the ten years leading up to the 1999 Open, three players won the Open twice: Curtis Strange, Ernie Els, and Lee Janzen.

Many of these golf greats established lasting legacies with their performances in the Open.

Jones battled fierce heat of over 100 degrees while competing in the 1930 Open at the Interlachen Country Club in Minneapolis. Following the first round, Jones had to have his tie cut from around his neck because the sweat-soaked knot could not be undone, but he persevered to beat MacDonald Smith by two strokes to win the third leg of his Grand Slam. Not to be forgotten was Jones's drive on the seventeenth hole with two holes to play. He had a three-shot lead over Smith, but his drive could not be found. Facing a potentially devastating situation where he would have to go back to the tee as per the lost ball rule, Jones received help from Prescott Bush, the grandfather of President George W. Bush, who served as president and secretary of the USGA. Bush ruled the ball had gone into the water, thereby penalizing Jones just one shot, but not the distance. Jones took a drop at the spot where Bush said the ball entered the hazard and made a double bogey. He finished his day with a birdie at 18 to claim victory. He completed his sweep of the majors by winning the U.S. Amateur at Merion, which was considered a major at the time; the British Amateur and British Open were the other two. Having won the Grand Slam, Jones retired from competitive golf at the ripe old age of 28.

Ben Hogan played his first Open in 1936 and did not make the cut. He went on to win four in his career, but none would be as memorable as his 1950 victory at Merion Golf Club in Ardmore, Pennsylvania. A little over a year earlier, Hogan and his wife, Valerie, had been driving east of Pecos, Texas, in light fog when they had a horrific crash with a Greyhound bus. Hogan mangled his left leg and broke his collarbone, pelvis, and a rib in the accident that nearly killed him. His chances of playing golf again seemed remote. Gradually he came back, but effects from the accident could be seen at the Open where Hogan limped in pain around the course. Somehow he managed to get through thirty-six holes on the final day, executing a miraculous 1-iron shot to the eighteenth green followed by a two-putt to get into a playoff with George Fazio and Lloyd Mangrum. Despite having to deal with the distraction of having his 1-iron and spikes stolen, Hogan went out and shot 69 in the playoff to win his second Open.

Arnold Palmer sat in fifteenth place facing a seven-shot deficit when he teed off on the final day of the 1960 Open at Cherry Hills Country Club in Englewood, Colorado. Hoping to make something happen, he decided to try and drive the green on the 346-yard first hole—and he pulled it off. He missed his eagle putt, but his reckless abandon helped him shoot 65, good enough to beat Nicklaus by two shots and expand the legions in "Arnie's Army."

Congressional Country Club in Bethesda, Maryland, hosted the 1964 Open, which marked the last time thirty-six holes were played on the final day, Saturday, leaving Sunday open for a possible playoff. Temperatures were close to 100 degrees and the humidity was unbearable, turning the tournament into a survival of the fittest.

Ken Venturi, a 33-year-old pro from San Francisco, began the day six shots behind second-round leader Tommy Jacobs and posted a 66 in his morning round. But the heat had already begun to bite into Venturi. He began to shake while walking up the seventeenth fairway and debated whether or not he would be wise to play in the afternoon round, forfeiting any chance to win the tournament. A doctor gave Venturi water and salt tablets after his morning round and warned him about the dangers of continuing. Ignoring the warning, Venturi continued accompanied by his doctor, who administered ice packs to Venturi as he continued to wilt in the heat. Somehow Venturi managed to shoot an even-par 70 in the afternoon round to win by four shots over Jacobs. A young Raymond Floyd played with Venturi that day and when Venturi sank his final putt, a visibly moved Floyd reached into the cup to retrieve the ball while Venturi raised his arms in the air and said, "My God, I've won the Open."

Nicklaus's first Open championship came at Palmer's expense when he won a playoff at Oakmont in 1962. The famed rivals fought it out again at Baltusrol in 1967 and Nicklaus won again with a final-round 65. But the lasting snapshot of Nicklaus came in 1972 at Pebble Beach. Playing No. 17 on the final day, he cut a 1-iron through the wind. The ball struck the pin and stopped six inches from the hole, helping Nicklaus earn his third Open championship.

Nicklaus fell victim to one of the great shots in Open history in 1982 at Pebble Beach.

On the brink of collecting his fifth Open victory, the Golden Bear sat in the clubhouse tied with Tom Watson, who stood on the tee at 17 reflecting on how to play one of the toughest par-3s in golf. All he needed to do was hit a 209-yard shot to a two-tiered green with a strong breeze from the Pacific Ocean blowing in his face. Watson chose a 2-iron and he hit it into the heavy rough left of the pin. Facing what appeared to be an impossible shot from a downhill lie to a sloping green, Watson refused to cower, telling his caddie: "I'm not going to get it close—I'm going to make it."

Using a sand wedge, Watson boldly slid the face of his club through the tall grass underneath his ball. The ball popped up, took two bounces on the green, and rolled into the hole. Watson began to move before the ball reached the cup then danced around the green pointing to his caddie while yelling, "I told you." He parlayed his good fortune with a birdie at 18 to beat Nicklaus by two shots.

Johnny Miller accomplished a remarkable feat at the 1973 Open at the Oakmont Country Club in Oakmont, Pennsylvania. He followed a third-round 76 with a 63 on Sunday, hitting every green in regulation en route to a one-shot victory. His final-round score remains the lowest in Open history and tied the record for the lowest-ever Open round.

Irwin secured his third Open title in 1990 at Medinah Country Club in Medinah, Illinois, by virtue of a sizzling 31 on the back nine of the Sunday's round to earn a spot in a Monday playoff with Mike Donald. Irwin's final stroke to his final-round masterpiece was a forty-five-foot putt on 18. When Irwin won the playoff he surpassed Floyd as the oldest player to win an Open at age 45 and the fifth player to win the championship three or more times.

Being a great golfer has never insured one of winning the Open. Take Sam Snead, who won more golf tournaments than any other player in history, taking eighty-one PGA Tour titles, three Masters, three PGA Championships, and a British Open. But Snead never managed to win a U.S. Open.

Snead's first attempt to win one came in 1937 at Oakland Hills Country Club in Birmingham, Michigan, when the 24-year-old shot an opening-round 69. He finished the tournament five-under par prompting golf legend Tommy Armour to tell him, "Laddie, you've just won yourself the Open." But Ralph Guldahl posted a 69 to win by two shots. Guldahl went on to win the 1938 Open at Cherry Hills in Englewood, Colorado—the last time the winner of a U.S. Open won wearing a tie—and Snead was well on his way toward a career of Open heartbreaks. In 1939 at the Philadelphia Country Club, Snead needed to make a par on the seventy-second hole to win. Unfortunately for Snead, he did not know all he needed was par, so he played aggressive and made a triple bogey to finish fifth. He later talked about the disappointment he felt, noting, "That night I was ready to go out with a gun and pay somebody to shoot me."

Adding to Snead's Open frustrations was his loss to Lew Worsham in 1947 at the St. Louis Country Club. Snead missed a two-footer for par on the eighteenth hole of a playoff to lose.

Despite never winning an Open, Snead played some wonderful golf in coming up short. He ranks on the all-time Open top-ten lists in sub-par rounds; rounds played; years played; and top-three, top-five, and top-ten finishes. But Snead hardly had the market cornered on Open heartbreaks.

Byron Nelson, who won the 1939 Open after Snead folded on the final hole, bogeyed the final hole of the 1946 Open at Canterbury to fall into a three-way tie with Mangrum and Vic Ghezzi. Mangrum won the playoff and Nelson retired at the end of the 1946 season.

When Palmer made the turn at Olympic in 1966 and his scorecard read 32, he disregarded the rest of the field and decided his opponent was Hogan. Palmer already had set the British Open record with a 276 at Troon in 1962. If Palmer shot a one-over 36 on Olympic's back nine, he could break Hogan's U.S. Open record of 276.

Palmer refused to play the final nine holes conservatively and paid dearly, shooting 39. In most cases Palmer still would have walked away with the championship after shooting 71, but Billy Casper shot 32 on the back nine to force a playoff that Casper won the next day. Palmer never won another major.

No golfer has ever won five U.S. Opens, but Jones might have had he not called a two-shot penalty on himself in the 1925 Open at Worcester Country Club in Worcester, Massachusetts. Widely praised for his integrity, Jones downplayed what he had done by saying, "You might as well praise a man for not robbing a bank as to praise him for playing by the rules."

Chen Tze-Chung, better known to the golfing world as T.C. Chen, felt the pendulum of the golf Gods swing both ways during the 1985 Open at Oakland Hills.

Chen put himself into the Open record books on the second hole of the opening round by recording a double eagle on the 527-yard par-5, the only double eagle in Open history. The shot propelled the former sailor in the Taiwan navy to the top of the leaderboard. Chen had extended his lead to four shots after four holes on the final day before one of the Open's most famous snafus occurred. Chen hit a perfect drive on the fifth hole, but his wedge shot to the green strayed into deep rough. When he tried to chip out, the ball seemed to hang in front of him until he hit the ball a second time on his follow-through, earning a one-stroke penalty for the "double hit." Chen made a quadruple bogey on the hole to lose the lead and, basically, the tournament. The costly shot earned Chen the Tour nickname of "Two Chips" Chen, while to this day golfers around the country refer to double hitting a shot as "T.C. Chenning it."

Orville Moody is the most unlikely winner of an Open in the last half century. A former army sergeant with a cross-handed putting style, Moody had never won a PGA Tour event when he won the 1969 Open at Champion in Houston. Oddly enough, Moody never won another title in fourteen years on Tour.

Moody has plenty of company on the list of unlikely players to win the U.S. Open.

Sam Parks Jr. was a club pro at South Hills Country Club in Uniontown, Pennsylvania, just up the road from Oakmont, site of the 1935 Open. Club pros aren't known for making runs at the U.S. Open, but the intrepid Parks did not feel like an underdog. He knew

Oakmont from playing the course during his college days and he'd practiced on the course almost daily during the month leading up to the Open. He believed he could win and did, finishing at eleven-over 299 to claim the championship.

In 1954 at Baltusrol, Ed Furgol caught everyone's attention with an unorthodox swing stemming from a childhood accident that permanently bent his arm at the elbow. Furgol could not hit the ball far, but his deadly accuracy led him to a one-shot victory over Gene Littler. The dark-horse win came during a year when two significant additions to the Open were made. Every hole was roped off from tee to green to help control the growing crowds and, most significant, the Open was shown live to a national television audience for the first time.

Other Open long-shot victories included those by Cyril Walker, a 118-pound heavyweight who beat Jones by three shots at Oakland Hills in 1924; Johnny Goodman, a 23-year old amateur, who beat Guldahl by one shot in 1933; and Tony Manero, who shot 282 at Baltusrol to win in 1936.

Andy North is a breed apart in Open lore. He would fall into the "nobody" category for winning the Open save for the fact he won the championship twice.

North won the 1978 Open at Cherry Hills after overcoming the anxiety of knowing the tournament was his if he didn't self-destruct, an inevitable occurrence when such thoughts enter the conscious mind. North's fate came down to having to sink a four-footer on the final hole to avoid blowing the four-shot lead he had enjoyed with four holes to play. Not once, but twice, North stood over his putt on 18 only to nervously move away. If he missed he would have been thrust into a playoff with J. C. Snead and Dave Stockton. North finally gained his composure and sank his bogey putt for the win.

Chen's collapse helped deliver North's second Open victory in

1985, bringing his win total on Tour to three and causing many to classify North's wins as lightning striking the same place twice. A more fitting legacy would remember North as the perfect U.S. Open player: a guy who knew how to protect par and minimize damage.

Gary Koch believes some golfers are better equipped for the U.S. Open than others.

"If you take the premise that the USGA thinks par is a good score, there are certain players whose games are more suited to shooting a score around par than they are shooting real low scores," Koch said. "Andy North, who I played golf with at the University of Florida, is a classic example. Andy was never a guy to shoot a lot of real low scores. That was just not in his makeup, whether it was in his personality, he wasn't aggressive enough, or his ball striking wasn't good enough, I'm sure there were a number of reasons why. But he enjoyed a more difficult golf course, when par was a good score. So you go into a U.S. Open with that mind-set to make a lot of pars, and that's how you tend to play anyway, yeah, you've got a chance to do real well."

U.S. Open–type courses are every bit as much a part of the tournament's history as the players themselves. Baltusrol and Oakmont have hosted the most Opens with seven each. Bethpage State Park's Black Course provided the longest course in Open history, playing 7,214 yards, while Shinnecock's 4,423 yard course was the shortest in 1896. (Shinnecock played to 6,944 yards when it hosted the 1995 Open.)

Typically the very nature of an Open brings the inherent understanding that creating shots from seemingly impossible conditions is part of the landscape. Many of these conditions are brought on by the USGA, which runs the Open, and not the PGA, which runs the other Tour events.

Among the USGA's duties today are to conduct golf's national championships. Included in these are the U.S. Open, the U.S. Women's Open, the U.S. Senior Open, the ten national amateur championships, and the state team championships. The USGA also helps conduct three international competitions: the Walker Cup and Curtis Cup matches, and the Men's and Women's World Amateur Team Championships.

The USGA is a nonprofit organization run by golfers for the benefit of golfers. Other services and duties performed by the organization include providing a handicap system for scoring that allows all golfers to compete on an equal basis, maintaining equipment standards, helping to preserve golf history, writing and interpreting the rules of golf, and producing the rules of amateur status.

Despite all the USGA's goodwill, it seems every year that at least one player expresses displeasure with the state of the course where the Open is played. Hazeltine Golf Club, host of the 1970 Open, is perhaps the most vocally-abused course in Open history. Dave Hill, who finished second behind Tony Jacklin, lashed out when asked to comment on the course, saying all it lacked was "eighty acres of corn and a few cows."

"Every year the masochists or sadists of the USGA try to get the greens as absolutely hard as they can and grow the rough as high as possibly allowed," Larry Guest said. "This makes conditions extremely difficult. The players always bitch and complain about the conditions, but they wouldn't miss [the Open] for the world. That's why the ones who don't have a spot will go out and subject themselves to thirty-six-hole qualifying rounds in June someplace where it's usually 98 degrees. So they know what they're getting into. But one U.S. Open victory is probably worth ten regular Tour events. Everybody remembers Andy North for winning two, and Orville Moody. Nobody earns that kind of legacy for winning the Milwaukee Open one time."

Koch laughed when asked about players complaining about Open conditions.

"If there's ever going to be stuff to complain about, it's going to be at a U.S. Open," Koch said. "The rough's longer than the players are used to seeing, the greens are usually harder, they're usually faster, and the fairways are usually narrower. And remember, you're talking about a group of guys who play on some wonderfully conditioned golf courses most of the time in perfect weather conditions as they rattle around the country. And yeah, the U.S. Open's setup is a lot harder than what they're used to seeing. Some guys react well to it, others don't."

The perception that the USGA is out to show up the professionals is perpetuated annually, but this perception is not necessarily reality.

"Having been around the USGA the last several years doing the U.S. Open telecasts, I don't get the impression that the golf course setup is intended to embarrass anybody," Koch said. "I think the philosophy, and this is just from what I hear and what I observe, is 'This is the national championship and it needs to be difficult in order to separate it from other events.' But at the same time, if a guy plays well, he should be able to shoot a good score somewhere around par. And that's kind of their philosophy that par is a good score."

There always will be some debate as to which is the most important tournament for a professional to win, the U.S. Open or the Masters.

"I think winning the U.S. Open just carries a certain panache," David Whitley said. "And there's the appeal that anybody can play in it. It sort of lets you dream, like, 'Hey, if I just get hot this one or two weeks, I can be teeing it up next to Tiger Woods, Justin Leonard, all these great names. But I think every major has a different appeal, that's just one of those matter-of-taste things. Nobody will match the Masters for the history. You go to Augusta, walk around and see it and feel it, it is unique and different. Even the most cynical people I know change when they go to Augusta. You can still buy a pimento cheese sandwich for a dollar there. It's not about the money. You couldn't even buy the wrapper for a dollar at the U.S. Open. When that's your starting point, that makes the Masters unique in comparison to any sporting event."

Koch believes preference is a matter of taste.

"I think which of the two tournaments a player favors is going to vary with every player," Koch said. "There's a uniqueness you find at the Masters you don't find at any other event. Consequently, some guys get enamored with the atmosphere and history of that event and they want to win it more than any other. Personally, the U.S. Open is the national championship of our country and to me the most important golf tournament there is."

Lee Janzen clearly has a favorite.

"It says United States Open on it," Janzen said. "And being an American-born golfer, I just know that it has more special meaning than any other majors. I remember watching it as a kid, and the Masters hasn't been around as long. This is our national championship. I think that the Masters has a shorter field. They don't let all the good players in. I'm not putting down how well you have to play to win the Masters, I just think [the U.S. Open] is the best tournament to win."

Payne Stewart believed the factors making the U.S. Open the most special among tournaments to win made the pressure to win one even greater.

"Well, at any major, there's more pressure than at the rest of the golf tournaments we play throughout the year," Stewart said. "And I think that is because of—there's only four so-called majors a year.

They're generally the most prestigious tournaments to win. And the United States Open, it's our open championship. Just as you hear the Europeans talk about the British Open; that's their open championship. Well, this is ours. And I'm an American, and it's a proud—it was a very proud moment for me in '91, when I got to hoist that trophy. It was very special. And the feeling you get, you can't really describe it, unless you understand the competition we go through."

CHAPTER FOUR

NO. 1 VS. NO. 2

FOLLOWING HIS VICTORY at the AT&T, Payne Stewart blended into the busy scenery of the PGA Tour.

He missed the cut at the Nissan Open and bowed out in the first round of the Andersen Consulting Match Play Championship before the Tour's Florida swing in March. Playing in the Honda Classic in Coral Springs, Florida, he finished second by two shots behind Vijay Singh then tied for thirteenth at the Bay Hill Invitational in Orlando before tying for twenty-third at the Players Championship.

Despite the marked improvements Stewart had seen in his game, the golfing universe was blinded by the aura cast by No. 1 vs. No. 2, Tiger Woods and David Duval. They represented the Tour's next generation. If Stewart wanted to win another U.S. Open or any other tournaments on Tour he had the daunting task of eclipsing these formidable opponents.

Prior to the 1999 Masters, the first major of the season, the much-anticipated showdown between Woods and Duval captured the imagination of all golf fans. No matter what the sport, the public longs for a great athlete to have a great rival. Joe DiMaggio had Ted Williams, Bill Russell had Wilt Chamberlain, Larry Bird had Magic Johnson, even Seabiscuit had War Admiral.

Duval and Woods looked like the contemporary answer to the black-and-white days of Arnold Palmer and Jack Nicklaus. During the heyday of that storied rivalry, Nicklaus and Palmer could be found on the course the same day forty or fifty times a year. Palmer won seven majors and sixty Tour titles and Nicklaus won eighteen majors and seventy times on Tour. From 1963 to 1966 they flip-flopped winning the Masters. Palmer was in his prime and Nicklaus was entering his when this rivalry captured a nation. When would Duval-Woods finally make the neck-and-neck journey down the final nine on the last day of a major? A battle where the stakes were high and shots were exchanged in "take that" fashion while America watched, glued to their televisions. Both were under the age of thirty and perched for the long-awaited showdown to happen.

Duval had a unique swing, thanks in large part to the wisdom of his father. Daddy Duval considered altering David's strong grip and his unorthodox swiveling-head action on the downswing, but after factoring in the results of his son's flowing, natural swing, he wisely concluded a hands-off approach would be best.

Duval arrived on the Tour in 1993 with great expectations after a stellar career at Georgia Tech. Included in his amateur accomplishments were the 1989 U.S. Junior Amateur Championship, making the cut at the 1990 U.S. Open, and the summer after his junior year he held a two-shot lead after 54 holes at the BellSouth Classic. Duval became the third player in NCAA history to be named first-team

All-America four times; Phil Mickelson and Gary Halberg also accomplished the feat.

Duval had the look of an assassin with his wraparound sunglasses and matching cool demeanor. The killer look produced the nickname "Darth Vader" for the black-armored villain of *Star Wars* fame.

"David is a complex guy," said *Palm Beach Post* golf writer Craig Dolch. "His image doesn't befit him, but I don't think he really cares. He just doesn't let a lot of people in. There's a lot of depth to him. He reads a lot—and we're not talking Tank McNamara. He has other interests besides golf."

Added Doug Ferguson: "Most golfers don't read Ayn Rand. He was literary and a good thinker. One of the best things about him was that he truly listened to a question [posed to him by the media]. And if it was kind of a dumb question or he didn't understand it, he would ask you what you meant by the question. Sometimes by doing that it sounded like he was dressing somebody down."

Rooted behind Duval's steely veneer was a private person carrying some hurtful baggage collected during his youth. Duval's twelve-year-old brother, Brent, was diagnosed with a blood disorder known as aplastic anemia and died from a graft-versus-host reaction shortly after receiving bone marrow from David. David was just nine at the time and grew inward, harboring deep thoughts about whether he had contributed to his brother's death.

Included in the casualties of Brent's death was Bob and Diane Duval's marriage. Duval's parents separated and later divorced. David found solace on the driving range at Timuquana where he could mash golf balls for hours on end.

Duval had the look of a champion from his swing to his tough mental makeup. Anyone who knew anything about golf forecast he would be a big winner on Tour. But finding the winner's circle did not come easy.

While Duval had been much heralded before joining the Tour, any hype he received paled in comparison to the advance billing accorded Eldrick Tiger Woods.

Woods had been a prodigy since appearing on the Mike Douglas Show at age 2. At age 3 he'd carded a 48 for nine holes and by age 5 he appeared in *Golf Digest* magazine.

Long before Woods knew who David Duval was, he identified that conquering the Golden Bear would be his career goal. Even before he reached his teens, Woods's bedroom wall was decorated with a Jack Nicklaus poster, which conjured images of green jackets, Claret Jugs, and U.S. Open championships. Conquering Nicklaus would earn Woods recognition as the best to ever play the game.

Nicklaus served as a measuring stick for greatness in the depths of Woods's consciousness.

Woods already had scored several victories against Nicklaus on his self-imposed scoreboard. At age 10 Nicklaus shot a 51 on the first nine holes he ever played; Woods shot a 48 on nine holes at 3. Nicklaus won his first U.S. Amateur championship at 19 and claimed his second at 21; Woods won his first U.S. Amateur at 18, added a second when he was 19, and collected a third at age 20 to become the first ever to win the event three times.

After winning the 1996 Amateur, Woods turned pro for the remainder of the 1996 season. Nike saw Woods as the perfect pitchman for their line of golf products and heaped a five-year, $40 million contract on him prior to his first professional tournament, the 1996 Milwaukee Open. Woods won twice in his first seven tournaments, earning enough money to place 23rd on the money list and enough to bypass PGA Tour Qualifying School. Suddenly golf had a star with drawing power capable of luring people to the sport who had never been interested in the past.

Said Stewart after Woods shot a final-round 66 to beat him in the 1996 Disney Classic: "It's the first time I've played with him. He's the shot in the arm the Tour needs. He's going to be out here a long time, and y'all are going to be writing about him for some time."

If he hadn't already had an auspicious enough beginning, Woods trumped all expectations at the 1997 Masters, turning the golf world on its ear with a record-setting performance. Woods made a mockery of Augusta National, winning by twelve shots en route to claiming the coveted green jacket to earn his first major at age 21, a year earlier than Nicklaus, who won his first major, the U.S. Open, at 22.

While the golfing world marveled at Woods's brilliance, the perfectionist in Woods told him he needed to make major changes to his swing. Consider the magnitude of such an assessment. Golfers from those at the most elite country clubs to those on the public links all wanted to be like Tiger because of the swing he wanted to change. A swing Woods had used to win four times in his first fifteen Tour events. Either Woods had major stones for daring to try and build on what most of the golf public thought to be perfection or perhaps he'd simply lost his marbles. At any rate, Woods went to his coach Butch Harmon seeking to build a swing that could "hold up" over a period of time.

"Even though I had a lot of success, I wasn't happy with the way I was swinging," Woods would later say. "If you look at it, it was either I was winning or I was way down the list. And when you're hot, I mean anybody can play with a swing when they're hot. That's not a problem. But it's when you're off, are you able to still shoot 69s, 70s? I didn't have the swing for that. I didn't have the game for that. I didn't have the shots. So it's just a gradual process, always try to get better."

Harmon told Woods such a project would be risky. He also told him the rewards would be worthwhile and that patience was needed. No golfer, not even the great Tiger Woods, could hope to groove a new swing overnight. And given the lofty platform on which Woods already stood, he could expect to raise many questions about the state of his game. Why wasn't he dominating the Tour like he had in his first fifteen tournaments? Was he a flash in the pan? Could he get it back? Had Woods gambled and ruined the best swing in golf?

"I think there certainly was an awareness among those of us who watched [Woods] that there were deficiencies in his game even though he was able to run away at the Masters," Koch said.

Woods went for it and while the Tiger was away, Duval played.

Duval teed it up in eighty-six tournaments on the U.S. Tour before claiming his first victory at the 1997 Michelob Championship. Finally acquiring a taste for victory, he went on a tear, winning the next two tournaments, the Disney Classic, and the season-ending Tour Championship. Duval's taste for victory carried over into the 1998 season when he captured victory four times, earning a Tour-record $2.6 million and winning the Vardon Trophy for the lowest scoring average.

"The greatest thing about Duval was, A, his power, and, B, his simplicity," Ferguson said. "You could just see the fact he was very good. He had a tremendous, big power fade of a drive. And it looked even better when he had that head turn ahead of the ball when he swung. I remember one year he made a statement, it was simple but profound. 'I hate making double bogeys.'"

Duval strived to avoid blowing up on any given hole.

"He never put himself in a position where he was going to shoot an ugly number," Ferguson said. "He never carried a sixty-degree wedge because it was only going to tempt him to hit shots he had no business hitting.

"He was not Mickelson, or Tiger, who were amazing with their wedges, but he was a very good wedge player. His philosophy was always, 'I'm not going to take a 3-iron and go at that flag. I'm going to go at the middle of the green.' And when he missed the green, he didn't try to hit a flop shot. He would hit it up there to six or eight feet, because he could make those putts."

Ferguson remembered observing how popular Duval had grown.

"At a gala dinner at the President's Cup, they had Greg Norman, Tiger, and Duval," Ferguson said. "David got the loudest applause of the night. I think people liked the fact he was a bit of a mystery man. You never saw his eyes wearing those glasses. You never saw him smile. It wasn't because he was angry. It was because I think he was good and he knew it. After shooting low numbers and winning all those tournaments, he was like, 'That's what I'm supposed to be doing.' And he didn't see it as this big deal that everybody else did."

Woods won just once during the period between July of 1997 and February of 1999. The questions came, the frustration mounted. Woods stayed the course until the day finally arrived when the transition period finished running its course. Woods's previous swing consisted of a roaring hip-and-shoulder rotation on his downswing that could produce an epic drive or major trouble when his arms couldn't keep up with the rest of his body. Working with Harmon brought about a more efficient swing. Control came with the package without short-circuiting the power.

Duval opened the 1999 season with a victory in the Mercedes Championship, shooting a five-under 68 on Sunday and setting a new tournament scoring record on the Kapalua Plantation course. Duval's nine-stroke margin of victory over Mark O'Meara and Billy Mayfair was the largest on Tour since Woods's Masters victory.

"He's kicking everybody's butt," Woods said. "Including mine."

Golf's popularity had grown, a fact many attributed to Woods, who had a multiracial heritage and a charisma that drew viewers to the sport; more Americans than ever were heading to the links. And more than ever before, they watched on TV, leading to a lucrative new $400 million, four-year TV deal for the PGA Tour. For the first time, every round of the forty-seven official Tour events would be televised.

The Mercedes Championship personified America's new obsession with golf. Due to the time difference in Hawaii, the tournament played out in prime time live on ESPN, which had increased its golf coverage by 45 percent in 1999. Corporate America's thirst for the Tour was seemingly insatiable. Reflecting the corporate climate were the purses. Total prize money hit a record $132 million in 1999, which represented a 40 percent increase from the previous year.

And here was Duval, the guy in the funny glasses who could take it to Tiger Woods. America watched and marveled at Duval's dismantling of the Tour. Even if Duval was playing the best golf, Woods remained the No. 1 ranked golfer in the world according to the Official World Golf Ranking, the complicated system for ranking players worldwide. Points are calculated in a rolling fifty-two-week cycle and are counted double for the current year. Each major is worth fifty points to the winner, thirty for second place, twenty for third, all the way down to one point for everyone who makes the cut. Points for other tournaments are based on weighting of the tournament as determined by how many of the top one hundred players are in the field. Bonus points are awarded to any tournament with the top thirty money winners on its respective tour in the field.

With golf's emergence all over the globe, these rankings began to take on added importance in 1998 when, for the first time, the USGA created a new exemption for the U.S. Open by taking the top twenty in the world rankings. Augusta National followed suit by announcing the top fifty players in the world at the end of the year would be invited to the Masters.

After winning the Mercedes, Duval took a week off to go skiing in Sun Valley, Idaho, before resuming his executioner's work of the Tour's best.

Duval's assault on the No. 1 position continued at the Bob Hope Chrysler Classic, where he trailed by seven shots when he teed off for the final round of the five-day tournament. In chilling fashion Duval cobbled together eleven birdies and an eagle to put up an unbelievable score of 59.

Making the feat all the more impressive was the fact his round contained no miracle shots, or even a long putt. Duval's most dramatic sequence unfolded on the par-5 eighteenth, his final hole of the ninety-hole tournament. After a 320-yard drive, Duval had 225 yards to the pin. He hit a 5-iron shot that landed on the front of the green and rolled to within six feet. Only when Duval sank the putt that broke left did he show any emotion. He pumped his fist, raised his arms, and smiled.

Talk about snakebit, how about Steve Pate? The only way he could lose was if Duval shot 59; Pate lost by one shot.

The tale of the tape for Duval's historic day: He hit eleven of thirteen fairways in regulation, seventeen of eighteen greens in regulation, and he had only 23 putts.

Duval's 59 allowed him to join Al Geiberger and Chip Beck in the elite group of players to have broken 60 in a Tour event. Geiberger shot 59 in the second round of the Memphis Classic in 1977 and Beck shot 59 in the third round of the 1991 Las Vegas Invitational.

Having added the Chrysler Classic to his list of wins, Duval had won nine of his last twenty-eight tournaments and was fifty-two strokes under par after playing a hundred and sixty-two holes in

1999. Still, Woods ranked two-tenths of a percentage point ahead of Duval in the World Ranking.

Then came the Player's Championship in March.

Duval grew up near the TPC at Sawgrass and played the course like only he could see the light. He won by two strokes over Scott Gump thanks to the way he played the ever-dangerous par-3 seventeenth known universally as the "island hole." A fitting description since successfully playing the hole translated to being able to land a lofted shot onto a green surrounded by water. The frayed nerves of a golfer trying to avoid disaster on his final two holes of the day always added to the drama of watching players hit to the seventeenth, particularly on Sunday when the outcome of the tournament was on the line.

Stewart had been in the hunt when he stepped to the tee at 17 and proceeded to dunk two balls into the water en route to a quintuple bogey to send him from third place to twenty-third with a final-round 78.

In stark contrast, Duval hit a pitching wedge to within six feet of the pin and made the putt for a birdie.

Woods needed to finish in sixth place or higher to retain his No. 1 ranking. Instead he bogeyed 18 for a final round 75 and tenth place. Duval had moved into the top spot in front of his hometown fans, and ceremoniously, on the same day as his father's first win on the Senior PGA Tour at the Emerald Coast Classic. Woods had been ranked No. 1 for forty-one consecutive weeks.

Duval and Woods "were No. 1 and No. 2 and they were friendly to each other," Mark Lye said. "And I just thought it was going to be a great deal between them. I was waiting for [Phil] Mickelson to get on in there, too. And he did, but he never reached what David Duval did.

"David was dominating in a lot of stats. He was long, he was accurate. He was a decent putter and a great chipper. You put those numbers together and you're going to do it. . . . He was the man. He'd won a bunch of tournaments. He was on fire."

Added media responsibilities accompanied Duval's newly earned No. 1 ranking. Woods acted as though he didn't mind having some of the media focus shift from his shoulders to Duval's. Since joining the Tour Woods had been bombarded by the media. Duval's ascent to the throne meant he would be the one who had to balance his preparation for tournaments with all the new external trimmings of being No. 1.

Financial opportunities were part of the spoils for being in the top spot. And fame is another by-product, but could be a plus or a minus depending on the player. Clearly, one of the big negatives of being No. 1 was the responsibility to serve as a spokesman for the Tour. When a player is No. 1, he instantly becomes the voice of the PGA Tour. If a hot topic is on the front burner, he is the guy at the podium in the media tent addressing questions about that topic.

Duval put on a good company face when asked about the new role.

"That's part of our responsibility as professionals," he said. "[Being No. 1] doesn't bother me, no. I embrace it. I believe it's my responsibility now. I firmly believe it's my duty to be here."

Duval sounded like a man trying to convince himself he was comfortable in the top spot. Nobody bought it. While Woods seemed to embrace the role of being No. 1, Duval resembled a long-tailed cat in a room full of rocking chairs.

"Those guys are such opposite guys," Dolch said. "David, it took him longer to get to the top. Tiger came out and went there right away. Tiger seemed more comfortable with the attention; he was used to being the man in the spotlight. Whereas David, he kind of recoiled. You could just sense he felt a lot less comfortable. He just seemed kind of perplexed by all the attention he got."

Lye said the collateral damage of being No. 1 never suited Duval.

"David's not a socially gifted person as far as being comfortable in a situation like Tiger would be or Jack Nicklaus or Arnold," Lye said. "He doesn't handle the press fluently. He's not a bad guy. He's just not a guy you can wrap your arms around. I like the guy. He's liked by the players."

Ferguson believes Duval confused some by saying he didn't like being No. 1.

"I don't think that's even close to being accurate," Ferguson said. "He takes great pride in his game. He wanted to be the best player. . . . But he didn't understand why, after all these years and he's No. 1 and suddenly his opinion mattered and before it didn't when he was only winning a couple of tournaments."

Heading into the Masters, the much hyped showdown between Woods and Duval quieted to a certain extent to favor a storyline about Duval claiming his first major at Augusta.

After Duval's victory in the Players Championship, he won the following week at the BellSouth Classic near his college stomping grounds in Atlanta. The win gave him four wins in the young season.

"I'm just amazed," said Tour pro Steve Stricker. "Who would have thought he'd win four times before the Masters? Nobody should be able to do that, not the way the game is today with so many good players out here. . . .

"Sooner or later, you'd think he'd start thinking about it all and come down off that cloud, but it doesn't look like that's going to happen. The rest of us have to keep working hard just to stay close."

Said the reigning U.S. Open champion Lee Janzen: "He's beating us, that's the negative. The positive is he's showing us the sky is the limit."

From the players' perspective, Duval looked like the favorite to win at Augusta.

"David is getting into a little bit of an intimidation factor," Fred Funk said. "And there's just no question that he's going to keep winning. I'd never make one guy the favorite here, but how can you not say he's the guy? Everyone is talking about him, and it's pretty neat to see."

Mark Calcavecchia told the *Atlanta Journal-Constitution* that having four wins in a decade would be nice for most pros, but "four in three and a half months? That's unbelievable. He's got to be the man to beat this week."

Calcavecchia even dared to mention Duval in the same breath as the sacred Golden Bear when he said: "I hate to compare him to Nicklaus, but I really think he has the greatest mind since Nicklaus."

The buildup for the Masters began to resemble the hype reserved for a championship fight along the lines of Ali-Frazier. Wrote *Time* magazine's Robert Sullivan:

> This week the two greatest golfers in the world, David Duval, 27, and Tiger Woods, 23, will play in the Masters, the greatest of golf tournaments. It offers the tantalizing possibility of a head-to-head shoot-out between two of the game's rocket launchers, and the kind of Jack Nicklaus vs. Arnold Palmer face-off that can make golf absolutely riveting television. Alas, there are eight dozen more golfers in the field. Let's hope they don't get in the way.

Much to the chagrin of the golfing public, the highly anticipated confrontation between the No. 1 and No. 2 players in the world never materialized Sunday on the back nine of Augusta National.

Jose Marie Olazabal didn't buy into the hype. Olazabal, who had won the 1994 Masters, shot a one-under 71 on the final round to win the 63rd Masters by two strokes over Davis Love III and three over Greg Norman, the Masters all-time whipping boy given his number of near misses. Duval had the best round of the day in the windy conditions, shooting a two-under 70 to finish at three-under, five shots more than Olazabal; Woods shot a final-round 75 to finish nine shots behind.

And as usual Stewart wasn't a factor at the Masters, where he finished in a tie for fifty-second place; his best ever finish at Augusta had been a tie for eighth place in 1986.

Despite their showing at the Masters, Duval and Woods looked like the real deal and the perception couldn't have been faulted that the AT&T might have been the last hurrah for Stewart, a golfer playing a sport ready to be dominated by two emerging superstars.

CHAPTER FIVE

DONALD ROSS AND
PINEHURST

Payne Stewart had a special affinity for the Sandhills of North Carolina. Dr. Richard Coop had seen the special way Stewart viewed Pinehurst No. 2 and could sense his excitement about playing the U.S. Open there.

"Strangely enough, Payne was an iconoclast in many ways," Coop said. "But he loved tradition in golf and he loved what Pinehurst stood for. We'd been down and played it a few times, because I live just sixty miles away at Chapel Hill. He loved the golf course and he loved the ambiance, he loved the tradition."

Any mention of tradition at Pinehurst began with Donald Ross. The famed golf course architect died in 1948, but his legacy lives on the fairways and greens at the many golf courses he designed. Well over a hundred United States national championships have been played on courses designed by Ross, yet Pinehurst No. 2, the course best defining his work, had never hosted the U.S. Open.

Ross grew up in Dornach, Scotland, a town located at the northern coastal region of the country, where he learned about the game of golf and was influenced greatly at Royal Dornoch, a course ranked by many as the premier course in the world. He became a fine player and in his late teen years went to St. Andrews to an apprenticeship under four-time British Open champion "Old" Tom Morris, to learn the finer elements of club-making and "keeping of the green." A year later Ross returned to work at Dornach, where he maintained the grounds, performed his duties as a club-maker, and continued to play the game he loved. The social divisions existing at many golf courses today obviously didn't exist when Ross worked at Dornach.

Ross immigrated to the United States in 1898 and in 1899 was hired to build and run the Oakley Golf Club in Watertown Massachusetts, near Boston. The assignment led to Ross meeting Leonard Tufts, whose father, James, owned the American Soda Fountain Company. Leonard had an asthmatic condition, which enticed the Tufts family to buy a large tract of land in North Carolina to serve as a health-centered winter retreat. He called the place Pinehurst after purchasing the name from an individual entering the name in a contest to tag a real estate development in Martha's Vineyard. Some locals felt like the Payne family took advantage of Tufts, who paid the Payne family an average of $1.25 an acre for the 7,480 acres purchased [Note: The Payne family had no relation to Payne Stewart]. One local man was quoted as saying the property wasn't worth more than eighty-five cents an acre. The land was considered "pine barrens" since the pine trees familiar to the area had been stripped in the name of turpentine, pitch, and tar.

The Tufts family closed the deal on their purchase in July of 1895. The physical plan for the Village of Pinehurst was prepared by the firm of Frederick Law Olmsted, the landscape designer acclaimed for creating New York City's Central Park. By New Year's Eve of 1895, the Holly Inn had been constructed.

Early in Pinehurst's existence, Tufts advertised the area as a healthy destination for those with consumption and sufferers were greeted to the area with open arms. "Consumption" or "white plague" referred to a wasting of the body from a chronic illness and later was called tuberculosis. Only after consumption had been identified as a highly contagious disease did Pinehurst roll up and stash away the welcome mat for consumption sufferers.

Sitting among the scrub pines, Pinehurst was a geographic anomaly. Though the land sat a hundred miles west of the Atlantic Ocean, it's base was composed of sand, a foreign soil base compared to what Ross was familiar with in the Northeast.

The Tufts family hired Ross in 1900 as golf professional for the first 18 holes built in the area. He would later redesign Pinehurst No. 1 and design No. 2, No. 3, and No. 4 for the Tufts family. Ross built No. 2's first nine holes in 1901, remodeled the original nine in 1903, and added the back nine in 1907. In 1923 he remodeled two holes, then remodeled the entire course in 1933. In 1934 two holes were redone and in 1935 he remodeled the entire course again.

Originally Pinehurst's courses had sand greens composed of a four-to-six-inch base of a sand and clay mix. Sand was then sprinkled on top to slow down the speed of a rolling golf ball. Sand greens required little maintenance other than having water sprinkled on them from time to time to keep them firm. Water would be delivered to the holes via a mule-drawn water cart equipped with a water-filled drum.

Some of the changes to Pinehurst instituted by Ross could be seen when Pinehurst No. 2 hosted the 1935 PGA Championship. Employing his extensive knowledge of turf management, Ross oversaw a transition of the course's greens from oiled sand to Bermuda grass. Golfers were left to deal with the domed greens that made them feel like they were putting on a linoleum floor.

According to Ross expert W. Pete Jones, Ross can be credited with designing three hundred and eighty-five courses, far less than some accounts attributed to him. In the 1920s, he was the most prolific creator of golf courses in the United States. He had as many as twenty-five crews working for him all over the country while serving simultaneously as Pinehurst's director of golf. Courses he designed or redesigned hosted eight of the thirteen U.S. Opens from 1919 to 1931. Along with his unique designs, Ross initiated developments in turf grass that changed the face of the golf layouts throughout the country.

Michael Fay is the head of the Donald Ross Society, a society that today has approximately 1,600 members. The society's creed is as follows:

Create awareness among members of Ross courses that they are caretakers of classics; to proceed with caution before making changes; and to zealously protect what they have if their course is in its virgin state.

Well acquainted with Ross, Fay believes Ross's high energy level enabled him to produce the quantity of courses he did.

"First of all, he was extremely organized," Fay said. "He understood that you had to be organized to be able to get the contracts at these different places. Now most of these contracts came to him; he didn't have to go out and compete for them. But he had the right people in the right place to make sure that the courses were going to be built correctly. He had the right horses in the right places and the right contacts to get the jobs because everybody who was anybody came to Pinehurst in the twenties. And he was well known. And I think he was the only guy who was truly in the golf course creation

business. . . . I think he was a very good businessman. He understood what he had to do to get the jobs done, how to maintain it and
punch up his reputation. And at the same time keep the same people
working for him for long periods of time. Those people stayed with
him pretty much through their entire careers. So I think he must
have been well respected."

His course designs put a premium on the golfer's ability to be creative in handling greens, with plenty of slopes and areas around the
greens being pitched and tilted, so offline shots rolled away into
swales and depressions.

Ross worked from his lodging in Pinehurst and, due to travel
constraints of his era, did not see many of his creations come to life.
He would simply send along instructions to accompany the blue-
prints for the different courses around the country. In addition to
Pinehurst No. 2, the most famous courses holding a Ross bloodline
include Seminole Golf Club in North Palm Beach, Florida, and
Oakland Hills outside Detroit.

The famed golf architect's test for any course called for length
and accuracy from the tee, an accurate iron game, and a certain
amount of creativity when chipping and putting. These were pro-
portional challenges in which no one phase of the game was empha-
sized over another. Above all, he sought to create a challenging
course that would be competitive for all levels of golf talent, which
can be assumed from the following comments Ross made about
designing a course:

"There should be two ways to play a hole, one for a physically
strong player, and one for the man not so strong.

"It's best not to make the first two holes or so too difficult. Give
the player a chance to warm up a bit and get the swing of his stroke
well under control. Then give him some real nuts to crack."

Ross favored a game played along the ground. One of his trademarks was to take mounds outside the green and run them through the green to create ridges, which created putting areas much more difficult than those of modern architecture. He also gave golfers two or three lines of play to any green where the ball could be run up onto the green. His course designs did not favor a game in the air. If a golfer should try to bring the game in the air to a Donald Ross golf course, he would often find frustration with the hard, fast greens that are not set up to accept shots that come in through the air.

"To play a Donald Ross course you have to be more creative and clever than when you're playing the ones designed by most of the modern-day architects," Fay said.

Ross loved Pinehurst like no other place, a fact many attribute to the region's topography; the rolling terrain and sandy soil reminded him of Dornach. He continued to tinker with the No. 2 course until the end of his life. Some believe Ross had a compelling obsession to perfect No. 2 and make the course the best in the Southeast. Speculation cited the root of the obsession to be Ross's devastation from not being hired to design Augusta National. Lore has it that Ross had reached an understanding with famed golfer Bobby Jones to design the course that would become Augusta National, site of the Masters. But after Jones saw Cypress Point Golf Club on the Monterey Peninsula in 1929, he fell smitten with its designer, Dr. Alister MacKenzie, and hired him for the job he had told Ross was his. Jones was said to carry a great deal of anxiety about having to tell Ross of the change. A reasonable explanation for the change could be found in Ross's preference to be a solo act and Jones's desire to participate in the course's creation.

Shunned, Ross was left with a compelling desire to make Pinehurst No. 2 the best golf course in the Southeast.

Whether touched by the area's similarity to home or driven by perfection, Ross rooted down in a cottage next to the third green on No. 2.

Ross's style of golf architecture was greatly affected by the era. On the positive side, golf course designers of Ross's era had the opportunity to choose the parcel of land where they wanted to create their masterpieces. Modern golf architects normally find themselves in a situation where they must build a course to fit an available track of land. Adversely affecting course construction during Ross's era was the lack of equipment to move dirt from one area to another. Ross employed a mule and drag-pan for most of the earthmoving he did.

The greens at Pinehurst No. 2 were crowned, giving a golfer the feeling of hitting to an inverted soup bowl, and planting the seed that if a precise iron shot was not hit trouble followed. The "turtle-back" characteristic of Ross's greens was a typical characteristic of top-dressed Bermuda-grass greens on his courses in the South. Over time the top dressing brought on an accumulation of sand, which caused the greens to differ from their original design; particularly at Pinehurst where they top-dressed more often. Many of the courses Ross designed in the North varied from those in the South by having inverted, saucerlike greens.

"I think he was out polishing and adding to and taking away from the No. 2 course from the time he first built it," Fay said. "Make no mistake, Pinehurst No. 2 is one of a kind. There's no other golf course like it that Donald Ross built anywhere else. I mean there are some features at the other courses that are like No. 2, but the greens at the No. 2 course are really unique, especially having eighteen of them on one golf course. Basically, I think it became his pride and joy as time went on."

In 1902, Pinehurst No. 2 began hosting the North and South Open Championship, a highly esteemed professional tournament.

Ross's brother Alex was the first champion in 1902; Donald finished second and went on to win the event in 1903, 1905, and 1906. Big-name golfers to win the North and South Open included Walter Hagen, Byron Nelson, Ben Hogan, Sam Snead, Cary Middlecoff, and Tommy Bolt.

Hogan's win in 1940 came at a pivotal point in his career. Seeking his first victory since becoming a professional in 1932, Hogan arrived in Pinehurst driving a jalopy with smooth tires and just thirty dollars to his name. In those days the North and South Open held the same esteem among golfers as a major does today.

Said Henry Picard, a former Masters champion and two-time winner of the North and South: "Back then the pros wanted to win the North and South more than any other tournament, except the U.S. Open."

Hogan lacked the confidence of a champion when he teed off on the tournament's final day, a chilly Thursday, holding a seven-shot lead heading into the remaining thirty-six holes. Despite shooting 74 for his first eighteen holes, Hogan still held a six-shot lead. "Benny" Hogan, as he was known in 1940, felt the heat of Gene Sarazen and Snead creeping up, but managed to birdie 16 and par 17 and 18 to beat Snead by three shots in claiming his first professional victory.

"I won one just in time," Hogan said. "I had finished second and third so many times I was beginning to think I was an also-ran."

Among the many victories that followed, Hogan would add North and South Open championships in 1942 and 1946.

Pinehurst No. 2 continued to hold a regal place in golf history, hosting the 1951 Ryder Cup that saw the United States defeat Great Britain 9½ to 2½. But this was a turning point in the course's history.

Many of the golfers playing in the Ryder Cup matches in 1951 did not stick around for the North and South Open that was played the following week because they didn't think the purse was enough.

Richard Tufts, who was the son of Leonard Tufts and ran Pinehurst, did not appreciate the snub and shortly after Tommy Bolt shot 283 to capture the 1951 North and South Open, Tufts canceled the tournament many felt to be on even footing with the Masters.

While Pinehurst continued to host the Men's North and South Amateur Championship, which dated back to 1901; began the Men's North and South Senior Amateur; and hosted other highly esteemed amateur events in the years following the 1951 North and South Open, one has to wonder what status the tournament might have achieved had it continued to be played until golf became a huge television sport.

Today Pinehurst is revered among golfers nationally and even worldwide. A typical morning will see corporate types gladly plunking down the $320 green fee to play No. 2. If a thought bubble could be read above their heads, it would no doubt read: "I've died and gone to golf heaven." Their faces stepping onto the course are reminiscent of the face of one's wife preparing for a shopping spree at Ann Taylor. But that's where No. 2 and the Village of Pinehurst are today. Tough times in which a loss of identity nearly occurred were experienced en route to Pinehurst reestablishing itself as a golf Mecca.

Problems began when relatives of the Tufts family sold their Pinehurst stock to Diamondhead Corp in 1969. Under the ownership of the land-development company, the face of Pinehurst changed from the way the resort had operated for the first seventy-five years of its existence. The worst of the changes came in a wave of prospective buyers to pick over available houses, lots, and condominiums. A once stately grand ballroom suddenly felt like Studio 54. Not exactly a great fit for the down-home neck of the woods were Pinehurst sits.

Over the course of the next fifteen years, Pinehurst lost its luster and appeared headed for ruin. By March of 1982, a consortium of banks holding overdue loans took over from Diamondhead. The grand old resort still had a pulse, but clearly it was in intensive care. That's when a savior arrived in the form of ClubCorp, a Dallas-based company that owned or operated many golf clubs all over the world. ClubCorp purchased the resort in 1984 for $15 million, a purchase that included the six courses, the Carolina Hotel, the club-house, the tennis facility, the gun club, and riding stables. And fortunately for Pinehurst, Robert Dedman, the president of ClubCorp, had a soft spot for Pinehurst. He understood the significance of the resort and its golf heritage, which led to the infusion of money needed to bring life back to the resort.

"He just loved the game of golf, he loved Pinehurst," said Beth Kocher, executive vice president of Pinehurst.

Kocher belonged to the three-person acquisition committee for ClubCorp that came in to work as operators of the resort in 1984.

"It was bad," Kocher said. "The first thing we said was 'What are we doing here?' We owned two thousand acres of land with an assortment of buildings. It took a year just to figure out what we had."

Restoring the Carolina Hotel, the signature building of the resort, became the first order of business.

"Before Diamondhead came along, the residents of Pinehurst would patch the holes in [the Carolina's] tin roof," Kocher said. "Diamondhead never repaired it.

"I had three pairs of socks back in those days. One pair to walk around in, a pair to wear to bed, and shower socks. Every time it rained the entire lobby [of the Carolina Hotel] was covered with big buckets to catch the water."

The old roof was covered and the restoration continued one floor at a time until the Carolina was brought back to its present pristine condition. Among Diamondhead's other sins was how it chose to handle No. 2.

"They had misunderstood No. 2," Kocher said. "They actually made changes to the course. They tried to make No. 2 a modern course. I don't think they really cared about the history of No. 2. They were in a totally different business. They were into selling lots. To their way of thinking, the only purpose for golf courses was to sell real estate."

Upon first examination of No. 2, Brad Kocher, also on the management team, told his wife: "We're having a few problems."

Little grass could be seen. Major work needed to be done to the irrigation system. Until the new management team took over, the resort primarily had been a winter destination and was closed in the summer; No. 2 never was open for play in the summer.

Blind luck led to a fortuitous find in the trunk of a car where the plans for No. 2 were discovered, thereby allowing the historic course to be returned to the condition Donald Ross intended.

Pat Corso, Pinehurst's president and CEO, joined the effort in 1987 with an eye toward once again making Pinehurst a marquee destination for competitive golf. Once again luck smiled on the project.

Corso wanted to find an insider, a person with contacts who could go out and schmooze with the top people on the PGA Tour or at the USGA. His pursuit led him to Don Padgett Jr., who was the director of golf at Firestone Country Club in Akron, Ohio, which happened to be owned by ClubCorp. Corso knew the Padgett name from growing up in Indiana and was astounded when Padgett suggested the man for the job was his father.

Corso smiled at the recollection.

"I told him, 'Your dad? I thought he was dead," Corso said.

In fact he was very much alive as the director of golf at Desert

Highlands in Scottsdale, Arizona, and the perfect person to breathe life back into the status of Pinehurst golf. Padgett Sr. had been a member of the PGA since 1950; was a past president of the PGA of America; served as the chairman of the PGA Championship in 1976 and the Ryder Cup matches in 1979; and had worked as the director of golf at PGA National in Palm Beach Gardens, Florida. Padgett Sr. was plugged in where connections to the game of golf were concerned.

"He knew everybody in golf," Corso said.

Once Padgett was hired, Pinehurst began a legitimate journey back to the head of the class for the golf world that would culminate with the procurement of the 1999 U.S. Open.

"We had begun a pilgrimage," Corso said. "We began attending every Open. Don was amazing the way he could talk up Pinehurst. He liked to hang around the driving range and putting greens at the various tournaments. He believed you could see everybody you needed to see at those two places."

Padgett understood the value of relationships. When he worked the crowd he made sure anybody from Pinehurst who accompanied him would be introduced to the influential people for the PGA Tour and USGA.

"Seemed like Don introduced us to all of them," Corso said. "The best way I can describe him is he was like a magnet. Everybody in golf knew him and when they stopped to talk to him he'd tell them all about the good things that were going on at Pinehurst."

Baby steps were taken at first before the Pinehurst management team went after the big fish. They hosted the U.S. Women's Amateur in 1989.

There were some queries about Pinehurst making a bid for the Tour Championship in 1988 and 1989, but Padgett convinced the management team to pass.

Payne Stewart reacts after making a birdie putt on the second hole during the second round of the 1998 U.S. Open Championship at the Lake Course of the Olympic Club in San Francisco, California, Friday, June 19, 1998.

(AP PHOTO/ERIC RISBERG)

Payne Stewart waits for his ball to stop rolling after his initial putt ran by the cup on the eighteenth green during the second round of the 1998 U.S. Open Championship at the Lake Course of the Olympic Club in San Francisco, California, Friday, June 19, 1998.

(AP PHOTO/KEVORK DJANZESIAN)

Payne Stewart, left, applaudes as Lee Janzen looks away after winning the 1998 U.S. Open Championship at the Lake Course of the Olympic Club in San Francisco, California, Sunday, June 21, 1998.
(AP PHOTO/ERIC RISBERG)

Tom Meeks (USGA/JOHN MUMMERT)

Ron Philo (DAVID BURGHARDT)

Oil painting of Donald Ross presently hanging in
Donald Ross Grill. (PINEHURST INC.)

Reigning U.S. Open Champion, Lee Janzen,
watches a shot Tuesday at practice.
(THE CHARLOTTE OBSERVER)

Phil Mickelson (*left*) is
congratulated by Payne
Stewart after Stewart sinks
a twenty-foot putt to win
the 1999 U.S. Open.
(THE CHARLOTTE OBSERVER)

Tiger Woods pumps his fist after sinking a birdie putt on No. 16 that brought him within one shot of the lead. (THE CHARLOTTE OBSERVER)

David Duval tees off on the second hole during the third round. (THE CHARLOTTE OBSERVER)

Phil Mickelson tees off at No. 9 on Sunday. (THE CHARLOTTE OBSERVER)

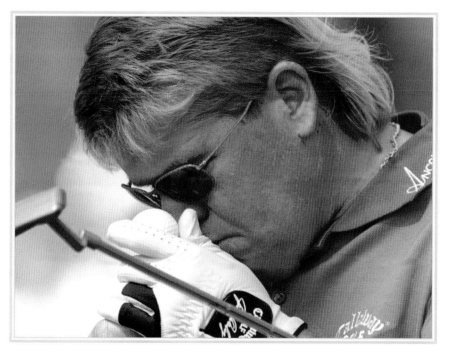

John Daly fires up a smoke after a bogey on the seventh hole on Friday morning.
(THE CHARLOTTE OBSERVER)

David Duval hits out of the sand on No. 6 at Pinehurst for the U.S. Open on Friday afternoon.
(THE CHARLOTTE OBSERVER)

Vijay Singh checks the skies before teeing off on No. 9. (THE CHARLOTTE OBSERVER)

Payne Stewart gets a hug from his caddie, Mike Hicks, after sinking the winning putt on the eighteenth green of the Pinehurst No. 2 course at the U.S. Open in Pinehurst, North Carolina. (THE CHARLOTTE OBSERVER)

Payne Stewart celebrates the winning putt on the eighteenth green of the Pinehurst No. 2 golf course at the U.S. Open in Pinehurst, North Carolina.
(THE CHARLOTTE OBSERVER)

Payne Stewart gets a hug from his wife after winning the U.S. Open in Pinehurst, North Carolina.
(THE CHARLOTTE OBSERVER)

Payne Stewart is all smiles after receiving the U.S. Open trophy on Sunday after winning with a spectacular twenty-foot putt. Stewart clung to a one-stroke lead to hold off Phil Mickelson for the U.S. title. (THE CHARLOTTE OBSERVER)

"We knew we would have the one chance to impress and we wanted to be ready when that opportunity came," Beth Kocher said.

Showtime arrived in 1991 when No. 2 hosted the Tour Championship won by Craig Stadler. Pinehurst put its best foot forward again in 1992 by once again hosting the Tour Championship, which Paul Azinger won.

Despite the fine showing during the Tour Championship, which moved in 1993, and despite the fact Pinehurst No. 2 was considered to be one of the best courses in the world, there appeared to be serious reasons why the U.S. Open had never scheduled a tournament there and never would.

Fay remembered a meeting of the Donald Ross Society that convened at Pinehurst in the early 1990s.

"We were at the Pinehurst Hotel and brought in people from all over the country, a good-sized group from the Donald Ross Society," Fay said. "I had three speakers that year, Harvie Ward, Peggy Kirkfeld, and David Eger. And the theme among them was these were three people who had won the North-South at Pinehurst No. 2.

"Harvie Ward gave a nice little speech, went on for about five minutes, had everybody rolling in the aisles. Peggy Kirkfeld gave her normal delightful talk on Ross and her experience with him while she was coming up and whatnot. Then came David Eger, who was in charge of site selection for the USGA. He gave us about thirty or forty minutes about why there was never going to be a United States Open at Pinehurst No. 2. Two years later they announced No. 2 had it."

Fay said there was nothing malicious about Eger's remarks. He simply stated the reasons for the USGA's misgivings about No. 2.

Pinehurst's location had a lot to do with the snub for many years.

Until 1972, the U.S. Open had always been played at a course located in a medium-sized population area. When the Open was played at Pebble Beach in 1972 (and again in 1982 and 1992), it was the first time an Open had been played in an area so remote.

In 1986 and 1995, the Open was played at Shinnecock Hills, also a relatively remote location, but at Shinnecock and Pebble Beach, the Opens worked well, which made the consideration of Pinehurst viable. However, while Shinnecock (located at the east end of Long Island) and Pebble Beach (in Monterey), were close to population centers, the Pinehurst Resort and Country Club was located in tiny Pinehurst, North Carolina, roughly seventy-five miles southwest of Raleigh and a hundred miles east of Charlotte.

In addition to the location, Pinehurst could not grow grass the way the USGA desired the grass to be grown for an Open. The USGA wanted firm, fast greens with deep rough along the fairways for the courses hosting an Open. Such conditions were difficult to accommodate the third week in June in the South when Bermuda grass needed an ample amount of water to survive, which adversely affected the greens when striving to achieve a hard and fast surface. The Atlanta Athletic Club had hosted the 1976 Open and the greens had been so slow players were able to attack the course with an ease unfamiliar to a U.S. Open.

Available housing and transportation for players, officials, and spectators served up yet another negative. And finally, there was the weather. The USGA could just imagine Open players basting like Carolina barbecue in the summer temperatures.

"There were a lot of legitimate concerns," Fay said.

Added to those concerns were the negative vibes from P. J. Boatwright, the USGA's director of rules and competition prior to Tom Meeks.

"I remember very distinctly during the times when the U.S. Open and Pinehurst No. 2 came up while P. J. Boatwright was alive, he'd say, 'You can't hold an Open at Pinehurst because you can't grow the rough up around the greens because they have these roll off areas,'" Meeks said. "Nobody ever said, 'Well P. J., why don't we have an Open where we don't have high rough around the greens?' Nobody ever said that to him because P. J. was the authority. And if he said you can't have an Open at Pinehurst No. 2 because you can't grow rough up around the greens, everybody accepted that. After P. J. died we realized we could hold an Open there."

Pinehurst No. 2 had been awarded the 1994 Senior Open, but the 1999 U.S. Open was awarded to No. 2 prior to the '94 tournament being played.

Pinehurst long has felt like family to staff and their families at the resort. When Beth Kocher got word that the announcement about No. 2 hosting the Open would be made at Pebble Beach, she gathered the staff.

"Pat Corso and Brad [Kocher] had flown to Pebble for the announcement," Beth said. "I called a meeting in the dining room and told them, 'As we're standing here right now, they're announcing we've got the U.S. Open.' The staff was thrilled. For all of us it was like the dog that chases the car and one day catches it. The feeling was almost overwhelming. Like, now that we've got it, what do we do?"

The USGA and Pinehurst had negotiated several items.

"The most prominent of these issues was the greens," Corso said. "In order to host the Open, we needed to change the greens. They weren't going to play on Bermuda. Jerry Pate shot lights out [on Bermuda greens when he won the '76 Open] and that was something they didn't want to happen."

The USGA preferred firm, speedy, slick greens where golf balls rolled like marbles on the kitchen floor. Having greens that could reach the preferred speeds during the summer heat of the South had previously been unthinkable.

"I think it's obvious that the fairways and approaches in the South are as good as anywhere, but the putting surfaces are normally the best during the early spring and late fall," Don Padgett told the *Atlanta Journal-Constitution*. "We had to convince them that we could get firm and fast greens in June before they ever thought about coming here."

Corso, Padgett, and the rest of the Pinehurst contingent agreed to work with the USGA on finding the right grass to be used on the greens to insure the speed would be up to U.S. Open standards. Eventually they decided on Penn G-2, a heat-resistant strain of bentgrass developed by Joe Duich, a professor emeritus of turfgrass science at Penn State. Accordingly, Penn G-2 was installed on the greens of Pinehurst No. 2 in 1996 during a refurbishment. The end result was greens resistant to heat and humidity and able to hold a smooth but firm putting surface.

Said David Fay, the USGA's executive director, when asked about Pinehurst No. 2: "Pinehurst is the St. Andrews of America. It's been a national treasure for nearly a century. And it has certainly earned the right to host [the 1999 U.S. Open]."

"Essentially [the decision to award the Open to Pinehurst No. 2] came down to No. 2 being just too good of a golf course not to hold an Open there," Michael Fay said.

Corso credited winning the Open to relationships.

"It's not about marketing, about big presentation boards and multimedia," Corso said. "Relationships are the key. Who would believe that the way to get a U.S. Open is to spend an afternoon on the putting green at the PGA, Masters, or U.S. Open with Don Padgett talking to whoever happens to stop by? I met all of the people I know from the game of golf that way."

QUALIFYING AT LAST

SURE, PAYNE STEWART had to deal with the disappointment of not winning the 1998 U.S. Open after having the tournament within his grasp, but other golfers from around the world would gladly have made a pact with the devil to merely tee it up at the U.S. Open. A group of golfers including quality amateurs like Bill Stewart had been or professionals not earning their cards, all of whom dared to dream. They believed in themselves and their games; if they just had that one chance . . .

Ron Philo was one such dreamer.

Philo grew up on the Redwood Golf Driving Range in Scotia, New York, performing the menial chores of retrieving and washing the golf balls that were the lifeblood of the business his father had inherited from his father.

Philo's grandfather had worked at General Electric as a purchasing agent in Schenectady, New York, and like many Americans in the

1940s he caught the golf bug, which led to his buying the property that had once been a pig farm and turning it into a place where golfers could hone their skills.

Philo was seven when his family moved to Scotia.

Working at the driving range "certainly wasn't forced upon [Philo and his sisters]," Philo said. "It's just what we did. My father always compared it to being on a farm. We farmed golf balls. Essentially, owning a driving range was very much like owning a family farm."

The kids' chores began early in the morning while their father mowed the soil fertile from the previous land users. Ample time for mashing golf balls until the club felt like another appendage could always be found if the kids weren't attending school or doing chores.

"Hitting balls was just something we did," Philo said. "I don't ever remember a time when I didn't hit balls."

Philo played on the high school golf team at Scotia Glennville in Scotia and tried to qualify for the U.S. Open his senior year. Unlike any other tournament in the world holding such prestige, the U.S. Open is just that, open. In theory, Joe Six-pack can pay his $100 entry fee, go to the local qualifier, and play his way into the national championship of golf in the United States. He failed in his first attempt to qualify.

After high school, Philo went to the U.S. Military Academy before ending up at Florida State University, where he thought he'd play golf before his path got diverted. Grades became his priority, leading him to graduate school. During this period Philo worked as a PGA apprentice for a longtime friend of his father's, Bob Duval, who is Tour pro David Duval's father. Later, when Duval accepted a job as the pro at Timuquana Country Club, a new club in Jacksonville, Florida, Philo accepted Duval's offer to become his assistant.

"My goal at that time was to go to work for Titleist, Taylor

Made, or Callaway," Philo said. "I was thinking about going to the factory and working at the corporate office of a golf program or working for the Tour, but not really any kind of work where I would be on the road. I wasn't thinking about that kind of life."

Eventually golf reeled Philo back into the fold.

"After working for a couple of years with Bob and doing a lot of playing—and David obviously was there and becoming a great player at the time—well, that kind of atmosphere is contagious," Philo said. "You get to playing better and the next thing I knew I was playing better than I ever had. I was shooting in the 60s all the time and people at the club were offering me money to go play. I hit the road to play, went to Tour school, couple of years later I ended up on the Nike Tour. I qualified for the Nike school in 1993."

His best finish on the Nike Tour had been second place at a tournament held in Pensacola, Florida. Nevertheless, golf had become his livelihood, whether teaching the sport or playing it. So attempting to qualify for the U.S. Open most every year after his failed first attempt became like his work on the driving range, it was just something he did.

"The fact is it's the national open," Philo said. "If you play competitive golf, you try to play in the biggest, the best competitions you can play. That is about the biggest and best tournament that everyone has access to play in; one of the tournaments that everyone has a fair and legitimate opportunity to participate in."

Golfers eligible to participate in U.S. Open qualifying events include professional golfers and amateur golfers with up-to-date USGA Handicap Indexes not exceeding 1.4 under the Men's USGA Handicap System. Approximately 750 golfers advance to the sectional qualifier; additional professional golfers and esteemed players are added to this field through exemptions to the sectional based on

USGA Executive Committee selections determined by a player's playing record.

When Philo made it through the first stage of qualifying for an Open he elected to play the second stage at Woodmont Country Club in Washington, D.C.

"David Duval would tell me, 'You need to go where the Tour is playing, because [the qualifier there] has the most spots,'" Philo said. "Woodmont Country Club was the qualifier to go to because the Tour was in D.C. the previous week."

Philo arrived at Woodmont knowing if he completed the thirty-six hole qualifier with one of the lowest score totals he would have a spot in the U.S. Open for the first time.

"This was the first time I'd made it to the second stage after probably seven or eight tries," Philo said. "So I got up there and lo and behold, it was like being in a Tour event. Everybody there just came the week before from the Tour event. And I think I was a little starstruck. I couldn't believe all the players that were there going through the same thing as me. I remember being paired with Russ Cochran, David Frost was there, Hal Sutton was there. It was just a who's who. Every other name on the list was somebody I recognized from the Tour. I think I just broke 150, which isn't anywhere close."

Philo continued to try and earn a spot in the U.S. Open through qualifiers at Woodmont.

"I played there for three or four years in a row," Philo said. "One of those years I thought I had a chance. I birdied the final hole to shoot 30 on the final nine holes for a 138. I thought I'd gotten in. Usually a pair of 68s is what it takes. A pair of 68s will get you in. Anything over that and you're holding your breath. But that year [Woodmont] wasn't a Tour site. We were only playing for six spots, so I thought 138 had a chance. When it's a Tour spot there are more spots, but there are more quality players trying to fill those spots."

Philo earned a spot in a playoff and lost.

Some might have quit after getting so close and still coming up short. Not Ron Philo.

"Getting close certainly feeds your confidence," Philo said. "Like I'm not showing up for the second phase just because I got there. You feel like if I can get to this point, I can earn a spot. I can play my way into the tournament. It's not unrealistic to think I can get there. So you keep trying. I figured 'What the hell.' I'm going to try again next year. It's part of what I do."

Philo's intrepid spirit and perseverance never wavered despite never having qualified for an Open; and he'd been trying for so long. Nevertheless, toward the end of May 1999, Philo knew the time was near when he once again would try and play his way into the U.S. Open. Now thirty-three, Philo had been trying to earn a spot in the national championship most every year since his senior year in high school. Each of the attempts had ended in failure.

Philo had recently taken the head professional job at the Country Club of Vermont, a new club in Waterbury, Vermont, in addition to running the Ron Philo School of Golf in Amelia Island Plantation, Florida. He needed to decide at which local qualifier he wanted to begin his bid. Having grown up around Albany, New York, he went to Skyler Meadows and ended up being the medalist at the local qualifier.

"That was probably the sixth or seventh time I made it to the second phase, the sectional qualifier," Philo said.

U.S. Open qualifiers had been a part of Philo's summers since he was a young man, so he took his advancement in stride, nothing to get too excited about. Other things occupied his mind, like his new job and heading to Florida to pick up his wife, Kim, and their two children, a six-year-old daughter and a one-year-old son so they could spend the summer with him. Like many times in the past,

Philo would try and qualify for the Open at the sectional played at the Woodmont Country Club.

He flew down to Jacksonville from Vermont, picked up his wife and kids, loaded up the minivan, and headed north on I-95. Maryland served as the perfect layover since it was the approximate halfway point between Jacksonville and Waterbury. The Philos had a twelve-hour drive on Friday before arriving in southern Virginia to a stay at a friend's house. Their friend had connections at the White House and arranged a Saturday morning tour. Afterward they did some sightseeing before Philo went to Woodmont to play a practice round. Familiar with the course from playing there on many occasions, Philo only played nine holes, then chipped and putted. He repeated the process on Sunday, playing Woodmont's back nine only.

"I felt confident going into that one," Philo said. "I really enjoyed playing at Woodmont, I liked the golf course. I'd played some good rounds there before. I remember being paired with Chris Perry, who was playing really well at the time. I'd played with him on the Nike Tour so I was familiar with him and he was good friends with a friend of mine, Lee Rinker. I remembered thinking how well Chris was doing and I thought, 'This is good, because I know I can play with Chris.' There certainly was some comfort there with the familiar surroundings and playing with a player I'd played with. I knew that if I played my best I could qualify."

And if he didn't?

"Certainly the Open had been going on for however many years without me, and I knew that if I didn't qualify it's not the end of the world," Philo said. "Nothing earth-shattering happens. You always go back and look at your rounds afterward and say, 'If I'd only have done this or that, I would have qualified.'"

Regardless of Philo's performance, good or bad, a van trip to Vermont with his family awaited the following day. And how did Philo's pursuit of qualifying for the Open play out on the home front? Some wives might not be so understanding of their husband's continued pursuit given his inability to qualify after so many tries.

"This is what I do," Philo said. "This is what I was doing when Kim met me. This is what I've always done. She's been with me through good events, bad events. She's there to support me. And my whole family does this so it's just what we do. Playing in golf tournaments is part of what I do. It's part of what I do for a living. It's part of what I do for my life, my sanity, what I like to do."

Approximately seven hundred fifty hopefuls like Philo convened at seventeen sites to play for eighty-nine available berths in the ninety-ninth U.S. Open. Rounding out the field of one hundred and fifty-six golfers in the Open were the fortunate sixty-seven who were exempt from qualifying.

Playing Woodmont's North Course during the morning round of the qualifier, Philo hit his approach shot to the first hole within ten feet.

"The putt wasn't that hard but I missed it," Philo said. "I should have made it."

Philo kept his nerves intact, but his approach shot to No. 2 finished thirty feet from the hole. He sank the putt.

Philo shot a six-under 66 in the morning round.

"I think we were only playing for six spots," Philo said. "At the turn, 66 was the low score. I knew anything under 70 was going to get in. That's just one of the things about it. When you're at that site and you know everybody is very competitive, 66 is only halfway home. Shooting a 66 and a 72 is the same thing as two 69s. Everybody playing is capable of shooting two 69s and certainly everybody there was capable of shooting 66."

Philo continued to play well in the afternoon round.

"Every time I hit a good shot, I made the putt," Philo said. "I didn't have any times when I hit a good shot and didn't make the putt after No. 1. Then the rest of the day, every time I hit it within ten feet, I made the putt. I birdied all the par-5s from up close to the green, just the way you're supposed to, just a very commercial day. The way you're supposed to do it, nothing extraordinary about it, like you drew it on a map. You hit it here. You hit it there. You putt it in."

Philo stood on the eighteenth tee knowing he had an excellent chance of claiming one of the six available spots if he could avoid a train wreck on the 370-yard par-4 with a dogleg right.

"The day before on the eighteenth hole I hit an iron off the tee," Philo said. "The caddie I had picked up from the club asked me why I chose to hit an iron off the tee when I'd been driving the ball so well.

"I remember telling him, 'I'm hitting the iron in case I don't need to make anything better than bogey here. I just don't want to hit it anyplace where if I hit it too far or too straight, I end up in a tree and I end up making a stupid score here.' What I remember most about the day is getting to the eighteenth hole on the thirty-sixth hole of the day and pulling out a 3-iron and telling my caddie, 'This is why we played an iron here yesterday.' So long as I don't do anything stupid, I'm pretty sure I'm going to get in."

Philo hit a decent 3-iron shot off the tee, hit the green in regulation with a 9-iron, and two-putted for par. Afterward Philo felt satisfied, but his enthusiasm was tempered with the confidence from his feeling he should have earned the spot.

"I felt like this is the way you're supposed to play," Philo said.

Philo especially wanted to play at Pinehurst No. 2. He had caddied for his sister Laura during the final two rounds of the Women's North and South at Pinehurst when she won in 1995.

"I was thinking I'd really love to play the Open there," Philo said. "It's such a great golf course. Historic, Donald Ross, really what the Open was all about."

Kim and the kids were at their friend's house after the qualifier when Philo stuck his head in the door and said, "We're in, we're going to Pinehurst."

Kim had called to find out how I did after the morning round, so she said, "I knew you were going to get in."

The Philos hopped into the family van the following morning and drove straight through to Vermont. Ron went back to work giving lessons.

Twenty-seven players, all of whom were professionals, qualified from a group of well over a hundred golfers at the Columbus sectional qualifier at the Lakes and Brookside Country Club. Chris Smith, who had never won in six years on the Tour, shot the low thirty-six hole total. Typical of such qualifiers, there was plenty of drama at Columbus, where it came down to ten players in a playoff for the final six spots. Tim Herron and Keith Clearwater sank birdie putts on the first hole while former Masters champion Larry Mize, Chris Tidland, Stephan Allan, and Bob Gilder all made par, thereby eliminating Fulton Allem, Steve Gangluff, Jim Johnson, and David Ogrin. Seasoned professionals Lanny Wadkins, David Frost, Ian Woosnam, and Craig Stadler all failed to qualify at Columbus.

Casey Martin, who played on the Nike Tour, failed to qualify in Chardon, Ohio, despite riding in a cart, which some players felt to be an advantage.

"I'm pretty beat," Martin said afterward. "My leg is killing me. The heat was definitely a factor. Riding in a cart was no advantage today. I'm in pain. I laugh at people who think a cart gives me a competitive edge. They should feel what I feel."

Fuzzy Zoeller, who won the Open at Winged Foot in 1984, and Tour regular Len Mattiace, qualified at Canoe Brook's Country Club in Summit, New Jersey; and Gary Halberg, a longtime touring professional, qualified in Littleton, Colorado.

CHAPTER SEVEN

PINEHURST NO. 2
STRAIGHT AHEAD

DEFENDING U.S. OPEN CHAMPION Lee Janzen didn't hesitate to answer when asked for his opinion regarding who he thought would win the 1999 U.S. Open.

"How about Payne Stewart," Janzen said, recalling what he told the media. "You see certain guys who play better at U.S. Opens. They hit the ball straight, they know how to recover. Payne Stewart was one of those guys. He always played well at the Open. Nobody was talking about him being one of the favorites."

Janzen might have liked Stewart's chances, but nobody else had the previous year's runner-up on their list of favorites.

"Payne hadn't really done squat," Doug Ferguson said. "He hadn't won since the Shell Open [in 1995] prior to his win at Pebble Beach. And what happened to him at Olympic where a guy reappears and it gets away from him, you don't expect to see him again."

Stewart viewed his chances differently.

"I think in his mind he wasn't sneaking under the radar," Mike Hicks said. "But he wasn't getting a whole lot of attention even though he was off to a real good start [in 1999]. In his mind he knew he was a lot better off going into that week than he had been the year before prior to the Open. His game was much better."

Tracey said Payne was happy about not being a pretournament favorite.

"It took some of the pressure off him," she said. "If you looked at it, though, it was kind of ridiculous [given the way he'd played throughout his career at Opens]."

Perhaps most underestimated when procrastinators failed to put Stewart among their favorites were the areas of emotion and resolve.

"Most people never get a second chance," Stewart said. "You live for the chance and pray you can get in the same situation again, but it usually doesn't happen. That's just the reality of it. I've waited a year. I want to take the trophy back home."

Stewart looked forward to playing the Open on an anti-Open course such as Pinehurst No. 2.

"You're going to see us play a number of different types of golf shots," Stewart said. "It's not a golf course where if you drive it out of the fairway, you just immediately grab your wedge or sand wedge and chip it back out to the fairway and proceed from there. You can get playable lies out of the rough, but that's kind of what the golf course wants you to think: 'Oh boy, I've got to lie and get this one on; I'm going to have to whip it right on the green.' And that's when all the excitement begins. You're really going to have to—this is a golf course you have to think and think about where you want the shot to finish, think about where you don't want to be, and if it gets hard, firm, and fast, wow, it will be exciting. It really will, it will be a lot of fun."

Having Hicks as his caddie gave Stewart a heads-up about what to expect from a summer round in Pinehurst. Hicks lived in the Sandhills region and warned Stewart to be prepared to play in extreme weather on a course different than any on Tour.

"Well, he was telling me how hot it was going to be, 'Man, it's hot over there in North Carolina, it's a hundred degrees,'" Stewart said. "But I don't know where there is a place that you can create the chipping that you have to do [at Pinehurst]. . . . You better have your feel [on chip shots at No. 2]. And I feel like I do."

Tiger Woods cited Stewart's chipping ability as one of the main reasons Stewart consistently contended in Opens, noting how the successful players at No. 2 would have an imagination.

"I would definitely put myself in that category," Stewart said. "I've always had a lot of imagination. It started probably when I was a kid. My father and I, we'd go out and he'd put me in different situations and I'd try to get out of them the best that I could. And I always found a lot of fun in that."

Following his disappointing finish at the Masters, Stewart played in one of his favorite tournaments, the MCI Classic at the Harbour Town course in Hilton Head, South Carolina. Twice Stewart had won at Harbour Town and he played well again, finishing second to Glen Day, who gained his first PGA Tour victory. The twenty-fifth second-place of Stewart's career denied him the feeling of winning a tournament after seventy-two holes. But it did validate the direction his game was heading, particularly his putting.

"By the time he got to April at the MCI he had what I considered a perfect putting stroke," Arnie Cunningham said. "He'd really mastered [the SeeMore System]. He putted lights out that week."

The mechanical parts of Stewart's game were in order, but the question lingered: Could he finish the job on Sunday?

Janzen, the man who had deprived Stewart of many a happy Sunday afternoon, readied to defend the championship he'd won the year before at Olympic. In the months following his win Janzen and a friend faced a long layover in San Francisco en route to Taiwan. Faced with occupying one's time under such a situation, the options are limited to travelers: read a book, sleep, or go to the bar.

Janzen asked his friend what he wanted to do to kill some time. When the question drew a blank, Janzen came up with an idea. They hailed a cab and paid a visit to Olympic, site of Janzen's 1998 U.S. Open triumph.

"We looked the course over," Janzen said. "You can walk down a hill and almost see the whole course."

Perhaps Janzen went to Olympic looking for karma; positive vibes can go a long way on the golf course. More than likely the unpretentious defending champ simply wanted to show his friend the course where he'd won his second Open. Either way Janzen clearly entertained thoughts of winning back-to-back Opens. History suggested the chances of such a feat were remote, but Janzen felt confident.

"I knew only one guy had repeated as Open champion [Curtis Strange, 1988–89] in more than forty years," Janzen said. "But my game was pretty good at the time and I loved Pinehurst. I played it just before the Open and was prepared to play a hot course with fast greens and a south wind."

In addition to the confidence provided by winning two Opens in six years, Janzen had a good experience at Pinehurst No. 2 when the Tour championship had been held there in 1992. Not only did he finish second to Paul Azinger, he still had the yardage book he'd used that week. Janzen planned to reacquaint himself with his notes during a practice round.

"I was really excited about playing [Pinehurst No. 2] because it was at the top of my list for favorite courses," Janzen said. "I'd had that good experience [in 1992], so I started getting excited about the Open being played there once they announced it."

A grizzled veteran in comparison to his status when he won his first Open, Janzen's preparation for playing in the Open focused on fundamental work early in the season to make sure his grip, setup, posture, and stance were in order. He didn't want to get to Pinehurst and realize he needed to make any major alterations to his swing, which would take away from his playing the golf course and establishing a playing rhythm.

For any pursuit there will always be bumps along the road. Janzen's bump came less than a month away from his defense in the form of a car accident in Fort Worth, Texas. Janzen was sitting at a traffic light the Monday prior to the Colonial when his courtesy Cadillac was rear-ended by a late-model pickup.

"I looked into the rearview mirror and got hit," Janzen said. "I had on a baseball hat and I started looking for it when I realized it wasn't on my head. It had flown all the way into the back of the car. The whole trunk was smashed in. Funny thing, my clubs weren't crushed."

Janzen didn't think about what effects the accident might have on his game. Instead he stepped from the car to ask the driver of the pickup if he had bothered to even touch his brakes. Initially, Janzen didn't feel any effects from the accident, but he was driven in a car to the hospital where he was put on a board and suited with a neck collar for precautionary measures. Shortly thereafter, his neck and lower back began to stiffen. Janzen felt disappointed at the disturbance. He'd finished third the week before at the Byron Nelson and thought his swing had arrived at the place where it needed to be and now this. He worked with a therapist on Tuesday and Wednesday to help combat the stiffness then decided to play in the Colonial.

"I continued to play, but it took me about four months to totally get back from all the stiffness," Janzen said.

Having won the Open twice made Janzen an exception among the many splendid golfers on Tour, prompting an examination of why he had been so successful.

"I think I like playing strategy," Janzen said. "Always playing the smart shot, and I think I control the distance of my irons very well, which I think is very crucial in the U.S. Open, the greens are very hard. I hit the ball pretty high and spin the ball a lot. I'm able to land the ball very close to where I think you need to land it on each green and make it stop. Fortunately, I putted very well [in both Open victories]. They weren't my best putting weeks I ever had, but they certainly were very good."

Some Tour players thrive in tournaments where attacking the course and putting up extremely low numbers is necessary to win while others, such as Janzen, were at their best when the course played to a higher degree of difficulty and the protect-par mentality came into play.

"I love playing tournaments where less than ten-under wins," Janzen said. "I'd much rather play in a tournament like that where conditions are very tough."

Patience is a virtue most Open champions share. Open courses might allow a golfer to master a succession of holes, but invariably the punch to the gut sat lying in the weeds just one T. C. Chen away.

"I've had my moments where I've been patient," Janzen said. "Like anybody else, certainly there are times when you're not patient; you let things get to you and when you do, you don't perform as well. But I know that helps. You have to remind yourself it's an extra hard week to do it. It's going to be hot. I think any of the majors wear your patience in the practice rounds because you're seeing the course for the first time. Even if you've seen it before, you're playing under forced conditions. You have usually thirty thousand people in the practice rounds, which is unusual. Sometimes it seems like you sign every one of their tickets or hats. I can't imagine Tiger and Freddie and Greg Norman, the bigger-name players, what they must go through those weeks."

Aside from his goal to repeat, Janzen held a lesser goal.

"I didn't want to miss the cut like I did in ninety-four," he said.

Tiger Woods and David Duval were the obvious favorites at Pinehurst given their top ranks.

Woods had looked sharp breaking his four-month victory drought by winning the Deutsche Bank Open in Heidelberg, Germany, by three shots at the end of May, and followed with a win at the Memorial. Meanwhile, Duval generally appeared unmotivated after the Masters. He took three weeks off and looked as though he were going through the motions during tournaments in New Orleans and Houston. But he did make a strong showing at the Memorial to finish third in his final tune-up before the U.S. Open.

With the head-to-head showdown between Woods and Duval still a figment of the golfing world's imagination, ABC Sports decided to make the showdown a reality.

In May of 1999, ABC Sports announced a made-for-TV live exhibition—the "Showdown at Sherwood"—they'd scheduled between the world's top-ranked players the week before the PGA Championship. The $1.5 million purse would dish $1.1 million to the winner and each player would donate $100,000 to the First Tee program and another $100,000 to the charity of their choosing.

But long before the made-for-TV event would take place at the Sherwood Country Club in Thousand Oaks, California, the U.S. Open would be played in Pinehurst, North Carolina, at the famed Pinehurst No. 2 course.

"Certainly I think people kind of expected that [rivalry] to occur [at the Open]," Koch said. "Tiger had been playing pretty well and David had been playing extremely well. . . .

"But you know, it's funny, most U.S. Opens, I know the one's I've been involved with, you have all these dream matchups. You know, you'd like to see so and so go at it and so forth, well, most of the time they don't happen. They really don't. I don't know whether it's the pressure of the event, the circumstances, the difficulty of the setup, but it just seems oftentimes that the potential is there for a great duel between a handful of guys and it just doesn't seem to work out that way."

If ever a course looked perfect to facilitate a Woods-Duval showdown, the course designed by famed golf course architect Donald Ross fit the bill.

Added incentive for Woods to do well at Pinehurst No. 2 was the fact his pursuit of Jack Nicklaus had fallen behind the pace deemed necessary to surpass the greatest golfer of all time. Heading into the 1999 U.S. Open, Woods had just one major under his belt. At 23, Nicklaus had won the Masters and the U.S. Open and was a few months shy of adding a PGA Championship to his growing resume. By age thirty, Nicklaus had seven majors and had not yet entered his most dominating stretch on the Tour. Nicklaus had posted a score on the career leaderboard: seventy PGA Tour victories and eighteen majors.

Woods would enter the Open at Pinehurst No. 2 at age 23. Would this be the title Woods needed to right his ship toward accomplishing his career goal of besting Nicklaus?

Woods's history at U.S. Opens suggested otherwise.

His first Open appearance came in 1995 at Shinnecock Hills. America watched while golf's messiah flailed at the deep rough, showing great frustration at the results, and generally looking like a, um, tiger that needed to change its stripes to survive the most severe test of golf.

Woods played his final Open as an amateur at Oakland Hills in

1996 and led the first round until he played the last five holes at nine-over.

Following his 1997 Masters victory, Woods went to Congressional for the Open at the height of "Tiger Mania." Everybody had conceded he would win. The only suspense came in the expected margin of victory. Fans and media fawned over Woods and he looked unprepared for the attention. Though he made a tournament leading seventeen birdies, he was done in by a slew of double bogeys and finished in a tie for nineteenth. Woods followed by tying for eighteenth place at Olympic in 1998, which had been his best Open finish to date.

Woods's take on his Open history was simple: "In my first four Opens, I simply wasn't good enough. My good shots were great, but my bad shots were atrocious," he said. "You might get away with atrocious shots at some events, but at an Open, you just disappear when you hit wild ones. I spent the last two years trying to develop a much more consistent game, and I think that's coming along."

Woods's game, mind, and body all seemed in order. And he liked what he'd seen of Pinehurst No. 2. At age 16, he had dominated the field during a North and South Junior Amateur at Pinehurst No. 7.

"Boy, my life has changed a lot since then," Woods said, adding, perhaps, the understatement of the century. "I guess for one thing, I've got a little more in my pocket now."

The list of other potential contenders included: Justin Leonard, whose surgeonlike touch around the greens looked like a good fit at Pinehurst; Phil Mickelson, known as a long, strong iron player with a devastating short game; Ernie Els, a two-time Open champion with the smoothest swing in the game; and Vijay Singh, a consistent player who showed flashes of brilliance.

Davis Love III, who had grown up near Pinehurst, had perhaps the highest comfort level of any golfer in the field.

Born in Charlotte, Love often played Pinehurst No. 2 during his teenage years when his late father, a teaching professional, ran a *Golf Digest* instructional school at Pinehurst in the summer. He'd won Pinehurst's 1984 North and South Amateur at No. 2 and he'd attended the University of North Carolina at nearby Chapel Hill.

At age thirty-five, and ranked third in the world, Love was forecast to attain far more than the one major he'd accrued at the 1997 PGA Championship at Winged Foot. Among the frustrations was the Open that had gotten away at Oakland Hills in 1996 when he bogeyed the final two holes to lose by a stroke.

"There are a lot of people who put themselves in position to win and they win," Love said. "And there are guys who put themselves in position to win, and it gets away from them. . . . I need to get there enough times where I win them from ahead, I win them from behind, when somebody gives it to you and when you snatch one away."

If sentimentality favored anyone, Love would have been the guy.

"I've had a lot of great memories around here, especially spending time here with my dad, growing up," Love said. "Number two is kind of where I learned to play a big course for the first time. It's a course that most people hope to play someday, and I've been lucky that I've gotten to play it a lot. I've been lucky to slip out there a bunch in my formative years."

Love remembered how Jack Lumpkin, his longtime teacher, had taught him to fade the ball off the tee at Pinehurst on a hole where the fairway ran adjacent to a road. If he didn't fade the ball it would have hit the road, literally.

"Obviously, Pinehurst is one of our U.S. homes of golf," Love said. "I'd like nothing better than to win my first U.S. Open there."

Pinehurst No. 2 would be a horse of a different color for those expecting to see a traditional Open course.

"It's not going to be what any of us who've ever played it in the past have been used to," Love said. "You're not going to be able to get the ball on the green as much as you want to. You're going to have to be patient and hole a lot of putts for par."

Love likened the strategy needed to play Pinehurst to that of playing Augusta National.

"You'll see some shots played around the greens a lot like you see at the Masters—bump and runs or putts from just off the edge of the green," Love said. "The greens aren't very big, so [the preferred option might be to] get it on the green front-middle and try to two-putt."

Pinehurst No. 2 appeared to be just the remedy for breaking an odd streak of Open history. Since World War II, Great Britain native Tony Jacklin was the only European player to win the Open, accomplishing the feat in 1970. Along the way there had been some close calls. Curtis Strange defeated England's Nick Faldo in a playoff in 1988. Ian Woosnam of Wales finished a stroke behind Strange in 1989, and Colin Montgomerie had lost out in a three-way playoff in 1994 and finished second in 1997. Could a champion evolve from a highly qualified 1999 European contingent? Lee Westwood had dazzled with his overall game; Montgomerie hit the ball straight, had Open experience, and had posted recent wins at the Benson and Hedges and Volvo PGA; and Olazabal was the Masters champion.

"I think [Jacklin] is motivation for every British golfer and every European golfer to try and emulate [winning the Open]," Montgomerie said. "It's been almost thirty years now. It's been too long, really, we feel."

The Europeans had a lot of pride, the same pride that fuels their valiant Ryder Cup efforts, and were quick to point out far more Americans than Europeans play in the U.S. Open. The flaw in that logic came in the fact the Americans were far outnumbered in the

British Open and had taken home the Claret Jug sixteen times during the same twenty-eight years.

The only non-Americans to win the U.S. Open since Jacklin's victory were David Graham of Australia in 1981 and Els of South Africa in 1994 and 1997.

Freak luck obviously contributed to the lopsided balance sheet. More to the heart of the matter were the different styles of European and American golfers. Most European golfers were weaned on links courses where fighting the wind was a major part of their golfing education. Most U.S. Open venues were better suited for players who could hit a ball high and straight without straying into the deep rough, which clearly characterized the American players more than their European counterparts.

At a U.S. Open "It's important to be able to go from point A to point B and from point B to point C," Olazabal said. "I think the Americans do that better than the Europeans, with maybe the exception of [Montgomerie], who is straight off the tee and a very good iron player."

The Europeans' chances seemed enhanced playing a U.S. Open on Pinehurst No. 2, a course more closely resembling those that hosted British Opens.

"The way the [course] setup is, it brings a lot more people into the mix," Duval said. "You have options of advancing the ball [from the rough, unlike at other Opens]. I think it's a lot more wide open."

Typically the Europeans might stray off the tee, but they excelled in their mastery of the short game, which included imagination and versatility.

"The only reason [there was talk of a European winner] was because it was a very un-American setup," Mark Lye said. "You had to play the ball on the ground if you missed the green. And so in that way everyone thought perhaps a European would show very well.

Also the rough wasn't the typical American, U.S. Open rough. That rough was very playable."

Shots at Pinehurst No. 2 would prompt golfers to hit anything from a bump-and-run shot with a 3-iron to putting from way off the green and even using fairway woods to chip.

"I've always said that the U.S. Open doesn't suit my game," Olazabal said. "Because my driving is not all that accurate . . . I've had tournaments where I drove the ball well for two or three days, but I don't think I've been very, very pleased with my driving ever in my life. I can't deny that the short game [will] play a part in this tournament, which hasn't happened for the past few years anyway."

Added Westwood: "I think it gives more people an opportunity to win. You don't have to be quite as straight. The tee shots aren't as demanding, and it brings into play the short game more."

Montgomerie touted the chances of Olazabal, who wasn't the straightest player off the tee.

"He has a chance to use his enormous talent around the greens and [his] imagination, which this will take," Montgomerie said.

Such comments from his peers brought about speculation Olazabal might become the first golfer in twenty-seven years to win the first two legs of the Grand Slam. Olazabal quickly tried to silence the suggestion any golfer, including him, could capture the Grand Slam.

"It's the closest thing to impossible to win the Grand Slam in a single year," Olazabal said before adding, "I would like to be wrong."

Olazabal conceded the short game would be a key element for the winner, but Pinehurst No. 2 would require more than just a quality short game.

"I still believe that driving plays a very important part," Olazabal said. "And I don't think I'm the only guy who has a pretty good short game. There are a lot of players here who have pretty good short games."

Montgomerie felt the Europeans needed to be opportunistic at Pinehurst No. 2.

"We've been quite close [to breaking the streak]," Montgomerie said. "It's a matter of being patient and trying to walk through when that door is ajar."

CHAPTER EIGHT

PREPPING FOR AN OPEN

UNLIKE SOME OF THE "TRICKED-UP" courses hosting other U.S. Opens, Pinehurst No. 2 didn't need to alter its character in preparation of the Open. Even the rough remained relatively short by Open standards. Instead of the customary five-inch rough, Pinehurst No. 2's Bermuda rough ran approximately three inches.

Bermuda grass typically grows straight up and down, leaving little support at the top portion of the rough, which sends most balls that land in the rough straight to the bottom every time.

"Three inches was adequate," Fred Ridley said. "If you hit the ball in the rough you might have had a shot, but it wasn't like being in the fairway. So you couldn't spin the ball."

Coming into play was the mind-set that if the rough were lower, players would view their options differently.

"I think the reason that was attractive was that these greens were so firm and fast and you had all these runoff areas that the committee thought it would be somewhat exciting to see players get in the rough and take a rip at it with the ball going anywhere," Ridley said.

Pinehurst No. 2 looked different around the greens, too. Not only did they leave the rough shorter, they elected not to grow the rough up around the green thereby keeping the character of the course intact. Donald Ross's intention around the greens was to force golfers to use plenty of creativity to combat the sloping greens and surrounding areas that pitched and tilted just so, routing errant shots to roll away into swales and depressions.

"If you've got rough everywhere and you hit the ball out and miss the green, it's just going to hit the rough and stop," Ridley said. "But at Pinehurst there were very few greens where you had any rough around the greens. For the most part the ball just rolls off and the rough doesn't start for twenty or thirty feet off the green. So you're going to have a tricky little shot if you miss the green."

Pinehurst No. 2 wasn't going to serve up the typical U.S. Open course, but those familiar with the storied course knew it would extract its pound of flesh.

Michael Fay talked to a friend who played the course shortly before the Open and was told, "I got really tired of chipping after I putted."

Harvie Ward received a similar forecast about the storm fast approaching the best golfers in the world.

"I had a couple of friends who were pretty good players who came over to play [Pinehurst No. 2] and they were hitting 9-iron and pitching wedge to the green and couldn't find a ball mark," Ward said. "They said the ball was bouncing as high as the flag."

Ward spoke at a dinner shortly before the Open and told the audience, "I don't think anybody's going to break par, I think par is going to be an excellent score."

Paul Jett, the superintendent of Pinehurst No. 2, was in charge of preparing the course to meet USGA standards.

"The USGA tells us how wide they want the fairways, how deep they want the rough, and how fast they want the greens," Jett said. "Our job is to give that to them."

Jett dispelled prevailing views about the USGA in regard to their approach toward prepping a course for a U.S. Open.

"There's a misconception that the USGA comes over and dictates maintenance, takes over," Jett said. "Nothing could be further from the truth. They tell us what they'd like and we know how to prepare our course best, so the end result is up to us."

How Pinehurst No. 2 arrived at those results began long before the weeks leading up to hosting the Open. Part of that preparation involved comparing notes with other Opens. Jett went to the 1997 and 1998 Opens at Congressional and Olympic to observe and to get a feel for the business of prepping a course ready for the U.S. Open and how to operate during the week of an Open.

"I saw two different maintenance regimes," Jett said of his experience observing the two Opens leading to No. 2's. "At Congressional they must have had a hundred and twenty people on their maintenance crew. They walk mowed everything. I think it was the first time I'd seen fairways walk mowed."

Jett considered walk mowing every fairway excessive, particularly after watching Olympic's crew handle the '98 Open with far fewer workers. Jett also observed how much preparation time was available prior to the first tee time and what the crews did after play had been finished for the day.

"I tried to relate it to Pinehurst No. 2 to think about how we would do things," Jett said. "It helped give us a plan about what I should be thinking about."

A maintenance obstacle Jett's crew needed to tackle resulted from the fact several holes at No. 2 doubled back parallel to other holes on the course. Congressional and Olympic had no parallel holes. Because of this facet to Pinehurst, Jett's crews would not be able to begin mowing a hole immediately after the final group passed through.

The schedule called for the course to be mowed twice daily. Jett had a pet peeve he addressed in his mowing instructions.

"In the morning I had the mowers go one way all the way up the fairway toward the greens and in the afternoon they ran from green to tee," Jett said. "I didn't want to put stripes in the fairway. That was a personal thing. I didn't want [NBC analyst] Johnny Miller to talk about the way the fairways were mowed affecting a lie. I figured [mowing the fairways in one direction] would eliminate one comment off the books."

Advance troubleshooting took Jett to Augusta National where he talked with Marsh Benson, Augusta National's director of golf maintenance. From this meeting came the idea to have five two-man crews stationed on the course with the capability of handling any number of problems that might arise.

Jett stationed eight-to-ten workers around the course specifically to rake wire grass on the mounds, three to rake the dirt cart paths and twelve to handle whipping. Whipping is the process of using an extended piece of fiberglass resembling a whip to clear impediments from the course. The whipping crews would start at the first tee and hand whip the entire course, clearing stray grass dropped from the mowers or any other objects that might have found their way onto the course to potentially impact a player's shot. Jett had observed on TV how the tee boxes for par-3s often resembled a strip-mined piece of land given the number of divots. Addressing this, Jett stationed a worker on every par-3 and some par-4s to pick up the divots and fill the spots with sand.

Jett had thirty regular workers on the payroll until six weeks prior to the tournament when he brought aboard ten additional workers in the form of interns. He had to cull a list of hungry college turf students eager to work at an Open.

"We ended up with students from Texas A&M, Clemson, Mississippi State, Virginia Tech, it was a highly qualified group," Jett said.

Fifty volunteers were added the week of the tournament.

"They did whatever had to be done," Jett said. "I was pretty much at the course from sunup to sundown."

The USGA asked that the fairways be maintained at three-eighths of an inch and the rough be consistent at three inches from the edge of the fairway to the rope line. Despite the rain that would come, the greens would vary from 10.5 on the stimpmeter, a device that measures the speed of the greens, to 12 on Sunday, which is a treacherous speed, particularly on Pinehurst No. 2's sloping greens.

"Generally, I believe the golf course is in excellent condition," Jett told the media prior to the first round.

Tim Moraghan, chief agronomist for the USGA, explained that keeping the rough cut at three inches was not a change of policy, rather a decision based on the location of the 1999 Open.

"This is warm-season grass, Bermuda grass, a little thicker," Moraghan said. "It has a tendency to grab the club a little more; harder to play out of. We have an issue, too. I think if we had the traditional U.S. Open rough in a cool season scenario, where the height of cut was above five inches, we could have a lost ball, five or six feet off the edge of the fairway. And I don't think we want to do that."

Moraghan stressed the USGA was not out to embarrass anybody.

"We try to make it more equitable for the player," Moraghan said.

"Let them try to advance the ball more than twenty yards, but I don't think that's going to be a change of philosophy at all. We'd like to set it up like we'd like to have it played."

Jett believed Pinehurst No. 2 would hold up during the week, noteworthy given the age of the course and the advances in golfing technology.

"I think to me—I believe this golf course could stand for a long time, just because of the greens," Jett said. "Nobody is going to get scared playing this course from tee to fairway. The fairways are ample width, I guess, twenty-eight to thirty yards that USGA normally makes, they play fairly wide, because obviously, they're pretty flat. But with the penalty of a bad iron shot around—from the fairway into the green—I believe this golf course would stand for many, many years, no matter how good the players got, because you're never going to get every shot exactly where it needs to be hit. With certain pin placements and different conditions you have to be so precise with the irons; and then if you're not, then the chipping game has to be exceptional."

With rain in the forecast some believed Pinehurst No. 2 would be defenseless against the world's best golfers attacking the greens. Jett and his crew had the capability of mechanically vacuuming the water from the putting surface through a system called SubAir that could be attached to the end of the drain lines.

"But the surface that we would like to have would be one where we can control the amount of water that goes on, preferably through a hose in the morning and in the evening, and not have uncontrollable amounts of rain put on the golf course, which will, no matter how well it drains, soften it more than what I think it needs to be for this week," Jett said.

Preparing the course is only part of the preparation for a spectacle such as the U.S. Open, particularly given the unusual arrangement

Pinehurst had with the USGA to run the tournament. Most U.S. Opens are totally controlled by the USGA. To help get the state of North Carolina unified for the event an eighteen-member "President's Council" was created to help sell corporate support.

"This is a great corporate event," Beth Kocher said. "It allows a corporation to bring in two or three clients, wine and dine them, play some golf, and watch the best golfers in the world."

By the time visitors began arriving at Pinehurst, there were two hundred and thirty-eight corporate clients underneath three hundred twenty thousand yards of canvas tents.

A quality transportation plan had to be made to get upward of forty thousand people in and out of the Village of Pinehurst each day. The Department of Transportation of North Carolina played an integral role in developing this plan. Fans were shuttled in by bus from the north and south ends of Pinehurst.

"We had held the '94 Senior Open [at Pinehurst] and that was like a dry run," Kocher said. "It wasn't like having the Open, but it helped give us some idea about what to expect. We went into the '99 Open in awe, knowing it was bigger than anything. But also knowing we had some solid people. There was a real air of excitement in the area since the U.S. Open hadn't been in the South since 1976. We had over five thousand volunteers come in to work the event with representatives from forty-seven states and seven countries. There was almost a fever."

CHAPTER NINE

OPEN WEEK BEGINS

THOUGH PLEASED WITH HIS GAME, Payne Stewart couldn't get it going and failed to make the cut at the St. Jude Classic in Memphis, Tennessee, the week before the U.S. Open.

"Payne wasn't into it," Mike Hicks said. "I could see he was looking toward the Open. We didn't talk a whole lot. It would have been one thing if he'd have been in contention and we were trying to win the golf tournament. But we were kind of floundering around the cut. I know I was thinking about Pinehurst and I think in the back of his mind he was, too, but he wouldn't admit to that. But I think he was."

At first Stewart planned to remain in Memphis until he talked to Tracey.

"I suggested that he head on to Pinehurst," Tracey said. "He didn't want to at first. His mother had actually gone to Memphis.

He was kind of down about missing the cut. I told him he could go to the course, take Chuck [Cook], and get used to the course."

Stewart took Tracey's advice to heart. When he called to tell Cook about his plan, Cook asked him to wait for him so he wouldn't have to change his flight to Memphis; they had planned to work on Stewart's game while he played in the St. Jude. Once in Memphis, Stewart and Cook boarded a private plane and flew to Pinehurst and Cook began to unveil a game plan for the Open.

"I told him No. 2 was a chipping golf course," Cook said. "I said, 'Nobody is going to hit a lot of greens, because these greens are like upside-down bowls. You're going to have to really chip your ball this week.' "

Examination of the golf course revealed the fairways were huge relative to most U.S. Opens and the rough was manageable.

"Let's just chip and putt," Cook told Stewart. "Let's don't even play the course, let's just chip and putt."

Stewart and Cook walked the course for two days playing all the angles on and around the greens.

Stewart chipped from all different spots. Cook took Stewart's yardage book and went to spots from where he deemed it would be difficult to get up and down. At first the exercise perplexed Stewart, who asked Cook, "What are you doing?"

Cook explained he wanted Stewart to be aware of the taboo areas around the green and how he was marking them in his yardage book.

"Mark them in red," Stewart said.

"Nah, I don't want you being afraid of it," Cook said. "I'm going to mark them in blue."

Cook and Stewart meticulously went to every green and marked spots from where Stewart would not want to play his ball.

"Like a spot on the eighth hole where you could hit the ball and if it didn't go far enough, it could roll back to your feet," Cook said.

Per Cook's instruction, Stewart was to aim at the middle of areas of the greens he marked in white.

"You aim at that white area no matter where the pin is," Cook told Stewart.

Referencing the par-4 no. 8 again as an example, Cook said the strategy was to shoot at the front right portion of the green.

"If he pulled it he'd still be on the green," Cook said. "If he hit a great shot he'd have an uphill putt. If he missed a little to the right he'd have a little chip up a hill. So there weren't any problems. We marked the whole golf course that way."

By the time the weekend of walking the course had run its course, Stewart had used nine different clubs to execute shots around the green: 2-, 3-, 4-, 5-, 7-, and 8-irons, along with his pitching, lob and, sand wedges.

Typical of Stewart's sense of fun was the "Pocket National" hat he wore while looking over the course with Cook.

Stewart lived on Pocket Lake in Orlando, where John Brendle and he created Pocket National, a neighborhood golf course. Not the kind with fairways, sand traps, and greens. Rather the kind of golf course kids played where they walked the neighborhood with one club and one ball, and each hole was a designated tree. Hitting a ball off said tree was the equivalent of rolling in a putt. Pocket National's nineteenth hole had no limits.

"Every kid who ever played golf has done this," Brendle said. "You wouldn't believe the number of people who played Pocket National. I called Payne the owner of the course."

Prior to the St. Jude Classic, Brendle, Cook, and Stewart played Pocket National. Cook was eliminated, leaving Brendle and Stewart to compete in a playoff hole for the championship. Stewart got to pick the tee and selected a tree on the other side of Brendle's house, which demanded a shot that had to pass directly over a large picture window.

"Added danger," Brendle said. "If one of us hit it, I was going to have to fix it. He had no worries. He was just putting the heat on me. He was fun like that."

Brendle won that day's championship and sent Stewart off with a hat decorated with a logo Brendle had designed at an embroidery shop. The logo had a sailboat with golf clubs adorning it.

"During the practice round [at No. 2] Payne wore the hat with the logo on it," Brendle said. "Someone asked him where Pocket National was and he said, 'Oh, it's down in Central Florida.'"

In addition to his Pocket National hat, Stewart donned shorts during his weekend practice round.

"Payne put on shorts just to irritate Tom Meeks, because before the tournament you're allowed to play in shorts," Cook said. "When Payne saw Tom Meeks he told him, 'I'm wearing these shorts because I can.'"

Stewart and Meeks had actually become friends during the Tour's Florida swing in March.

Meeks was teaching a rules seminar in Orlando when he had an opportunity to play golf at Isleworth, Stewart's home course, which is a sister course of Bay Hill. Meeks's group went out to hit balls on the driving range prior to their round when suddenly he saw an unfamiliar pair of shoes within his range of vision.

"I raise my eyes up and lo and behold, there's Payne Stewart," Meeks said. "He says, 'You and I have got to talk.'"

Through this brief exchange, they arranged to meet for lunch and play nine holes. Given Stewart and Meeks's shotgun wedding introduction at the previous year's Open, it was inevitable that sand-filled divots eventually became the topic of discussion during their outing. Stewart clearly favored players getting relief from such lies.

"I can tell you right now, we're not going to change that," Meeks said. "We'll put in any kind of sand fill you want us to."

"The problem I have with the sand-filled divots is I don't know how deep the divot is," Stewart said. "So how do I know how to play the shot?"

"Well, we're not about to change it," Meeks said. "Have you ever practiced hitting from a sand-filled divot? You can go to any practice range where they fill the divots or you can fill your own. Why don't you practice that?"

Stewart did not seem to embrace the idea, but their meeting had served both well and presented further evidence of Stewart's growth through his ability to forgive.

"After that nine holes I felt like I had gained a wonderful friend and I'd also gained the respect of a wonderful friend," Meeks said. "And I kind of think that he had the same feeling about me. That he thought, 'This guy is not the jerk I expected him to be. He's got some common sense, he's very proud of his job, proud of his organization, and he's going to continue to challenge us at the U.S. Open like he should.' "

Teasing with Meeks, wearing his Pocket National hat and having the confidence to prepare by only chipping showed how loose and relaxed Stewart felt while preparing to battle No. 2, but the aftertaste of his last tournament lingered.

Hicks and Stewart sat down to talk after Sunday's practice round. The pair had been together since the late 1980s, which made them the Tour equivalent of an old married couple. Hicks knew something was bothering Stewart. And he was right, Stewart hadn't gotten over Memphis.

"You didn't do a very good job last week," Stewart told Hicks.

"What do you mean?" Hicks said.

"The back nine there on Friday when you didn't say two words to me," Stewart said.

"We were both thinking about this week," Hicks said. "I know I was."

"I was, too, in a way," Stewart said. "But you still didn't do your job."

Hicks said such conversations were not unusual given the nature of the caddie/player relationship.

"I think [a caddie's job] is really figuring out his player's personality," Hicks said. "Not only knowing what to say, but when you can say it. Some guys can take constructive criticism right away. Some guys you have to give them a little cooling off period. Basically, it's getting to know the guy's personality. You're with them about as much time as they're with their wife.

"After say, two years or so, I could pretty much say whatever I wanted to him. He never once told me to be quiet or didn't listen. He basically wouldn't say anything to me, he'd just look at me."

Stewart had not questioned Hicks's work habits in several years.

"But we could talk to each other about anything," Hicks said. "He got that off his chest and we went forward. I'm glad he told me, because he was right. But it turned out to be a blessing we missed that cut or we would have been stuck there like everybody else."

Rain forced the St. Jude's final round to be played on Monday.

"By the time the guys got there on Tuesday we were playing our last practice round," Hicks said. "We'd seen it three times, so Wednesday we had off to rest."

Dr. Richard Coop continued to work with Stewart on the mental aspects of his game.

"I was mainly trying to work with him on his pre-shot routine, trying to get him to be more disciplined earlier in the week," Coop said. "I didn't want him to wait until he got to the first tee to get into his pre-shot routine and get into his discipline. I wanted him to play his practice rounds the way he was going to play the tournament."

Coop chuckled remembering how this philosophy led to a mild contest of wills between him and Stewart.

"We had a little head-butting session on Tuesday," Coop said. "He didn't want to do what I wanted him to do, so we had a little disagreement."

Rather than force the issue, Coop went passive-aggressive by turning his attentions on the range to another player who worked with him.

"Before I even went back to Payne I could see him from the corner of my eye and he was doing what I wanted him to do," Coop said.

Typical of Stewart and Coop's relationship, Stewart acknowledged Coop had been right.

"But not in words," Coop said. "Just a little sheepish grin, I knew and he knew."

Coop's prescribed pre-shot routine was simple.

"We wanted him to get an intermediate target to aim over, to get behind the ball and choose something down the fairway where he wanted to land the ball, then choose an intermediate spot about a foot, a foot and a half out in front of his ball," Coop said. "And we had a cleansing breath where he breathed in through his nose and out from his mouth, like a free-throw shooter."

Coop gave Stewart a trigger that served as a signal Stewart could use to prompt him to focus on the shot. While establishing a pre-shot routine sounds simple, getting Stewart to focus on anything continued to be a challenge.

"We worked on him letting go of his focus between shots," Coop said. "Try and get more relaxed, not be like Ben Hogan, frowning and being in total concentration. Payne was not that way. That approach wouldn't have worked for him. He did not meditate or anything. So we tried to take his natural thing, which was to come in and out of focus, and use it.

"We figured he had eighteen or twenty seconds. If he could just focus that long on hitting the golf ball, then he could let go a little bit. Eighteen or twenty seconds is kind of the pattern I found for most golfers. And Payne fit pretty nicely into that. You have a Berhard Langer, who is maybe up to a minute and ten seconds, and Jim Gallagher, who might do about seven or eight seconds. But most Tour players, depending on when you decide the pre-shot routine should start, it takes about eighteen to twenty seconds to really get focused and hit the shot."

Coop and Stewart also continued to work on Stewart becoming the best possible golfer he could be for seventy-two holes.

"We talked a lot about challenges," Coop said. "Golf is a game of challenges."

Recognizing the challenges, Coop would have Stewart write "C" three times at the top of his scorecard. Every time something went wrong he'd just cross through one of the Cs. Coop told Stewart Cs were part of the game and not to let them fluster him.

"Some days you have five or six, but most rounds, you have four or five," Coop said.

Coop believed the exercise helped promote a positive mind-set by recognizing every player faced challenges. The three Cs helped combat the feeling of "why me?"

"When you go back into the locker room, every player has a story about how many bad breaks they've got," Coop said. "Just understanding they're not by themselves is a big step. Physically, just checking them off is a reminder that it's a fairly normal thing to have a bad break. But calling them challenges instead of a bad break is a better way of doing it, more positive."

Coop sought other advantages to helping him play better.

"Payne was a little bit like that speckled trout, every fly that came by he was interested in it," Coop said. "Everything got his attention. I'd worked with a lot of football teams and basketball teams where they would sequester the players before a game. So I got to looking at golfers and they were always in a hotel. They were always out. They were always getting people tickets right up until the last minute, doing all these little things for friends coming in or family coming in."

Coop tried to convince Stewart to be more like the Orlando Magic, the team Stewart loved, telling Stewart he didn't think the Magic's coach would let his players be running around before the game getting everybody tickets.

"We walked backwards from team sports to golf," Coop said. "And we tried to make his major tournaments more like a Super Bowl or an NBA final. I had worked a lot with team sports, so I was able to give him some ideas he could use."

In line with this philosophy, Stewart stayed at a private residence—a condominium on Pinehurst No. 6, which he'd done in the past when he had experienced successful performances at majors.

Cook, Coop, and Hicks—aka "Team Stewart"—all felt Stewart was better prepared for the 1999 U.S. Open than he had been prepared for any tournament he'd ever played.

Stewart talked about facing the pressure of playing in a major following his practice round on Tuesday.

"I think [learning how to deal with pressure] comes just over time spent out here putting yourself in that situation," Stewart said. "I think you learn how to deal with it. I can't sit here and tell you that

I can go out, and if I happen to be leading the golf tournament on Sunday, that I won't feel any pressure. Sure, I'll feel pressure. I'm human. I think that learning how to deal with it over—through my past experiences—I think I'm better with dealing with it than I was years ago, say, at Shinnecock when Raymond won. I didn't understand. I wasn't prepared for it. I think I'm prepared for that now, being able to handle the situation when it presents itself."

Stewart seemed genuinely excited about the skills that would come into play in order to do well at Pinehurst No. 2.

"This [course] is a gem—it's a pleasure to play," Stewart said. "And when you're excited about going out and playing, you tend to play a little better, rather than being miserable."

Stewart expressed excitement about playing No. 2, but he offered another view to Meeks regarding No. 16.

"When I got to Pinehurst, someone told me Payne was out on the golf course, so I was kind of looking for him to say hello," Meeks said. "I finally run into him and I tell him good luck and so on, the general stuff. And he says, 'I don't like the way you set up 16.'"

No. 16 is a par-5 for the regular players, but Meeks and the USGA made the hole a par-4 for the Open, the longest in Open history at the time at 489 yards.

"That green was designed for a short iron and you're playing it now as a four-hundred-and-eighty-five-yard par four where I have to hit a long iron into it," Stewart said. "It wasn't designed for a long iron."

"That's interesting, Payne," Meeks said. "I'll tell you what I'll do. I'll move the tee markers all the way back to the back of the tee box, which will make it play five hundred and thirty yards, we'll play it as a par five, if you promise me you and everyone in this field will not go for this green in two, because it's not designed to be hit with a long iron. Will you promise me that?"

"You're impossible," Stewart said, walking away, halfway joking and halfway peeved.

"He realized I'd kind of stumped him again," Meeks said with a chuckle.

Other elite players who missed the cut at Memphis, allowing them to have an early look at Pinehurst No. 2, included former U.S. Open champions Tom Kite and Fuzzy Zoeller in addition to former major winners Bob Tway, Jeff Sluman, Mark Brooks, and John Daly.

Masters champion Jose Maria Olazabal played his way to the top of the leaderboard on Sunday at Memphis moving to eight-under for the day through fourteen holes and fifteen-under for the tournament. Then the skies opened, unleashing a torrential downpour that forced the postponement of the final round until Monday. For the players scheduled to play the Open, a postponement was the worst possible situation. Most had planned to fly to Pinehurst Sunday night and play a practice round on Monday.

"I don't like that, I don't like that at all," Olazabal said. "But, you know, those things happen, and, well, you have to take them. I have to find a way to feel comfortable."

Olazabal and other players had planned to board a charter flight to Pinehurst after Sunday's round; such a flight was not available on Monday.

Assuming everything fell into place the following day, Olazabal rationalized about his altered schedule.

"I should be [at Pinehurst] tomorrow evening, not too late, anyway," Olazabal said. "That would give me two rounds of practice next week. Obviously, it is not what we had in mind, but you know, I came to play this tournament here, and if the tournament finishes on Monday, I'm going to stay."

Ted Tryba stood at thirteen-under in contention with a host of other players at Memphis. His best finish for the year had been second place at the Nissan Open so a delay didn't hit him the same way it had Olazabal.

"I've played well for fifty-four holes," Tryba said. "I want to play seventy-two and win a golf tournament."

Packing his positive vibes while delaying his departure for Pinehurst, Tryba eagled the sixteenth hole en route to a five-under 66 to win the tournament; Olazabal tied for fourth.

Tryba planned to arrive at Pinehurst Monday night then play eighteen holes on Tuesday and nine on Wednesday, his tee time for practice rounds was 6:40 A.M. both days.

"It's one of those situations where I guess these golfers have a full-time job; no days off," Tryba said.

Tryba didn't sound too upset given the manner in which he was heading into the Open.

"I feel good," he said. "I've never gone into a U.S. Open playing this well. . . . I've never gone into there playing well at all. I feel confident that I can go in there and at least have a chance to compete."

Tom Lehman finished two shots out of the lead at Memphis and was chagrined about there not being another available charter flight.

"I was disappointed with the fact that it was just like, 'Sorry, you guys, you're on your own,'" Lehman said. "Getting to Pinehurst is not an easy proposition, especially at the eleventh hour, trying to get your three kids, wife, and cousin—six people from here to there is not easy. I was disappointed with the fact that it was like we're going to stay and play and you're on your own, kind of a scramble to get there. We had all planned on taking the charter and—to me, I was upset with that. There's not much you can do about that. It all worked out well. We all found our way there and everything is fine."

Bob Burns remained in Memphis to play the tournament before

electing to drive a rental car from Memphis to the Village of Pine-hurst.

"I didn't get there until Tuesday afternoon," Burns said. "I remember it was heck getting down there. I played one practice round on Wednesday. It throws your tempo off a little."

Greg Norman withdrew from the final round in Memphis after rounds of 66, 72, and 72, noting that once he fell from contention he wanted to have the extra day of practice.

"I had my reasons, but I basically saw what the weather forecast was going to be and one of the tour officials told me what was going to happen Sunday [if it rained], so I decided to go," Norman said. "I was a genius. I came home and I practiced my short game all day Sunday, bump-and-run stuff that we knew we needed up here. We did the same thing Monday. Now, let's hope it pays off. I thought it was more beneficial to my game to go home than to stay there and finish fifty-eighth."

Ron Philo wasn't on the PGA Tour. He didn't need to compare and contrast the benefits of staying at one tournament instead of preparing for another. So despite qualifying for the Open, life went on as usual for Philo. Bills needed to be paid, his family had to be cared for, and he continued to work. However, his qualifying did elevate him to local celebrity status at the Country Club of Vermont.

"Everybody was very excited," Philo said. "There haven't been many golf professionals from Vermont to participate in the U.S. Open. It was neat for the membership. They were very excited and supportive."

Several members of the club booked trips to Pinehurst to watch Philo while others pitched in to raise money to help Philo cover his expenses. Making arrangements to go to the U.S. Open might be second nature to a PGA Tour professional, but Philo came from another spectrum of the golf world. Fortunately he had a connection for making his arrangements.

Philo's sister, Laura Diaz, played on the LPGA and was represented by IMG, which allowed him to make a single phone call to her agent and they immediately had six different places to choose from for where they wanted to stay.

"We were able to rent a house for the week," Philo said. "We were very comfortable for the week."

The Philos flew into Raleigh, North Carolina, the Sunday before the Open. Because most of the Tour remained in Memphis, Pinehurst was a ghost town. And it would remain so through Monday. Philo walked the course with his caddie Sunday afternoon.

"I remember walking out there on Sunday and Payne Stewart was playing the eighteenth hole that evening," Philo said. "He was dressed in shorts. It was so odd to see him out of costume. At first you didn't recognize him until you got close."

Despite lacking the background of most of the golfers he'd be competing against at Pinehurst No. 2, Philo's career included playing in three PGA Championships and he'd learned from the experience and made his schedule accordingly.

"I didn't sign up to play a round on Wednesday," Philo said. "The thing I knew was the excitement of playing the practice rounds can wear you out. By the time you get to Thursday you've used up all your energy."

Philo signed up to play practice rounds on Monday and Tuesday mornings at 8:30 and found his name as the only one listed for the time.

"There were less than ten names total on the list," Philo said.

Philo's practice round on Monday wasn't memorable, but Tuesday's held a surprise. When he arrived at the course on Tuesday he found his caddie grinning from ear to ear.

"Did you see who signed up to play with us?" the caddie said.

"No, but I'm sure it must be somebody special from the look on your face," Philo said.

Tom Watson, Davis Love, and Fred Couples were signed up to play with Philo.

"That was something else," Philo said. "I'll never forget that."

But it wasn't the typical practice round with which Philo was familiar.

"The practice round was a little odd because when I play practice rounds I like to play golf," Philo said. "I like to hit the greens and try to make the putts and maybe do a little fooling around outside of that. Tom Watson played the practice round like that but Fred Couples and Davis Love, after they hit their shots to the green, they'd just get their caddies to pick up their balls then they'd just spend the whole time chipping and putting from around the green. That was very different for me. I remember I didn't drive it very well. I didn't drive it the way I was accustomed to and it didn't get any better that day. Otherwise, I just remember walking around and talking with them. They were telling some stories. It was a lot of fun."

Watson made a lasting impression.

"The most extraordinary thing I remember about the entire week happened after we had finished playing on Tuesday," Philo said. "I went into the contestants' dining area and I was sitting with my back to the door and Tom Watson, Davis Love, and Fred Couples were sitting around the table kind of facing the door. It was about one o'clock and my wife showed up holding my daughter's hand and holding the baby carriage. And Tom Watson immediately stood up as she came in the door. I had my back to her so I didn't even know it was her. As she came over he extended his hand and introduced himself. It was the most extraordinary act that spoke just volumes. Not only is this guy one of the greatest players ever to play the game, he's just truly a class individual, a gentleman. Introducing himself around like she wouldn't know who he is. I've played golf all my life and she's been around since she's been married to me, pretty obvious who he was."

Janzen arrived from Orlando on Sunday with his wife and their five-year-old son. He knew the feeling of arriving at an Open as the defending champion from his experience after winning the 1993 Open. He had a different mind-set following his 1998 victory.

"The second time around I really enjoyed it more," Janzen said. "I knew what to expect. I knew not to give back the trophy too early. I brought [the trophy] in on Wednesday before the tournament. They usually want to have it back months before that. But why shouldn't I keep it as long as I could? They didn't know where it was."

On keeping the trophy for a year, Janzen said, "I didn't do a Stanley Cup thing with it," meaning he didn't take the trophy around to different destinations like hockey players do the fabled trophy for winning the championship of the National Hockey League. "We just had the trophy somewhere at home," said the understated Janzen.

Over the course of the year leading up to the 1999 Open, Janzen did notice some changes in the trophy, which Payne Stewart had added some character to during his tenure with the trophy after winning the 1991 Open.

"When I got the trophy in ninety-three, there were some different markings," Janzen said with a chuckle. "I noticed they'd been repaired when I got it in ninety-eight. Payne had marked it. I told Payne, 'Hey look, they fixed that dent.'"

Janzen played a few holes on Sunday and practice rounds Monday and Tuesday.

"I've seen the course plenty of times," he said. "And unless some weather comes in and the course plays completely different than what I've seen already—I know the shots I'm supposed to hit. It's just whether or not I can do it."

Phil Mickelson arrived at the Village of Pinehurst carrying two five-hundred-pound gorillas on his back.

The first was the obvious: He and David Duval were the most talented golfers on the Tour to never have won a major.

Mickelson, who played left-handed, brought a superb blend of power—he was one of the longest players off the tee on the Tour—and finesse—Lefty's lob flop shot to the green was unmatched. At age twenty-nine, Mickelson had earned $10.7 million during his career and had the look galleries loved: dimples, an easy smile, and a thick head of hair.

Mickelson had grown up in San Diego a natural right-hander, but learned to play the game by standing across from his father and mirroring his swing, which turned him into a left-handed player. While approaching the final hole during his first-ever round of golf at age 4 Mickelson began to cry, not from anything that had happened out on the course, rather the youngster loved playing so much he didn't want to stop. This passion later translated to thirty-five San Diego County titles, a U.S. Amateur title, and a win on the PGA Tour's Northern Telecom Open as a collegian at Arizona State.

Despite Mickelson's passion and ability to go low, he often gambled and paid dearly for poor shots hit when taking those risks. And he did not have a particularly inspiring record on the final days of majors. Hearing Mickelson and "choke" in the same sentence was commonplace.

"You were never out of it when you were up against Phil," David Whitley said. "Because he can be up by five shots then he tries something that flops and you're right back in it. So much of his [coming up short in majors] is self-inflicted. He insists on going his way. You want him to just learn from his mistakes. Sort of like Payne Stewart squared. He's very cooperative [with the media] and very likeable. It's not like people are waiting to come down on him. Generally I think everybody was pulling for Phil. He's made a ton of dough, won a ton of Buick Invitationals. Mickelson had more talent than anybody other than Tiger but he couldn't win a major."

To the modern golf fan, winning a major has taken on a life of its own—like major leaguers who have had complete and full careers without ever having played in a World Series, à la Ernie Banks, or an NBA great like Charles Barkley, who had the misfortune of playing during the tenures of Air Jordan and Shaq. The longer a player deemed worthy of having the talent to win a major goes without winning a major the heavier the gorilla becomes.

Mickelson had declared a new emphasis on winning majors and earlier in the 1999 season addressed his lack of winning one and the label of "best player never to have won a major."

"I don't think [the label] is unfair," Mickelson said. "The majors take golf to the highest level. The greens are faster and harder than you see anywhere else. The fairways are narrower. The rough is deeper. The majors challenge you in ways that regular tour events don't."

Mickelson changed to a simple heel-shafted blade putter sized to the width of the hole and he took a hard look at his attacking approach to playing a golf course. Statistics told him he had been thirty-seven over par on par-3 holes during the 1998 season, which told him to set the reasonable goal of making four pars on the par-3s thereby removing the possibility of killing his round. Further, he told himself to gamble less with the driver—taking double bogey out of the equation.

The other gorilla weighing heavy on Mickelson rested back in Arizona, where his pregnant wife, Amy, awaited her coming labor and delivery of the couple's first child. How could any good father miss the birth of his first child?

Mickelson arrived late on Tuesday after going to a doctor's appointment with Amy. He would carry a beeper and a cell phone in his bag throughout the tournament just in case Amy went into labor. If this scenario developed Mickelson declared he would leave the U.S. Open and head back to Arizona—no matter where he stood— to be with his wife during the delivery.

"On the day I left for the tournament, we had the doctor check her," Mickelson said. "The doctor said, 'No, your cervix is tight, you're a good week away at least. So we decided that I should go ahead and go and it wouldn't be a problem.'"

Blisters were the topic of conversation where David Duval was concerned. And for what? A lousy cup of coffee.

Duval had been preparing a cup of coffee—the single tea bag variety—at a newly built Florida home when he grabbed the kettle and singed the flesh of his right thumb and forefinger. He immediately stuck his hand in the refrigerator then went to the hospital. Doctors applied antiseptic balm and wrapped the second-degree burns in gauze.

Duval's blistered fingers placed a big bull's-eye on his back to be the target for quips from the media, who inquired in jest whether future kitchen adventures would be limited by having someone cut his meat, pour his coffee, etc.

Duval pointed out that his kitchen endeavors looked tame when compared to his penchant for snowboarding. More important, he would not withdraw from the tournament due to the blisters.

"Absolutely no way I'm not playing," Duval said. "Hey, this is the U.S. Open. I'm going to play. I don't care what's happening. I'm going to play through the pain if that's what I have to do. With-drawing was never an option. . . ."

Duval putted on Monday for approximately an hour then walked the course with his caddie, Mitch Knox, packing only his 9-iron, two wedges, and a putter to familiarize himself with the greens and pitching areas. After finding some frustration at being able to grip the club with just three fingers, Tom Loss, a Seattle doctor and USGA rules official, convinced Duval that lancing his blisters would be the prudent move. He used a knife to do the job then heavily taped both fingers, treating his wounds with ointment and protective NuSkin.

"I may as well get used to it now," Duval said.

Afterward he did not sign autographs and was apologetic to fans for not being able to do so due to his injury.

"I'd rather sign ten thousand autographs and be 100 percent," he said.

Given the nature of how Duval had incurred his injury, he was fair game for the other players to rib.

"It was all in good fun," Duval said. "What can I say? As long as I can tee off on Thursday, it'll all be good fun."

When Duval wasn't discussing his blisters he made perhaps the most intelligent assessment about his approach to playing the course.

"I have yet to play in one that hitting it in the fairway and knocking it on the green doesn't work," Duval said. "Whether there is rough or not."

Tiger Woods didn't have a pregnant wife, nor had he physically handicapped himself in any fashion, but he had to deal with questions about an interview with his father that was published in the May-June issue of *Icon*, a bimonthly men's magazine. Earl Woods was quoted as making ethnic and racial slurs at Scotland.

Scotland is "for white people," Earl was quoted as saying. "It has the sorriest weather. People had better be happy that the Scots lived there instead of the soul brothers—the game of golf never would have been invented."

Later in the interview Earl said: "We wouldn't have been stupid enough to go out in that weather and play a silly game and freeze to death. We would have been inside listening to jazz, laughing and joking and drinking rum."

Earl maintained the quotes had been fabricated, but the author of the interview stood by her position that the interview was all on tape.

Tiger told the *Washington Times,* "I've heard about [the article], but I don't read any of those magazines. They've ripped me and my family too many times for me to get into it."

Dismissing questions about his father, Woods looked ahead at Pinehurst No. 2 and exuded confidence.

"With the fall-away cutouts around the greens, the key here looks like it's going to be chipping and putting," Woods said. "I've always thought my imagination around the greens was one of my greatest strengths. No predictions, but I'm feeling very confident. Winning two times in a row is always very good for your confidence, particularly when the next tournament is a major championship."

Generally, the players' echo heard after their practice rounds was one of confidence. Pinehurst No. 2 did not have the imposing feel of U.S. Open courses such as Olympic, Oakmont, Oakland Hills, Oak Hill, or Congressional.

"I was surprised to find the fairways a little more generous than normal," Colin Montgomerie said. "But the reason we call them generous is because they're not twenty-three yards wide. Just because they're twenty-eight yards does not mean that they're wide."

Mark O'Meara and Woods couldn't get over the un-U.S. Open–like rough.

"The rough is deep, but not as deep as past U.S. Opens off the edge of the fairway," O'Meara said. "There's going to be times you might be able to advance your ball, maybe get it on a green. In past U.S. Opens, it was usually a sand wedge out."

"I thought the rough would be higher, the fairways be narrower," Woods said. "The golf course is playing a little more friendly than I thought it would. I like it a lot. . . . The golf course from tee to green is very simple. It's around the green where it becomes complicated."

Added Jack Nicklaus: "You've got that many fellows that are happy with the golf course, there must be something wrong. But I enjoy it, too."

Duval understood the subtle dangers lying ahead.

Pinehurst No. 2 "gives the players a false sense of security that you can advance it onto the green," Duval said. "And it looks to me the reasoning is to get players to try to hit some shots that will run into the greens, because that's when you can get in more trouble."

Philo piddled around on Wednesday, eager to get started.

"I don't know if I was nervous or anxious," Philo said. "I don't know if nervous is the right word. Anxious sounds more like the right description, anxious to get going, not to get it over with, but to get started."

Philo had been at Pinehurst since Sunday in an environment basically foreign to him. The tournaments he normally played in might have a hundred spectators if well attended whereas thousands attend the U.S. Open practice rounds.

"I was ready to hit the shots," Philo said. "To try and do the golfing stuff instead of trying to figure out how to help people I know get tickets. A few of our members came. Obviously they want to get a little bit of your time. And there's a hospitality tent and you're invited to go here and invited to go there. I think I was anxious. Obviously I wanted to do my best. Certainly I was ready to go. My heartbeat was a little bit faster and all those things, which are the same as being nervous, so I probably was nervous as well."

The odds of a no-name like Philo winning the U.S. Open were remote. Philo wasn't thinking that way.

"Obviously you allow yourself to fantasize," said Philo, who played in three PGA Championships. "The first time I played in a major was the PGA Championship at Southern Hills. I was playing really well when I got there. I birdied the seventh hole to go one-under par. And when they started peeling my name off and putting it on the leaderboard for the eighth tee, I can remember kind of feeling the Bill Murray Caddyshack Cinderella Kid deal.

"[At the '99 Open] I'd just played with a bunch of other guys who were in the tournament. I had been the medalist at the qualifier so I told myself, 'I can shoot the same score these guys can shoot.' No. 2 was a golf course where you didn't have to be extraordinarily long. I wouldn't have to demonstrate any skills I didn't have. So I'm thinking, 'If you put it all together, you can put your name on that board on Sunday at the Open.' Obviously you can't help but go there trying to win the tournament. If you're not going to try and compete to win the tournament there's no reason to be there."

Meeks took a last-minute look around Pinehurst No. 2 on Wednesday to see that everything was in order.

"I like to go around the course one more time on Wednesday before I go to my meetings and dinner and get ready for the real show on Thursday morning," Meeks said. "So I'm going backwards around the course and I get to the seventh hole, a neat dogleg right. And lo and behold, here come Tom Lehman and Andy Martinez, his caddie, also a good friend of mine. I stop and they're just coming around the corner."

"How are you playing?" Meeks asked Lehman.

"I'm playing well, I can win this week if I get things going," Lehman said. "I feel pretty good about my game."

"I hope I don't make any mistakes like I did last year with the hole locations," Meeks said.

Lehman looked at Meeks.

"Don't be gun-shy," Lehman said.

Meeks read the remark as Lehman's way of telling him to set up the course as hard as he could and hopefully what happened the year before at Olympic wouldn't happen at Pinehurst.

"He was basically saying don't back off, you're doing what you have to do and it's the right thing," Meeks said.

While much of the late-arriving field practiced Wednesday, Stewart rested.

"He hit a few balls, putted, and we were out of there by eleven o'clock," Hicks said. "Then he rested all day."

Resting on Wednesday had become a custom for Stewart in majors.

"We noticed how well he did in '91 when he won at Hazeltine, his back was bad and he didn't do anything on Wednesday," Hicks said. "There was a pattern. When he played well in majors he rested on Wednesday, save for a few practice balls and some putting. I think that was a big part of his doing well.

"Tiger [Woods] will play Wednesday, but he starts at six in the morning and he's done at nine. He's always off the course on Wednesday by ten in the morning. I think that's very important in a major tournament so you can rest your mind and your body, because it's a grind. Especially a U.S. Open. There's no harder tournament that's going to test your game than a U.S. Open."

After finishing with Stewart, Hicks enjoyed one of the perks of the job when he and a friend went to Pinehurst No. 5 to play a round with Tour pro Ben Crenshaw and Crenshaw's caddie. Hicks offered a little chuckle about the golf that transpired.

"At one point all three of us were beating Ben," Hicks remembered.

What better karma heading into a major than having your caddie going toe-to-toe with a great player like Crenshaw.

Tracey Stewart arrived Wednesday. She and Payne hosted Chuck Cook and his wife for dinner that night. Payne prepared the meal.

"He loved to cook, he cooked great steaks, he could cook everything," Tracey said.

Payne conceded he wasn't a gourmet cook.

"But I do enjoy cooking. I like it," Stewart said. "It's a nice release for me."

So on the eve of the ninety-ninth U.S. Open rain soaked the Village of Pinehurst while Payne Stewart prepared spaghetti for his guests and tried to relax for the competition he'd so anxiously awaited.

CHAPTER TEN

LET THE OPEN BEGIN

PAYNE STEWART AWOKE at approximately 7:30 on Thursday morning, the first day of the U.S. Open, and began the ritual he had followed throughout his career by ironing his knickers. He then sat down with Tracey to a breakfast of mangos and muffins.

Fresh from the ironing board, Stewart put on the cream-colored plus fours. To complete the ensemble he added a white tam, a gray striped shirt and the W.W.J.D. bracelet given him by his son. At approximately 11:00, he headed to the course to warm up, giving him an hour before joining his playing partners Stuart Appleby and Jeff Maggert on the first tee at 12:10 P.M.

Falling in line with his routine, Stewart putted on the practice green, went to the driving range until he felt loose, hit a few bunker shots then finished with fifteen minutes on the putting green.

"That particular week I know he didn't know if he would win or not, but I know he knew he was going to be in there," Mike Hicks said. "Because in ninety-eight he did it with mirrors, he had maybe a B game going as far as tee to green. And it eventually caught up to him on Sunday.

"[Heading into the Open] he was putting well; he'd been putting well all year. The short game was good and he was real proud of his long game, so he knew that he was going to contend. He was very confident of his game."

Perhaps even more important than the golfing skills Stewart packed was the man inside the body with so much talent on the links. Though he considered himself a humble man, he recognized the fact that he remained a work in process. The new Stewart not only was a better person, he was better equipped to handle the mental games associated with being a golfer on the PGA Tour. Having his marriage, his family, and his game in order had made him a happy man and a much more dangerous player to compete against.

While Stewart prepped for his first round, much of the field was out on the course playing in the aftermath of the previous night's rains that had swamped the course and left the greens soft underneath a gloomy mist.

Due to the weather conditions, the USGA pushed up the first tee time during Thursday and Friday's rounds from 7:00 A.M. to 6:30 to help combat the possibility of afternoon thunderstorms, a staple for June afternoons in the South.

"If we run into some weather delays, we wanted to make sure that we've used all the available daylight and don't leave players out on the golf course Thursday and Friday," said Trey Holland, USGA vice president. "We'd feel bad if we had five groups that are out on Friday and we need to make a cut, and we had started at seven o'clock. We would have lost a half hour of daylight over the course of the day."

The other available option would have been to start players on 1 and 10, which was commonplace at PGA Tour events. However, Pinehurst No. 2 didn't make such an option easy since the tenth tee was located a good distance from the clubhouse. Besides, the USGA didn't like the idea of having players starting on the back nine.

"We're solidly opposed to that," Holland said. "We believe the Open championship should be played the way the golf course architect laid out the golf course, and we'll continue to use the No. 1 tee format."

Jumbo Ozaki, David Toms, and Brandel Chamblee were the first group to tee off on Thursday.

"When I'm at home and have a 6:30 tee time, I usually get out of bed about 6:20," Chamblee told ESPN Golf.

Such a decision would have been hailed as colorful at the U.S. Open, but hardly wise. Chamblee diligently reported to the range, where he and the rest of his threesome had to hit warm-up balls in the semi-daylight. This led to the odd sight of eager news photographers snapping away while their flashes illuminated the dawn like heat lightning.

"We really couldn't see where the ball was going on the practice tee," said Chamblee, who shot a three-over 73. "When it's that dark, the flashes really stand out. I was seeing spots for a while there."

Despite the damp early-morning weather, ideal conditions were created for the best golfers in the world to fire away at the pins when the sun peeked through the afternoon clouds. On the flip side, rain also made the course play longer. Soaked fairways felt waterlogged and the rough felt heavy with moisture. Few of the balls hit managed to travel more than a few yards past where they landed. Wet conditions can make clubs hard to grip and golfers uncomfortable in soggy clothes and shoes.

David Duval found the conditions to his liking and all the fuss about Duval's burned fingers became a moot point once he stepped to the tee at 7: 30 A.M. Thursday.

"I was not able to practice quite like I would have liked, but there are times when that's good," Duval said. "When I did finally hit balls on Tuesday, everything was where I wanted it to be."

Duval pushed his drive on 1 into the right rough. He recovered nicely by hitting his second shot onto the green and two-putted from seventy feet to make par.

Duval then showed why he held his lofty position on Tour. He landed a 7-iron eight feet from the pin on 2 and sank the putt to drop into red numbers. Twelve successive pars followed before he hit a 5-iron to within two feet on the par-3 fifteenth to make birdie, then hit a 7-iron less than ten feet away on the par-3 seventeenth and sank the birdie to drop to three under. A par on 18 capped Duval's 67, which contained no bogeys and required no heavy lifting to make his pars. He hit fifteen greens in regulation to tie for the lead.

"I was pretty pleased with all of it today," Duval said. "I felt like I drove the ball well. I hit my iron shots where I was trying to. The shorter putts I had for birdie, a couple of them looked like they might go in and did, and then I made a few of them."

Addressing the immaculate way he'd played, not missing fairways and finding no trouble, Duval spoke in a manner almost sounding arrogant.

"That's how I try to play," Duval said. "I try not to do those types of things. I find it to be less stressful. . . . If I'm driving it in the fairways and avoid three-putting, I think there's a good chance I'll be here Sunday night talking to you."

Duval conceded he would be content to turn in three more days like his opening round and called his performance the best he'd experienced at a U.S. Open when it came to ball striking. He cited the course for being forgiving in one area and punitive in another.

"The greens are more receptive," Duval said. "[But] we're in a position where we're having to hit anywhere from two to three clubs more into the greens now."

Despite any pleasure Duval derived from his round and the fact his burned fingers were not a factor, he respected the dangers ahead.

"It seems to me in the past Opens I've played that the golf courses the first day are set up to where if you're playing well you can make some birdies and put up a 2-, 3-, 4-under par score," Duval said. "And after that everybody tends to drift backwards a little bit."

Phil Mickelson played in Duval's group and experienced a more exciting round. Included in the excitement were birdies on 2 and 4 followed by some stellar work on 5, the 482-yard par-4 that featured a slight dogleg left and a sloped fairway in the landing area. The fifth hole was the longest natural par-4 on Pinehurst No. 2 (as opposed to the par-5 holes converted to par-4s for the Open) and ranked as the toughest hole on Thursday when the field of one hundred fifty-six players playing the hole averaged 4.494 strokes.

"Number five is a brutal hole," Mickelson said.

Mickelson hit a good drive and followed with a 5-iron that seemed to please him until he watched the sloping green treat his approach shot like a toddler going down a slide. By the time the ball quit rolling Mickelson stood looking at a shot twenty-five feet off the edge of the green.

Unfazed by the sour turn of fortune, Mickelson pondered his situation. Should he try something different than his famed flop shot? He considered putting the ball but noticed the grain of the grass running into him, which would offer resistance to a putt. Going against the grain he'd have to hit the ball just right to reach the green. If he hit it too hard he might send it racing by the hole and if he didn't hit it hard enough the grain would kill it, leaving him short of the hole. His deliberation led him to select an L-wedge, a club offering more loft than a sand wedge and a club he handled with the touch of a surgeon holding a scalpel.

Mickelson hit his shot just as planned and felt a wave of good fortune rush through him when his chip rolled into the cup for a birdie to move him to three-under after five holes. But waves have crests and troughs. The troughs came when he bogeyed 6 and 8 before riding back to the crest with birdies at 13 and 14.

Mickelson's seesaw fate put him at two-under heading into 18, where he hit, missed the green with his approach, and hit a poor chip on his third shot, leaving him a tricky fifteen-footer.

"Looking back [at the chip], it was probably a poor choice of clubs," Mickelson said. "Because I had some green to work with, I probably should have putted it. [But] I hit an L-wedge because it was downhill and I thought spin would help. But it ended up checking up short. I could have done either [wedge or putt], because the grain was down. I felt like I had been practicing that shot with the L-wedge and it would be fine."

It wasn't, but Mickelson didn't let the flubbed shot trouble him even though he faced a quick-downhill putt to save par. He stroked his ball and it crawled toward the hole, curling left at the end but managing to catch a part of the hole before it passed.

"I just wanted to work it down the hill," Mickelson said. "And when it got down there it snuck in the left edge."

The birdie gave Mickelson a 67, a share of the lead, and a healthy dose of optimism.

"I was really excited about this tournament," Mickelson said. "I'm really excited about the setup of the golf course. I think this is the best test of golf that I've played in a major championship in that it tests every area of your game. It tests every shot.

"I thought this would be a good opportunity for me to play well in the U.S. Open. I'm fortunate to have gotten off to a good start. Obviously, the course is playing as easy as it can with the greens being as soft as they are, but it's a tribute to how difficult the course is in that there really aren't any really low scores. I think we're going to be in for a long weekend if the greens were to dry out."

Immediately after his round, Lefty telephoned his wife for the latest report on her pregnancy. Mickelson acknowledged how pondering his coming fatherhood might serve him well.

"I have something to take my mind off a major championship," he said.

Mickelson, though excited about competing in the Open and how well he played his first round, remained adamant about his situation.

"If the beeper goes off I'm out of here," Mickelson said. "I have a once in a lifetime opportunity to be there, whereas the U.S. Open takes place every year. We're very fortunate to be able to have a child. We thought we were going to have problems. We just got lucky."

If Mickelson had to make a cross-country flight at a beeper's notice, he was an accomplished pilot and knew the time involved. To his calculations, such a trip would require five hours and fifteen minutes from the time he got beeped to his arrival at the hospital.

"I've got a plane standing by," he said. "I've got my copilot ready to file [flight plans] and we'll go."

Mickelson even guarded against false alarms by creating a code to use to protect against getting beeped accidentally. However, Mickelson made it clear that while he was ready to bolt, he held the U.S. Open in high esteem.

"I would much rather be home than be at a golf tournament, even this championship, but if I am going to fly across the country to be here and play golf, then I want it to be worthwhile and just a top-five finish isn't worthwhile," Mickelson said. "I'm here to win."

The element of time hung outside Pinehurst like a ship outside the harbor. Could Lefty play well enough to win the U.S. Open? And if his game was right, could he get in four rounds before getting beeped? These questions served up a tasty morsel for the media to feast upon.

"He sparked the whole debate about what was bigger, becoming a father or a first-time U.S. Open winner?" David Whitley said. "It's a no-brainer, really. You can't come out against fatherhood. You just can't say that. By the time he finishes his career he'll play in seventy or eighty majors. I don't think anybody in their right mind could have ripped him for choosing to leave, if that's what happened."

Whitley chuckled before pointing out, "If he had to go, say, in the middle of Saturday's round, how long could they keep his wife waiting to give birth after her water breaks?"

Tied for the lead with Duval and Mickelson at three-under were Billy Mayfair and Paul Goydos. Mayfair had sunk three sizeable birdie putts and Goydos had birdied three of the last six holes to reach the low number. The last time as many as four players were tied for the U.S. Open lead after the first round had been 1984.

Mayfair and Mickelson were close friends and had more in common than dining and practicing together, which they often did. Both lived in Scottsdale, Arizona; they each had attended Arizona State; each had won a U.S. Amateur title; neither had won a major; and each was about to become a father for the first time, though Mayfair's delivery date was later in the year. Mayfair knew Mickelson well enough to have access to his beeper number and he joked that if he remained among the leaders he might have to use it.

Stewart's facial expression looked uncharacteristically serious once he stepped between the ropes at Pinehurst No. 2

"Payne seemed to have the mentality for the kind of play demanded by No. 2," Scott Hoch said. "He was very jovial when he played everywhere else, but he never broke a smile or anything [at Pinehurst]. He was really into what he was doing."

Hicks knew Stewart well enough to recognize the look.

"Once the gun went off on Thursday, I could see it," Hicks said. "I had seen it before. He'd kind of gotten in this mode at the Ryder Cup and in '91 at Hazeltine, though he wasn't quite as confident back then. He was still young. He was still finding himself.

"As the years went on he would get in the Ray Floyd zone. And he couldn't do it very often, maybe a couple of times a year. That was all he could handle mentally. Payne couldn't get to that level every week, so when he did I knew it. And I knew to just get out of his way. Just like a jockey, if you've got a horse that is riding hard, you don't pull the whip out, you just ride him."

Stewart made pars on the first two holes then found trouble on 3, a 335-yard par-4 that called for accuracy in the fairway. While the shortness of the hole enticed some of the longer hitters to try and drive the green, the out-of-bounds on the left made such an attempt risky. Stewart selected a 3-iron and struck the ball perfectly, but his shot landed in a sand-filled divot. Talk about déjà vu, wasn't it just yesterday he'd let a similar shot sink his chances at Olympic? Stewart would be hitting from a mystery lie knowing that if he flew the green he'd have a difficult up-and-down.

A couple of differences existed between Stewart finding himself in a divot at Olympic a year earlier and Stewart finding himself in a divot at No. 2 in the early going of the '99 Open.

"To begin with, it's a sandy soil [at Pinehurst], so they don't have to put a lot of sand in the divots," Hicks said. "It was a totally different sanding job than at Olympic. There was just a small layer of sand [at Pinehurst]. Those divots were a little easier to hit from."

In addition to the different conditions, Stewart had practiced hitting shots from sand-filled divots and learned how to consistently pick the ball from the divot.

"Obviously, if you've been practicing the shot you're going to have a little more confidence if that situation arises," Hicks said. "He didn't get upset, he just played it where it was. I think at that point he was glad that he had practiced the shot and since it happened so soon in the tournament he was going to find out right away if he was able to handle the shot."

Stewart selected a pitching wedge and hit a shot that finished fifteen feet from the cup. He sank the birdie putt, showing an early indication of his resolve while surging into red numbers at one-under.

Stewart did a superb job of protecting par the remainder of the front nine to make the turn at one-under 34.

Any way one wanted to look at it, the par-5 tenth hole broke down to six football fields long at 610 yards. Golfers could not see the green standing on the tee and their second shots were to a blind target as well. Stewart hit well-placed shots with his driver and 3-iron before dropping a wedge shot two feet from the pin. He sank the birdie putt to move to two-under.

History continued to repeat itself when Stewart's ball found another sand-filled divot on 13. Once again he avoided disaster and finished off the hole by running in a fifteen-footer to save par.

"I hope I don't hit into any more divots this week, I've had enough already," Stewart said. "There wasn't a divot on the golf course when I was walking it on Saturday. But the areas we're playing from, everybody seems to play from the same areas, so that's going to happen and you've got to deal with it."

Stewart had strung together four consecutive pars when he stepped to the tee at the 205-yar par-3 fifteenth hole. Selecting a 5-iron from his bag, Stewart hit his ball to within twenty feet. Stewart stood still over his putt knowing that 2s at 15 would be as rare as dry socks on No. 2. He drew the putter back and made a smooth pass. The putt looked good from start to finish. When the ball split the center of the cup and dropped for a birdie, Stewart moved to three-under. Inside Stewart might have been throwing a ticker-tape parade, but on the outside he handled his good fortune by remaining in character. He acknowledged the cheers from the gallery without a smile; the stoic expression told anyone watching this was a veteran who understood there was much work to do.

Stewart made par at 16 then took a "good cut" with the 6-iron he hit to the 188-yard par-3 seventeenth. The shot finished four feet from the hole. If he sank the birdie he would have gained the outright lead at four-under.

A sneeze echoed from the gallery just when Stewart started his putter back, but Stewart remained locked in with his focus.

"I never heard [the sneeze]," Stewart said. "I hit it right where I wanted to. I played just inside the right edge."

A less than receptive cup grabbed Stewart's ball when it entered from the right side and rerouted it in a U-turn before ejecting it like a passenger in James Bond's Aston Martin. Stewart had to settle for par.

One final confrontation with Pinehurst No. 2 awaited Stewart before he finished the first round. After hitting his drive into the left rough on 18 he recovered nicely with a well-stroked 6-iron to the green, but the ball rolled up on the front of the green then rolled back down the slope. Stewart elected to putt on his third shot and left the ball ten feet short. He missed the par putt to finish with a two-under 68, one shot out of the lead.

"I was very, very pleased with how I controlled myself and how I felt out there today and I'm satisfied with my score," Stewart said. I think it was a really nice day to play golf out there today. I just think that the golf course is going to continue as the days progress to get harder and firmer and play more like Pinehurst is supposed to play or would have played last week before the rain. So to get off to a start like this, it's satisfying."

Stewart remembered being put on the clock for slow play during the previous year's Open and believed time would again become an issue considering the USGA's pace-of-play policy.

"Well, when I saw [the policy] I spoke to Tom Meeks and I said, 'Well, this golf course gets hard and dry and fast. I don't see the first groups playing in the amount of time that you've allotted for them to play,' " Stewart said. "I think the first group is supposed to play in four hours and thirteen minutes or twenty-three minutes, something like that. We played in five hours. We got to the fifth tee and there were two groups on the tee, one on the fairway, one on the green. There were four groups on one hole. So this is not going to be a golf course that we're going to be able to play at the pace that's been set for us."

Stewart waxed eloquent about the merits of No. 2, a course with which he'd grown smitten.

"This is a great golf course," Stewart said. "If you manage your game around here you can shoot in the red. If you quit thinking one time all of a sudden you're going to flip it over a green. Then you really got your work cut out for you. This golf course just tests everything. I think it's a great challenge for us this week."

Stewart and Hicks were pleased, but the experience gained from years on Tour told them to temper their enthusiasm.

"It was kind of old hat," Hicks said. "It wasn't like something we'd never been in before. So when we got done with round one, it's, 'We've got three to go. We didn't shoot ourselves out of it. We're right in the thick of it.' That's how you kind of look at those things. Every day at the end of the day it's, 'Where are we? Well we're right there.' Then you get to Sunday morning and you hope you're saying you have a shot at winning.

"You're happy to be in the situation you're in, but you don't start thinking about what can happen. What if? That's the worst thing you can do. You learn that over the years. You try not to let yourself think about, 'Gee, if we win this tournament.' "

Having gained a feel for the course, Stewart had an idea about what the leader would need to shoot to win.

"I think it will be in the red," Stewart said. "I don't know how far in the red, but I think it will be in the red."

When Stewart left the media tent he tended to his post-round routine.

"They all have the same routine," Hicks said. "He went out and hit some balls then he went to the putting green and hit some putts. That's basically it. The routine doesn't change whether you're at the U.S. Open or the Memphis Golf Classic."

Stewart's game always dictated how much time he spent on the range, which Hicks attributed to Dick Coop's philosophy.

"Say you hit a bad 3-iron during your round, you go and hit your 3-iron," Hicks said. "If your wedge game wasn't good you'd go work on your wedges. Work on whatever club you weren't hitting well. Go hit some of those. So that's what Payne would do. When Payne was on, he'd still hit some balls, but he wouldn't stay out there like Vijay [Singh], who just beats 'em, and beats 'em and beats 'em. If it's not broke, don't fix it."

Stewart arrived at Pinehurst packing a game with no flaws.

"That particular week we didn't spend a lot of time on the range once the tournament began," Hicks said. "We went down there and hit a few balls and a few putts and we were out of there."

A situation that suited Hicks just fine since he would commute the entire week from his home in Mebane, North Carolina, sixty-three miles away.

"The sooner we got out of there the sooner I got home," Hicks said.

Hicks chuckled when asked if Stewart had been sensitive to the fact he was commuting and cut his range work accordingly.

"Yeah, I think he was," Hicks said. "And it was easy for him to be because he was playing well. It wasn't like we had to stay out there all day."

After finishing at the course Stewart headed home with Tracey to figure out what they wanted to cook for dinner. He planned to spend a quiet night with his wife eating what they cooked, then watching the NHL and NBA playoffs on TV. The superstitious part of Payne and Tracey brought about the need to buy more mangos for the next morning's breakfast.

Tiger Woods teed off after Stewart, well after the rain had stopped. He promptly pulled his first drive into the rough then nearly hit his first putt into a trap before converting a nice up-and-down by sinking an eight-foot par putt.

Throughout the day Woods's drives were embarrassingly long compared to playing partners Lee Westwood and Corey Pavin, who constantly looked ahead forty to fifty yards from their drives to where Woods's ball sat mocking them. Unfortunately for Woods the old adage "It's not how you drive, it's how you arrive" applied to his game. He hit just nine greens in regulation during an opening round that saw fans standing ten to fifteen thick behind the ropes to watch the golfing prodigy.

More annoying to Westwood than Woods's drives were the distractions associated with "Tiger Mania."

"The spectators were fine, it was the people inside the ropes who were the problem," Westwood said.

In particular, photographers. When Westwood missed a short part putt on 6, he directed a steely-eyed scowl at a photographer next to the green.

"The photographers thought there was only one person in the

three-ball and were never in position when Corey Pavin and I were playing," Westwood said.

Westwood then made bogey on two of the next three holes.

Woods's worst shot of the day occurred on the seventh hole after a stray 9-iron shot landed in a greenside bunker. Attempting to escape, Woods's blast landed three feet past the sand then returned to his feet in taunting fashion. Luckily for Woods a solid putting stroke accompanied his erratic play and he sank a ten-footer on 7 to dodge a double bogey.

"I got out of it very lucky," Woods said. "I should have been making double there, but then again, I figured I also should have made an easy par, too, with a 9-iron in my hand."

Amid this chaotic round for Woods were flashes of brilliance like saves on 12 and 16 when he showed his imagination by using his 3-wood from just off the green to bump the ball close to the hole. At 11 he used a 9-iron to sculpt a towering shot that hung in the air like a zeppelin. A roar erupted when the shot dropped from the sky two inches from the hole.

Despite playing from lies all over Pinehurst No. 2, Woods went to the tee on 17 at even par. A wind blowing from the left prompted him to try and put the ball ten-to-fifteen feet left of the hole. He aimed at a camera tower in the background knowing if the wind pushed it he wouldn't find too much trouble and if it didn't he'd have a short putt.

Woods smoothed his tee ball with a 7-iron and felt like he'd hit the ball perfectly. The shot headed straight toward his target before the wind began to push the ball to the right. He watched and hoped he'd calculated the right distance. The suspense ended when Woods's ball just missed the pin then rolled backward before stopping six feet from the hole. He sank the putt to move to one under.

Woods unloaded a huge drive on the par-4 eighteenth that allowed him to use a pitching wedge for his second shot. Once again he hit his approach stiff then knocked in the putt for another birdie to finish at two-under for the day, putting him close to the lead for the first time on the first day of an Open. He had used just twenty-four putts, leaving him one stroke off the pace of the leaders and making him look particularly dangerous given the fact that he hadn't hit the ball well.

"I'm feeling very happy," Woods said. "If you saw me play today, you'd say no way he could have shot the number I shot. It wasn't a pretty round, but I scored, and that's something I've always been able to do. I just didn't hit the ball as good as I'd like. I didn't play my best, but I hung in there and made a lot of saves. In order to win a U.S. Open, you have to do that."

Though the softened greens were nice, Woods felt like the course played harder than if it hadn't been wet.

"Strictly because of the fact that your bump-and-run shot is gone, that's been taken away, and this golf course is designed for you to roll a ball up," Woods said. "You don't have that option anymore. It's taken away from you."

He'd watched Pavin hit his 3-wood on two occasions and the ball backed up before finishing in the slopes short of the greens.

"You don't see that very often around here," Woods said. "So I hit a couple of shots like that today that hit and bounced back off the green that normally would be bouncing up onto the green. That's taken away from you. You have to land the ball on the flat spot, and sometimes it can get away from you and scoot over the back and from there you're dead."

Daly, the Tour's uncontested longest player off the tee and resident enigma, had several adventures during his opening round.

He began his day with a booming drive on No. 1 that enabled

him to hit a sand wedge on his second shot. He landed the ball twelve feet from the pin and sank the putt to go one-under. Another prodigious drive followed on 2. Daly then hit a 9-iron to twenty feet from the hole and again sank the putt. Daly's driver led to an L-wedge from forty yards on 3. After sinking the five-footer for birdie Daly stood at three-under after three holes.

Daly's driver and putter stayed with him for the duration of the first round, but the lasting image of his opening round work came at 18 where he directed his drive into a row of trees along the right side of the fairway. The ball kicked off a tree and rolled across the fairway to the left side a hundred yards from the tee and approximately 350 yards from the pin. Daly elected to lay up with a 5-iron on his second shot, then hit a wedge to twenty feet and two-putted for a bogey to finish with a 68. The pro-Daly gallery offered up a huge ovation.

For a man whose previous four tournaments had included two missed cuts and two withdraws, Daly looked like he'd hit the lottery holding a lucky number 68. Pleasing him to no end was No. 2 allowing him to hit driver on thirteen of the fourteen driving holes. But history wasn't working on Daly's behalf. At Olympic the previous year, his opening-round score had been 69, but he finished at seventeen-over par in a tie for fifty-third place after shooting 75, 75, and 78.

"The thing with me is, I don't know who's going to show up tomorrow, that's the way the year has been," Daly said. "I can honestly say that. And it's a little scary."

To celebrate his day, Daly had a game plan for the evening.

"I'm going to go eat about six cheeseburgers at McDonalds, probably have a bag of Oreos and a big thing of milk, watch Sports-Center, and hopefully see myself on TV," he said.

Also in the hunt after the first round were a number of former major champions. Justin Leonard and Vijay Singh were in at 69, and Davis Love III finished at 70. Ernie Els shot 72, as did Colin Montgomerie, posting the low score for the European contingent.

Montgomerie had long been a target for hecklers in American galleries for comments he's made and his flabby, less than svelte appearance. Among the hecklers' favorites: "Nice tits, Monty."

But the oft-abused star closed the opening round in a manner that commanded respect by even his biggest critics. He finished with birdies on 17 and 18 to stay in contention.

"It'll make dinner taste all that much better," Montgomerie said. "It's changed my mood and all I want now is to get out again tomorrow and maintain that type of form. I couldn't believe the weather when I started. It's warmer and drier in Scotland. I still believe level par will eventually win this tournament. So to be two-over is pleasing."

When all the scores were turned in, twenty-three golfers had navigated No. 2 under par during a day in which the scoring average stood at 72.8.

Not everyone was happy with Pinehurst No. 2 after the first round.

Defending champion Lee Janzen shot a disappointing 74, and Masters champion Jose Maria Olazabal shot 75.

Olazabal made double bogeys on Nos. 5 and 18, the latter coming after a fluffed chip shot and a three-putt.

"I've made it tough for myself," said Olazabal, who appeared visibly upset. "I hit the ball all over the place and there's no way you can score doing that."

Every year the U.S. Open brings out the worst in the way of tempers, much like Little League games do parents. Sometimes it's vocal, such as a player criticizing the course's conditions—like Dave Hill did at Hazeltine. Others have been more demonstrative. Olazabal fell into the latter category, turning into the Jerry Springer guest who discovers his wife had two babies with his brother. Frustrated with his play, Olazabal took out his ire that night by punching a hotel wall.

Ron Philo played in the second-to-last group of the day hoping to find the same magic he'd found during the qualifier ten days earlier, that wondrous, fleeting day when the game came easy. Instead the magic wand could not be found and he finished with a 77.

"I remember missing all the same putts I made in the qualifier," Philo said. "All the putts you're supposed to make, I missed. I was hitting it well enough. I wasn't hitting it perfect, but I felt like with the ball-striking round I had I could have shot three or four shots better. That would have allowed me not to have to do anything extraordinary to make the cut.

The projected cut would be somewhere around seven or eight over par. Philo had backed himself into a corner where he knew he'd have to shoot even par or better the next day to make the cut. He retreated to the range to work with his father on his driving.

"By the time we were finished working, I felt like I was going to drive the ball well," Philo said.

The opening day of the Open ended with sixty-six players within five strokes of the leaders at 67. Players within ten shots of the leaders would make the thirty-six-hole cut, giving the appearance after one day that Pinehurst No. 2 would be crowded during the weekend rounds.

If drier conditions showed, another script might be written.

"The firmer the golf course gets, the more the guys who are playing well will separate themselves," Goydos said.

CHAPTER ELEVEN

STEWART, MICKELSON, AND DUVAL TO THE TOP

PAYNE STEWART HAD a 7:50 tee time Friday morning, but the early hour did nothing to diminish his wardrobe consisting of a white shirt, white tam, white stockings, and green, white, and, black plaid plus fours. The clean and classy look hid the fact they composed the uniform of a grinder on a day when Pinehurst No. 2 made grinding a necessity.

The weather and the USGA both made adjustments for the second round. An eerie wind howled through the Carolina pines, changing the complexion of the turtlebacked greens. Only a day earlier balls had stuck on the putting surface like darts at an English pub. Now they were welcomed with hard bounces on the suddenly sunbaked surface before rolling into Donald Ross purgatory in the surrounding hollows and swales. The USGA did its part by sticking pins in seemingly impossible places to reach. From the beginning of

Friday's round, Stewart seemed above succumbing to the pitfalls created by No. 2, the weather, and the USGA.

Stewart hit a solid 3-wood drive on 1 then missed the green, but got up and down. On 2 he missed the fairway, missed the green, and once again got up and down. When his approach shot spun off the green on 3 it was almost a foregone conclusion he'd once again convert the par. He did.

"I was very patient with myself out there," Stewart said. "I knew that I was coming into some holes that I felt that I could actually hit a green in regulation."

Stewart began to attack when he could on 4, hitting a sand wedge from eighty-five yards to a resting spot two feet from the hole and sinking his birdie putt. He found yet another sand-filled divot when his ball came to rest in the fairway on 5. He hit a crisp 6-iron from the difficult lie then sank his par putt.

Stewart looked in complete control when he hit a 9-iron to twelve feet from the hole on 7 and sank the birdie to move to four-under for the tournament.

Stewart's roll ended on 8, one of two par-5s converted to a par-4 for the Open. After hitting a booming drive that found the middle of the wide fairway on the 485-yard hole, Stewart looked at the danger facing him on his second shot and felt uneasy. The worst danger the uphill shot would encounter would occur if his ball went left where the terrain sloped drastically to trouble. The right side, though the lesser of two evils, was protected by a bunker ten yards in front of the green.

"I just didn't trust my swing going into that pin," Stewart said. "And the last place you want to miss that green is left. So I kind of came out of a 6-iron and missed the green to the right and didn't get that one up and down."

Stewart dropped to three-under after the bogey at 8, but relief sat on the horizon: No. 9.

The ninth hole had played as the tenth easiest hole on the course through thirty-six holes with a scoring average of 3.265. A straightforward par 3 with few mysteries to it, 9 looked like a hole where a golfer could catch his breath after the tough stretch of 5, 6, 7, and 8.

"I thought I made a good swing on 9," Stewart said. "I might have hit the wrong club. There was quite a bit of wind in our face. I hit the 5-iron, then I made another bogey."

But Stewart didn't have the experience Billy Mayfair had at 9.

Mayfair's tee shot hit close to the pin, took two hops, then rolled off the back edge into a collection area. He tried to putt only to have the ball roll back to him. He finished with a double-bogey 5.

Stewart finished the front nine with an even-par 35 to remain at two-under. Perhaps most important, he didn't get rattled by his consecutive bogeys.

Good karma doesn't have to come in the form of a birdie, which Stewart discovered on 12 after hitting his 4-iron approach into the right greenside bunker. Wielding his up-and-down magic, Stewart blasted from the bunker and sank a twelve-foot putt for par.

"That was probably one of the good points of the round, that spurred me on a little bit," Stewart said.

Stewart faced trouble again on 14. After hitting his drive into a fairway bunker on the 436-yard par-4 his approach shot fell short of the green. On the fortuitous side of the ledger, his ball avoided the swales and hollows around the green, leaving him with a decent lie. His chip stopped six feet from the hole and he sank the putt for another par save to remain at two-under.

Stewart cast the image of the consummate Tour professional through the manner in which he navigated the course, making par after par like the poster child for course management and patience. When he reached 15, the par-3 he'd birdied in the first round, he hit a solid 4-iron that left him an eighteen-footer for birdie. His putt broke right and fell into the cup, moving him back to three under and giving him a share of the lead. The cheers were growing for him. He clearly had become one of the crowd's sentimental favorites. Stewart waved to acknowledge the cheers, but continued to wear a mask of indifference when it came to revealing his emotions.

Stewart felt a big wind in his face when he looked down the sixteenth fairway that felt like a par-10.

"Wow, that's a long hole, really long hole to do into the wind," said Stewart about the second of No. 2's par-5s to be converted to a par-4.

Perhaps reaching back for a little something extra, Stewart drove the ball into the rough. For someone like Stewart who strove to manage the course properly, such a position dictated how he should play the hole.

"I had to take my medicine and just play it like a par-5," Stewart said.

After chopping out an 8-iron, Stewart hit a wedge to within six feet of the cup and sank the putt for par.

"Any U.S. Open course calls for great patience and this golf course takes a lot of patience," said Stewart referencing his work at 16. "You have to really think about where you want your ball to finish."

Stewart hit 17 in regulation and two-putted before landing his drive in the right-side rough on 18. The short rough didn't keep him from hitting a high-flying 8-iron onto the green, but he left himself with a long, uphill putt that he left eight feet short.

"That putt was slow from where I was coming from, kind of going back up the hill and through a little valley that holds a lot of moisture," Stewart said.

Unfazed by the knee-knocker to finish his day, Stewart calmly did what he'd done all day by splitting the middle of the cup to save par.

"You have to putt well," Stewart said. "You have to make the six- and eight- and ten-footers to save par. And I did that well today."

Stewart's 69 made him the only player in the field to have two rounds in the 60s.

"That really meant a lot to me to shoot under par today," Stewart said. "And I would have been disappointed if I'd been on the green on 18 at one-under par and walked off even par. That would have been disappointing. And I'm proud of what I've done out there. I didn't hit as many greens today as I did yesterday, but it's not as easy a golf course out there as it was yesterday. We had a lot of wind to contend with. It's very testy. Anytime you can go around and shoot under par at a U.S. Open, I don't care where we're playing it's a good score, so I'm proud of that. The way I got it was not what I envisioned, but it's what I came up with, and that's what you have to do."

Stewart felt like he was playing better at Pinehurst than he had the previous year at Olympic, which led to his addressing whatever mental damage he'd had to overcome from losing in '98.

"Well, how long did it take to get over [Olympic]? I kind of felt that I got over it in a relatively quick manner, I didn't want to dwell on it," Stewart said. "I've never watched the tape [from Olympic], and it's kind of like, why bother? Why bother seeing it? I know what I did. I don't need to see what anybody else did. And unfinished business, yeah, I got in position last year and I didn't play well enough to win the golf tournament. And I'm going to try to get myself back in position. I'm doing a pretty decent job of it right this second, but I still have thirty-six holes to play. As long as I can get myself in position and deal with it better than I did last year, I know my golf game is better than it was last year, so, yeah, there is some unfinished business."

Stewart had taken the previous year's loss in the right spirit.

"I could have crawled away and hid after what happened last year, or I could build on what happened and the position I was in and use it to strengthen myself, and that's the avenue I chose," Stewart said. "I've been here before."

A member of the media noticed the W.W.J.D. band Stewart wore on his wrist, which led to questions about his faith. Stewart looked comfortable discussing how he'd gained a higher faith and credited his children's influence for helping the process before he affirmed: "I've made my peace, and so what goes on the next two days I still have my peace with God. I have a beautiful family. My life is going to go on, and that gives me an inner sobriety, I guess. I go out there and I'm not worried about what's going to happen. I'm going to be taken care of."

Stewart represented calm on a day when No. 2 taunted many in the field.

Jose Marie Olazabal arrived for Friday's round wearing an equipment adjustment: a splint. The hotel wall had not agreed with his hand.

After trying a few practice swings Olazabal realized any chances he had to end the European U.S. Open drought no longer existed. Olazabal walked to the parking lot and drove off.

"I was upset with myself," Olazabal told the Associated Press. "I wanted to do well this week. After the way I played . . . I did something I should not have. Now I'm paying the price."

He released a statement through a USGA official about why he had withdrawn from the tournament.

"I have a broken bone in my right hand," Olazabal's statement read, explaining he'd broken his right fifth metacarpal. "I hit a wall. It was my fault."

Doctors told Olazabal the break was clean and he would be out three to four weeks.

"To me it's typical of Olazabal, who I think is one of the most decent people in this game," Doug Ferguson said. "He won the Masters and he was on a course that was this links-type course, which was supposed to give him an advantage. I think he put way too much pressure on himself and when things did not go his way he took it out on a hotel wall."

Olazabal's exit added to the Europeans' legacy of failure at recent U.S. Opens. A frustrating legacy that included Seve Ballesteros's disqualification in the 1980 Open when he missed his tee time and Colin Montgomerie prematurely accepting victory congratulations in 1992, then sitting by helplessly as Tom Kite stormed to victory at Pebble Beach.

In Olazabal's absence, Tom Lehman and Nick Price played Friday's round as a twosome. The sign that accompanied the group had Olazabal's name on it with a "WD" next to it—the Open's version of "no mas."

Greg Norman's response typified the lack of compassion for Olazabal in the wake of his action.

"I would have kicked the wall. I wouldn't have punched it," Norman said.

"I guess that takes him out of the Grand Slam," Janzen said.

"That's under the stupid-things-I-did-in-my-life category," Corey Pavin said. "I'm sure he feels pretty dumb about it."

Added John Daly: "This game is crazy. I've done crazy things with my fists. I've never hit any walls. But I've torn up a few houses and a few cars."

Tom Meeks had not repeated the Olympic fiasco with his selection of Friday pin placements, though some might have suggested otherwise.

After carting a 73 to go two-over for the tournament, Jim Furyk expressed frustration at the pin placements.

"Brutal would be a good word for a few of them," Furyk said. "[The pin on 1] was on the side of a hill. Go out and look at 14, that's a fun one."

Pavin called 14 "an optical nightmare."

"It looks like you can hit it an inch by the pin and it will roll forty yards over," Pavin said.

Pavin, who won the 1995 Open at Shinnecock Hills, managed to birdie 17 and 18 to make the cut and avoid the distinction of having missed the cut three consecutive years.

Tiger Woods called some of the pin placements "questionable."

"Just go out there and look at them," Wood said pointing his finger at 5, 7, and 16. "There are several where you say to yourself, 'That hole shouldn't be there.'"

A player's point of reference can affect how he views a course. As a rule, the leaders like the course better than those not making the cut. Still, it sounded odd to hear Stewart sticking up for the USGA and their pin placements after being told by reporters how some players had complained about the positions.

"I don't think they're questionable," Stewart said. "I think they're tough. The way that the USGA, from what I understand, sets the pin placements, they have six they consider easy pins, six medium pins, and six difficult pins. Now, if you pick a difficult pin and put it on a hole such as the eighth hole or the fifth hole, yeah, then it makes it very hard. But I don't know what we expected, because we did get rain. We had soft conditions [in the opening round]. They're not going to put the pins in the middle of the greens, I know that. The people that are complaining about the pins, then, they haven't played enough U.S. Opens."

Said Tom Meeks: "The only way to have an easy hole location was to put the pins in the center of the greens. The players knew we weren't going to do that. . . . The pin placements were hard because the greens are difficult. They're difficult because of the way they're built."

When Vijay Singh was told the USGA picks six easy pin placements, six medium and six difficult for each round he quipped: "I'd like to see where the easy ones are . . . come to think of it, I haven't seen the medium ones yet either."

Despite the hardships, players were enjoying Pinehurst No. 2.

"It was an A-plus; I think it was great," said Jack Nicklaus, who shot 153 and did not make the cut. "I think they [the USGA] would want to run back here as fast as they could."

Pinehurst No. 2's main attraction to the players continued to be the fact it was a thinking man's course.

"The USGA has got this golf course set up the way they wanted it set up," Hal Sutton said. "A lot of times when we get out there in a normal round of golf, it's almost mindless sometimes. It's a hundred and seventy yards and, 'Okay, give me the 6-iron.' Around here, a hundred and seventy yards is not necessarily a 6-iron; you may be shooting at another part of the green."

Other than Woods, Daly had the largest crowd lining the fairways to cheer him. Daly returned the favor by bombing three-hundred yard drives in all directions and mingling with his fans while chain-smoking Marlboros. Daly's lack of game on Friday turned him into an attraction—like the bearded lady at a county fair. Even if he played poorly, his fans could still watch him go bombing with his driver. Daly stood at even par for the tournament through thirty-one holes. But after botching a cut wedge at 14 to make double bogey, Daly's game came apart and he resembled a man trying to put shaving cream back into the can. He bogeyed 15, 16, and 17 en route to a 77. In twenty-four hours he'd gone from two-under to five-over, yet he continued to sing the praises of Pinehurst No. 2.

"It's hard, it's very hard . . . but you don't have to sit there and hit

2-iron and 3-iron off every tee like you do at most U.S. Opens," Daly said. "I think it's a fun golf course."

Daly ended his session inside the media tent by telling reporters he planned to follow the same post-round ritual he'd followed after Thursday's round.

"Round up some chow, get stuff-bellied, and go to sleep," Daly said.

Phil Mickelson's "will he stay or will he go?" situation remained choice fodder for the media covering the Open. Noted sports columnist Skip Bayless of the *Chicago Tribune* took the stance after Thursday's round that Mickelson should stay in Pinehurst for the conclusion of the Open even if his beeper sounded. This opened the door for others to blather on about the virtues of fatherhood and how Mickelson had his priorities in order.

Mickelson again played in the same group as David Duval and they continued to dazzle despite the difficult conditions.

The left-hander's fortunes did not change as drastically as they did during the first round. Once again he played 5 like a master, using an L-wedge to hit a bump-and-run shot to within five feet and sink the par putt. On the par-3 sixth hole, his tee shot landed in the rough beside the right bunker and he failed to get up and down when he missed a twelve-foot par putt. But he did get up and down at 9 after a long sand shot from the front bunker and a five-foot par putt.

"I'm really pleased with the opportunity this golf course presents," Mickelson said. "If I, or another player, misses a shot, we have the opportunity here to hit a great recovery and get up and down."

Mickelson birdied 10 then added another birdie at 12 when he sank a thirty-foot putt to go to four-under for the tournament. But his drive at 16 found the left rough and his next shot landed in the right-front bunker before he missed a ten-foot par putt. He nearly sank a forty-footer for birdie on 17 but lipped out and when the day was done he'd shot an even-par 70—including four saves on the six holes he didn't hit the green in regulation—to remain at three-under for the tournament.

"I thought 70 would be an exceptional score today," Mickelson said. "I would have taken 70 at the start and I'm pleased with 70 at the end. . . .

"In a major, it's very easy to get overly excited. It's very important to try to calm down. I'm on myself to try to stay on an even keel."

Duval began Friday's round with a charge.

On 2 he hit a 7-iron thirty feet to the right of the hole and drained the putt to go to four-under for the tournament; he sank a birdie putt of approximately the same distance on 5 to move to five-under. He'd played the first twenty-three holes of the tournament without making a single bogey. Then he missed the green at 6 with his tee shot, landing a 3-iron into one of the right-hand bunkers. When he blasted out he could only watch while his ball rolled over the green.

"I never expected it to stop," Duval said. "I thought there was a chance before I hit the shot. But when it came out where it did, I knew where it was going."

His ball rolled past the pin and slowed to a crawl when it approached the crowned edges of the green. Thursday's conditions likely would have added enough moisture to the ball's path to make the ball stop. But twenty-four hours had passed and the course had gone from saturated to scorched.

"I certainly wanted to hit it up next to the hole and make par," Duval said. "But I was making sure I hit it [too far] in error, as opposed to getting an opportunity to try it again from [the bunker]."

Duval chipped back up the hill to within five feet but missed the bogey putt to post a double bogey and fall back to three-under.

Looking like the No. 1 ranked player in the world, Duval responded to his double bogey by hitting 4-iron, 9-iron to within three feet at the 398-yard par 4 seventh, then sinking his putt to move back to four-under.

"I don't know what the bounce-back statistic is, but I think the reason that I tend to keep going fine after [a hole like 6] is because . . . I don't care when it's done, because there's nothing else I can do," Duval said. "I've got to play No. 7, and it presents its own challenges. It's just a progression."

On 8, Duval hit driver, 7-iron to fourteen feet and sank the birdie putt to get back to five-under. After joining Stewart as the only players to bogey 9 on Friday he made the turn at 34. He bogeyed 11 and 16, then sank a fifteen-footer on the par-3 seventeenth to finish at even par for the day.

"I drove pretty well, it seemed like each time I got to the fairway I didn't have a 9-iron or 8-iron in my hand, I was in between them," Duval said. "Seemed like I had a lot of those shots today. When you combine hitting a lot of knockdowns and three-quarter shots with that wind into these greens, you're going to make some mistakes and make some shots you would have preferred not to hit. I think that combination is why I've got so many squares and circles on my printout here."

But the challenges didn't diminish Duval's experience on Friday.

"It was fun when you executed a shot and got it on the green," Duval said. "I did enjoy playing today. I like the golf course and it's fun to be out there and today presented a lot of new challenges."

Halfway home at the U.S. Open and Duval remained tied for the lead. He'd never won a major, could he handle the weekend play and compete for a major title?

"I think I'm suited for it because I'm patient, and I feel like I'm efficient at what this tournament demands, which is hitting the ball in the fairway and knocking it on greens," Duval said. "I enjoy that mind-set and I enjoy that type of event. And I enjoy what it does to you as a player, how it makes you a little goofy at times. I think that's the beauty of this golf tournament."

The ever-calm Duval said he didn't feel any extra pressure.

"You can say I should have [won a major] so far or you could say I should very soon, but that's not going to help me either way," Duval said. "So we only have that opportunity four times a year, and you better be playing well when those weeks come around or you're not going to have any opportunities. So to feel like I have to any time right now, or this week, I just don't think that way."

Stewart's share of the lead after two rounds gave him the distinction of having led three of the four most recent U.S. Opens after two rounds. Combined with Mickelson and Duval, the trio had posted 14 top-ten finishes in the past twenty-one major championships played and did not have one win among them. Of the three, Mickelson accounted for ten of the top-ten finishes, with notable failures in the 1995 Masters, the 1995 U.S. Open, and the 1996 PGA Championship.

Tiger Woods loomed boldly in the background.

Woods and the U.S. Open had looked like oil and water over the years. Would he become his generation's Sam Snead? He easily had the most talent on Tour, but his game was ill suited to the normal demands of a U.S. Open golf course. Woods took advantage of the differences Pinehurst No. 2 held in contrast to other Open courses.

On 8, Woods pushed his tee shot way right into the pines at the base of a tall tree. Had this drive occurred on a hole of similar distance the year before at Olympic, he would have been lucky to find his ball in the deep rough and if he did find it the best he could have done was to hack it back to the fairway. Instead, Woods hit an 8-iron off a pine needle lie to split a ten-foot opening between two trees and landed his ball forty feet from the pin; he two-putted to record a par.

Friday morning at 16 looked almost comical given the frustration of playing the hole. The first twenty players to pass through did not hit the green in regulation. Then came Tiger.

Woods cut a four-iron into the elevated green that stopped six feet from the hole and two-putted for par.

Such spectacular displays by Woods had many believing the Tour's reigning wonder boy had the field right where he wanted it and the Open was his for the taking.

Open courses had flogged Woods the previous three Junes, forcing him to hit a 1-iron off the tee and generally taking him out of his game. The golfer who best protected par normally won the Open, not the boldest golfer. The combination of Woods's maturity and a different type of Open course made the idea of Woods claiming his first U.S. Open palpable.

"I love these conditions because it brings out the imagination," Woods said. "So many U.S. Opens, if you miss a fairway—get the sand wedge, hack it back out, try to make par from a hundred yards. If you miss a green—bring out the lob wedge, hack it out, and try to make a ten-foot putt for par."

Woods shot 71 to place him two shots behind the leaders heading into the weekend rounds. Tied with Woods for fourth place at 139 were Singh, Hal Sutton, and Mayfair.

"I'm very pleased just to be under par," Woods said. "I know how difficult it is out there, and everyone else does as well. But you have to hang in there. You have to keep grinding it out and making the pars, but the guys will come back. It's difficult to shoot under par. There will be a couple of rounds under par, but it will be difficult to do."

Which was due in large part to the greens at No. 2 that Woods called "more severe than Augusta."

"Because they're all domed," Woods said. "At Augusta you have flat surfaces to putt on. Here you really don't. You can't feed the ball off the slopes here. Most holes you can feed it off the slopes; no big deal at Augusta. Guys are hitting good shots ten feet away from the hole, and next thing they're twenty yards away, and that doesn't happen at Augusta."

Ron Philo teed off at 10:30 hoping to play well enough to make the cut for weekend play. The work he'd done on the range the day before helped ease his nervousness when he walked to the No. 1 tee and prepared to hit. Everything felt right and a healthy dose of confidence could work wonders. His swing then performed exactly as he'd hoped, producing a marvelous drive down the center of the fairway that left him a shot of 175 yards to the green. Philo further validated the positive vibes with his approach shot that finished fifteen feet from the pin.

"I'm like, 'Here we go,'" Philo said. "I was thinking if I could get those first four or five holes under my belt and be under par, then I'm not so worried about having to make the cut."

When Philo stood over his putt his mind ran freely, conjuring positive images of charging to a quick start after he sank his birdie. The optimistic imagery lasted right up until his putter made contact with his ball.

"The ball got about halfway to the hole and I knew it wasn't going in," Philo said. "It rolled over its mark, but it was going way too fast. It wasn't going to take the break. And it didn't slow down. The ball rolled off the front of the green."

Philo's ball came to rest forty feet away from the hole close to the edge of a bunker.

"I had no stance," Philo said. "I could barely hit the ball. I chipped it and it came back to me. Before I knew it I'd made 7. At that point my chances of making the cut were over. It was a matter of playing in and doing my best just to maintain my composure.

"You couldn't really attack the course. There weren't a lot of places where you were going to make up ground. There were certainly places you could make some birdies, but you were definitely going to make bogeys. It was just an extremely difficult golf course under difficult conditions."

Exposed were deficiencies in Philo's short game.

"That's where the golf courses, especially the major championship golf courses, challenge players more than any other tournament because you miss a lot of greens there," Philo said. "It's tougher to hit fairways, which makes it tougher to hit greens. And then they make the greens more challenging. When you do hit them it's harder to make birdie and when you don't it's harder to get up and down."

Philo shot 79 and missed the cut, turning from player to spectator for the weekend rounds.

"I certainly gained more respect for what the players who are winning out there are capable of doing with a golf ball," Philo said. "When you go out there and you play on those courses, you play at the same venue, but you can't play Pinehurst No. 2 the way it was for the Open, no matter what tees you play from or where they put the flags. People can even shoot the scores the players shot if they go and play Pinehurst No. 2 right now. But to do it in the conditions of the Open or any major championship is certainly an incredible accomplishment. You gain a lot of respect for what the players on Tour can do and how much effort is required to play at that level of skill."

Philo was just one of the many in the field to feel the wrath of Pinehurst No. 2 during the second round. Notables not making the cut included Ernie Els, Fred Couples, Mark O'Meara, and Norman, who hit just two greens in regulation. Lee Janzen just dodged not making the cut by chipping in on 18.

Scott Hoch, who grew up in nearby Raleigh, missed the cut when his putt lipped out on 18.

"The putt wasn't but about five feet," Hoch said. "It went in the right side, went all the way around and came out at three o'clock on the right side. It was brutal, but I wasn't playing well at the time."

Despite the proximity to his hometown, Hoch confessed to not being a big fan of No. 2.

"They tricked it up," Hoch said. "But in their favor, they pretty much had to because of the weather. Because the greens were softer than they wanted them to be. So they made more severe pin placements."

Also failing to make the cut was Lee Westwood, who had been one of the European contingent's great hopes for breaking the victory drought. Prior to the tournament, Westwood, who was one of the most accurate drivers in the world, pooh-poohed Pinehurst No. 2 when asked if the U.S. Open provided his best chance to win a major.

"I used to think so, when there was five inches of rough [at the U.S. Open]," Westwood said. "[At Pinehurst] I think it's a bit too short, a little bit too easy. Once you've knocked it up on the green that's about it."

His words came back to haunt him during Friday's round at 17. After missing a short putt to make double bogey a fan in the gallery chortled: "Is this easy enough for you?"

Only sixty-eight players stood at seven-over or better at the conclusion of the second round and only three players shot under par rounds Friday—John Huston and Jeff Maggert each shot 69 to join Stewart—and the scoring average had shot to 75.5 strokes.

Pinehurst No. 2 would only get firmer, faster, and less forgiving during the weekend. Already the sloped edges around the green were turning yellow, indicating a dry texture that enhanced the chances of errant shots receiving a checkered flag while rolling off the green. Par would look like an oasis in the desert.

Norman offered this forecast to the *Seattle Post-Intelligencer* before cleaning out his locker: "If it stays breezy like this, I doubt you're going to see an under-par winner."

Despite No. 2's difficulty, most of the players already were talking about making No. 2 a regular stop for the U.S. Open.

"It would be nice [for the Open to return to Pinehurst No. 2]," Woods said. "Because it would be a break from having five-inch rough eight feet off the green. It would be a nice break to have that, and to see guys use their short games and use their imagination, because so many U.S. Opens basically take that part of your game away from you. And it's basically you have to hack the ball out and try and make a 10-foot putt for par. And unfortunately I don't think that really tests a person's all-around game. And this course really does."

Paul Jett spotted Stewart Friday afternoon on the putting green. Stewart knew Jett ran the course and couldn't resist teasing him.

"You're going to put some water on those greens aren't you?" Stewart said smiling.

"No, they'll be just fine through Sunday," Jett said, sounding every bit the executioner at the gallows.

CHAPTER TWELVE

ALONE AT THE TOP AGAIN

CHUCK COOK STOOD on the putting green with Payne Stewart prior to Saturday's round and listened to Stewart taking it and giving it back to Tiger Woods.

"When I build golf courses I'm going to build them nine thousand yards long," Woods told Stewart. "Then you guys won't stand a chance."

Woods clearly meant to imply he would be out-driving him. Stewart would have none of that nonsense and didn't hesitate to respond.

"Yeah, but if it's a U.S. Open, you'll still have to drive it in the fairway," Stewart said. "Besides, by the time you're designing golf courses I won't be playing anymore."

Cook laughed at the recollection.

"Payne just handled it," Cook said. "He just came right back at him."

Saturday at Pinehurst No. 2 was not for the faint of heart.

The greens continued their transition from a stimpmeter reading of 10.5 on Monday to the desired 11½ to 12 reading the USGA wanted to attain by Sunday.

Paul Jett's crews were mowing the course twice a day.

"By the weekend we weren't getting a whole lot of grass in the mower blades," Jett said.

If the difficult pin placements for the third round weren't enough, early starters were punished by blustery wind conditions that died down considerably when the leaders teed off. But the wind picked up again, joining forces with occasional spurts of rain in the late afternoon. Pars became treasured commodities while birdies evolved into a rare and exotic species.

Stewart had Carolina on his mind, or at least on the fashion portion of his gray matter. He wore a Carolina blue tam and plus fours with white stockings, shoes, and shirt. Resembling Charlie "Choo Choo" Justice, Michael Jordan, or any other notable Tar Heel did nothing to help him avoid a less-than-auspicious beginning. His first drive of the day missed the fairway by six inches. He managed to hit the green with a 5-iron from the rough, but the ball rolled into the fringe leaving him in a position from where he couldn't get up and down. The bogey moved him to two-under for the tournament.

Stewart just wouldn't go away, though.

Demonstrating similar grit to what he'd shown in the previous two rounds, he hit a 9-iron approach shot to 3 where the precarious nature of fate smiled on Stewart and turned its back on his playing partner, David Duval. Stewart's ball landed at the top of a ridge and trickled down to within two feet of the pin. Duval's ball hit only inches behind where Stewart's had landed but the difference was just enough to send Duval's ball hiking back down the slope at the front of the green.

Stewart sank the birdie to go back to three-under, which wore like a protective suit of armor against the course and the elements; Duval headed in an opposite direction after the bogey. The No. 1 player in the world had gambled and lost in the early going and paid for his aggressiveness, making the turn at 40 after losing five shots to par on his first eight holes.

"I was never panicked about what was going on out there," Duval said. "As you can see by every player in the field, especially those on top, it's very easy to make a 5 or a 6. So there's no reason to panic.

"Even after I went five-over for the day after eight holes, I figured that if I could par in, the worst case [was] I was going to be three behind. I knew everybody was going to struggle. I just happened to be early. I just tried to focus on keep making pars."

Stewart stood at three-under when he blasted from a greenside bunker to fifteen feet at 7 then two-putted for par like, 'ho, hum, another par.'

"However I go about making par—whether it's two beautiful shots and two putts, or two ugly shots, a chip, and a nice putt—I accept it, I take my par and go," Stewart said. "Because you're never losing to anybody if you're making par."

But beginning at 8 Stewart had a hard time making par and he would need to dip into the reserve of strokes he'd built. His drive found the fairway but he hit a poor 4-iron into the bunker guarding the green of the difficult par-4. He couldn't escape this time. After hitting from the bunker to twelve feet he missed his putt for par.

"I hit a good putt there, actually, but I missed it," Stewart said.

At 9, Stewart pulled a 6-iron left of the green, chipped to within four feet, and missed the putt for his second consecutive bogey to drop to one-under.

"I could have righted myself a little bit on 9," Stewart said. "I hit a nice chip from the left of the green down to a very makeable distance to miss the putt. I should have made that putt."

Trying to escape the funk established on the previous two holes Stewart ripped a long drive down the middle of the tenth fairway before making what he deemed a mental error by pulling a 3-iron into the cross bunker approximately 100 yards from the green.

"That wasn't a very smart play," Stewart said. "You either take that bunker out of play or you don't get to that bunker. And I'm going to learn from that . . ."

Further trouble followed when he powered a sand wedge over the green.

"I didn't anticipate being able to hit the sand wedge that far out of that bunker," Stewart said. "And I caught it nice and clean and I made a mistake there. You hit it somewhere—where you don't want it to be over that green."

He managed to chip his ball back to eight feet, but again, he missed his par putt to remain on the bogey train.

This was not the kind of move Stewart wanted to make. He needed to get back on an even keel if he wanted to be in contention on Sunday; the tournament appeared to be slipping away from him. And the group in front of him contained the pair most likely to grab the prize in Tiger Woods and Phil Mickelson.

Woods wore white shoes, which had the same effect on the eyes as seeing Joe Namath wearing black shoes. The odd visual paralleled an odd beginning for Woods.

Woods's drive on 1 went left into the rough thanks to a gust of wind. He hit a sand wedge on his approach, but his ball carried a yard too far and rolled off the green into a difficult lie in the rough just above a greenside bunker. To balance himself he planted his back foot firmly in the trap with his front foot pushing forward in the greenside rough; he never looked comfortable in his stance.

Woods shanked the shot, sending his ball to the other side of the green where it rolled down the shaved slope. He bumped it back to within fifteen feet of the pin on his four shot then missed the left-to-right putt for a double bogey and a resounding "oooh" from the gallery.

More trouble followed at 2 after he'd hit what he believed to be a perfect 9-iron on his approach. The ball landed a yard from the hole, but there is a basic truth about Pinehurst No. 2: Landing a yard from the hole and stopping a yard from the hole were two different matters.

Donald Ross had to be smiling somewhere.

"Next thing I know I've got about a twenty-yard chip," Woods said.

Using his 3-wood from around the green like he had much of the week, Woods ran the ball fifteen feet past the cup and two-putted. In two holes he had gone from one-under to two-over for the tournament. Most would have understood if Woods went ballistic, instead he took the mature route, and recovered with a birdie at 4 en route to a 37 on the front side.

In years past "I probably wouldn't have handled [the double bogey, bogey start] as well as I did this year and I'm sure I'll get better at it," Woods said. "If I started off double bogey, bogey in a regular Tour event, I'd probably lose about five shots. At U.S. Opens you just expect it."

Stewart's woes continued at 10 when he recorded his third consecutive bogey. Mickelson now had a three-shot lead despite the way he had hit his driver. Lefty and his big stick fought like jealous siblings during Saturday's round resulting in countless pulled drives into the rough. He still managed to make the turn at 35 after a birdie at 8 moved him back to three-under where he'd started the day.

"I hit the ball awfully sloppy, drove it poorly, poor iron play, and

I just got up and down quite a bit to keep the round somewhat intact," Mickelson said.

Stewart desperately needed a par on 11 and made the first step toward that goal by blistering a drive down the middle of the fairway. He then hit what he thought to be the perfect 8-iron at the pin, but the shot had too much muscle behind it. Stewart watched helplessly while his ball flew directly over the flag into the back bunker of the 453-yard par-4. Feeling frustrated about taking two good swings and having nothing to show for it, Stewart selected his get-out-of-jail-for-free club—his sand wedge, and hit from the bunker to within ten feet. Miraculously he sank the putt he so badly needed to save par.

Sir Issac Newton's third law of physics, the one concerning propulsion, visited the back nine at Pinehurst No. 2 at this juncture. *Every action has an equal and opposite reaction.*

Stewart surged forward with six consecutive pars, including a near-miss birdie at 17 where his fifty-foot birdie putt slammed on the brakes inches from the hole, while Mickelson moved backward with bogeys on 11, 15, 16, and 17.

Along the way Mickelson and Woods were put "on the clock" by USGA officials for four holes. If their play did not speed up they would be assessed a one-shot penalty.

The slow-play warning came at 12. Woods had been standing over his second shot preparing to hit when the wind shifted.

"It went from straight into me to straight across, and I had the wrong club," Woods said. "I backed off, hit the shot correctly, made my par, and I was informed I got a bad time."

Playing on the clock was a particularly difficult situation during the third round.

"You've got some weird shots and it takes some time to figure them out, and you don't want to blow it, but you don't want to get a bad time," Woods said. "It would be tough to say, you know what, if I do it again I'm going to get a one-shot penalty, and to lose the U.S. Open by one shot would be pretty tough to swallow."

Saturday's easiest hole of the day was 18 with a 4.015-stroke average. Only the par-5 fourth hole had more birdies on the day with twelve while 18 had ten. An explanation for the players' ease negotiating the 446-yard par 4 came in the comfort of feeling the wind at their backs when they stood on the tee. To Mickelson, the wind felt like salve applied to an open wound.

Given the extra boost off the tee, Mickelson opted to keep his cantankerous driver sheathed on the final hole and pulled out his 3-wood. Caution rewarded him handsomely with a big drive down the middle of the fairway. Pleased to be playing from the fairway, Mickelson celebrated by cutting an 8-iron to within six feet of the hole, which was situated back left. The shot evoked laughter from Mickelson and his caddie, which Mickelson attributed to their sharing an inside joke.

"It was the first fade I tried to hit all week," Mickelson said. "This golf course sets up well left-to-right. I wasn't going to get to the pin left-to-right on that shot, so I took an 8-iron and hit a cut shot. I anticipate trying to hit a lot of fades all day tomorrow, because basically that came off good."

Mickelson sank the birdie putt, rolling his eyes and smiling with relief when the ball dropped. Despite hitting just eight fairways, he had shot 73 to place him at even-par for the tournament in a tie for the lead with Stewart at that point.

Stewart stood in the middle of the eighteenth fairway after his drive and had to endure the standing ovation extended Mickelson by a gallery sensitive to what was going on in his life. Stewart understood the situation, but the veteran of many a U.S. Open battle refused to be distracted by the salute. Looking deliberate, like just another day at the office, Stewart hit a 7-iron to fifteen feet then dropped the birdie putt to earn his own standing ovation from the appreciative gallery.

Stewart had shot a 72 that felt like a 66. Though he'd lost two shots to par, he finished with a one shot lead; addition through subtraction. Miraculously, Stewart had managed to hit 80 percent of the fairways through three rounds.

"I'm pleased with the way I dealt with everything today," Stewart said. "The putt I made on 11 was a major, major factor in my round of golf today. I made that one and then I kind of righted the ship a little bit and birdied there on 18, which leaves a very pleasant taste in my mouth."

Stewart's love affair with No. 2 continued; he talked about the course with reverence—a vastly different opinion than the opinion he'd formed about Olympic at the previous Open. Why the difference? Players were having trouble aiming at the flagsticks and nobody was breaking par, yet Stewart thought the setup at No. 2 fit the parameters for what a U.S. Open course should be.

"Why the discrepancy?" Stewart said. "I think that the conditions here lend [themselves] to playability. I think the conditions at the Olympic Club, with the severity of the sloping fairways with the firmness of how firm the fairways got—what would happen at Olympic Club if they shaved all the collars?

"All of a sudden that ball is going to be thirty, forty yards away from the green. That might be a lot more difficult than having that eight-inch rough that they claim to be four right there on the edge of the green. You don't know. But I just think that the severity of the slope of the fairways at Olympic club, and as firm as they got, it was just extremely difficult to put the ball in the fairway, which is—I don't know. It was tough. This course is tough, but fair. I'd question the fairness of Olympic Club."

Stewart's third-round success had put him back into the familiar position of leading the Open after 54 holes for the third time in the 1990s. In doing so, Stewart put himself in Sunday's final group for the second consecutive year. He loved the slot.

"I'm not going to sit here and say that it's not [different than any other tournament]," Stewart said. "That's just the fun of it. It's having to deal with the restless night's sleep that I'm probably going to have tonight. You've just got to deal with it. If I didn't enjoy this, I wouldn't ever have entered the golf tournament."

Stewart even managed a smile when a reporter asked if he was glad Lee Janzen was not near him on the leaderboard.

"That's a great question," Stewart said. "Yeah, that's all right, you know."

A U.S. Open—without Janzen on his tail ready to rip out his heart; life couldn't be better for Stewart.

"I love this golf tournament," Stewart said. "I enjoy playing golf when par gets its reward no matter how you make it. It's the mind-set I get when I come to this tournament. My adrenaline is flowing more. My concentration is better. All those things have gotten me to where I am right now."

Mickelson would be the player in closest pursuit of Stewart a year after Janzen had run down Stewart on Sunday at Olympic.

"Tomorrow is something that I have looked forward to ever since I've played amateur and junior golf," Mickelson said. "I've looked forward to having an opportunity to win the U.S. Open come Sunday. I've had the opportunity a couple of times in my career, and I've really enjoyed playing those final rounds, even though I have not broken through yet and won."

Woods shot 72 for a 211 total that placed him in a tie for third place. Along the way he'd overcome a slow-play warning and a rough start while looking relaxed throughout the day. From time to time

Woods even displayed a smile, like when his left hand released the club on his follow-through after hitting his approach to 16. Woods had gotten rattled when he heard the silence broken by someone teeing off on 18.

"It was so quiet out there, and then that metal-wood sound—it was just right there," Woods said. "Whoever it was made contact right on my downswing, and I flinched. I didn't even know they were on the tee."

The fact Woods's shot finished fifteen feet from the hole did nothing to diminish Woods's good feeling. He was in his element, which made him seem all the more invincible with one round to go.

"I love playing in the most intense pressure," Woods said. "How can you not? This is what we play for. This is why you play hard, why you practice is to get in these positions where you have to be so committed to a shot and be so mentally exact that it takes a lot of effort. And that's what we as players love. I absolutely love it and it's a lot of fun. Don't forget, I'm nervous. There's no doubt about that, but I love the pressure. It's a lot of fun."

Duval remained in contention by making par on the final ten holes for a 75, putting him three shots out of the lead at 212.

"I'm going to enter the final day three shots behind the leader, and not many people between us," Duval said. "I probably can't shoot much better than par tomorrow, maybe one-under. . . .

"I look forward to [Sunday]. Everybody is going to back up some more. The guy who backs up the smallest amount is going to win. I think it serves me well here. I'm pretty close to sitting on the winning score, I think. What do you think?"

Among the horror stories from Saturday's third round were Ted Tryba's 82, which came just six days after he had won the PGA Tour event in Memphis. Tom Kite shot 80; John Daly, 81; and Larry Mize, 84—each of the trio had won at least one major.

Janzen shot 76.

"I've been asked many times what's the hardest golf course I've ever played," Janzen said. "Now I have the answer."

Nick Price said the dangers of Pinehurst No. 2 were hard to describe.

"It's really a shame that television isn't three dimensional, so the folks watching at home could see how severe all these humps and bumps are around the edges of the greens."

Bob Burns, who won the Nike Tour's Player of the Year award in 1998, made eight consecutive bogeys in the third round when he shot 84. Burns did not hit a green in regulation during Friday's round.

"I went eighteen straight holes without hitting a green," Burns said. "I mean, I hit some, but they didn't stay on. It was amazing. It's a fun golf course, but most golf courses lose their fun when the USGA gets hold of them."

Among Burns's Saturday adventures was the one he experienced at the par-4 twelfth after pulling his tee shot left of the fairway. Once on the ground his ball continued to roll along the cart path until glancing off the tire of a golf cart where a USGA official sat. The ball bounced back into the rough.

"It was basically unplayable after that," Burns said.

Burns pitched the ball back to the fairway, hit his next shot over the green, chipped the ball and it rolled back to him, putted the ball and it rolled over the green into the rough.

"That green basically was a hog's back," Burns said. "It was like trying to stop the ball on the hood of your car. I ended up chipping out of the rough again, I'm on in 6 and I two-putt for an 8."

Daly's festive humor blew away in the wind Saturday. He did not talk to the media after finishing his round, stopping briefly in the locker room before dashing off in his car.

In general the uncharacteristic praise for the USGA from earlier in the week had subsided. The players had been suspicious of No. 2 when the USGA kept the rough short and did not extend the length of the course by miles. The suspicions were validated Saturday with pin placements near the edges of the greens and several of the holes were located at the peak of a mound, allowing balls to fall from any point of entry. Frustrations mounted when high, pure shots landed near the pins but didn't stop until they rolled off the green.

"It's not the hardest course I've ever played, but it's the hardest to get it close to the hole on the green," said former champion Tom Watson, who shot 77.

Birdies trailed bogeys Saturday by a ratio of four to one in the third round and just 41.6 percent of No. 2's greens were hit in regulation. The scoring average came in right at 76. Pinehurst No. 2 boasted of having three of the five longest par-4s in Open history and they offered plenty of trouble.

The fifth hole yielded an average of 4.6 strokes through three rounds; the eighth hole averaged 4.45 strokes; and 16 played to an average of 4.5 strokes and allowed just eight birdies.

Tom Lehman had been a member of the final twosome on Sunday for the previous four U.S. Opens. He'd led after fifty-four holes at Shinnecock Hills in 1995, at Oakland Hills in 1996, and at Congressional in 1997 before trailing Stewart prior to the final round at Olympic in 1998. But Lehman wasn't a factor at Pinehurst. He shot 73 on Saturday, leaving him at ten-over-par 220 and heading into Sunday's round with a much earlier tee time than the final group.

"If it hadn't been for the cloud cover and wind dying a little, it would have been the highest scoring day in [Open] history," Tom Lehman said. ". . . Somebody may be under par after three rounds, but nobody will be after four."

John Cook walked off 18 as the first player to finish the third round.

"Today I played this as a par 88," Cook joked. "I had twelve birdies and a bogey. A birdie today is out of the question unless you are off the green and chip in or hole a bunker shot or make a thirty-foot putt. You're not going to get close from anywhere on the fairway."

Cook's words proved prophetic in relation to Steve Stricker.

Minutes after Cook delivered his state of Pinehurst No. 2 address, Stricker ran in a forty-foot putt on the second hole. His encore came from a fairway bunker on 3. When he reached the bunker he found his tee shot sitting up in the sand approximately 136-yards away from the pin into the wind; he selected an 8-iron and swung.

"I heard the people going crazy," Stricker said. "I had a great lie in the bunker. I could tell [the ball] was getting closer. You can tell how the people are reacting when it's getting closer."

The ball hit a foot past the hole, spun backward, and dropped into the hole for an eagle 2, giving Stricker the shot of the tournament en route to a 69, the only subpar round of the day.

Stricker finished second to Vijay Singh in the 1998 PGA Championship. His third-round 69 at No. 2 matched the third-round 69 he'd shot the previous year at Olympic before finishing in fifth place with a 73, six shots behind Janzen. Stricker learned from those experiences.

"I was able to see how they won, basically," Stricker said. "It's hard to put in words, I guess. They stayed real patient. I could tell they were battling nerves, too. They got a couple of good breaks, but I think mainly they remained calm on the outside. I'm sure they weren't on the inside. But it looked like they were fairly patient. And I know when I got into contention, especially in a major tournament, that I'd really get ahead of myself and I'd start to walk a little bit faster, my swing would get a little bit quicker. And those are the things I'm going to have to deal with and slow down a bit."

Stricker's outstanding day put him in a tie for fourth with Singh and Duval, but his day could have been better had he exercised a little patience on 16 and 17.

"I felt like I was way too aggressive," Stricker said.

When Stricker first pondered his shot on 16 the voice inside him screamed "3-iron." Rather than going with his first instinct Stricker talked himself into hitting a 2-iron hoping to get the ball to the back of the green to the hole. He then experienced the sensation familiar to every player in the field when he watched his ball land on the green, then roll through the back left part of the green until it came to rest in the rough. Bumping his ball to within ten feet was the best he could do from the rough, laying the groundwork for his missed par putt.

"If I hit that 3-iron, it probably would have slowed down on the front of the green, and I probably could have two-putted from there," Stricker said.

Stricker didn't learn his lesson on 16 and tried to hit a 7-iron stiff on the par-3 seventeenth. The wind grabbed his shot and pushed it to the right side of the green. Again he bogeyed.

"I should have put it in the center of the green and tried to make a twenty-footer," Stricker said. "But maybe that's a lesson I learned today I can apply tomorrow."

Stricker played a lot more at ease than the previous August when he was in the running to win the PGA Championship in Seattle. The Wisconsin native had faced a similar situation to Mickelson's as his wife, Nicki, sat at home ready to deliver their daughter, Bobbi Maria.

"You know, I was pretty emotional about the whole thing last year for some reason," Stricker said. "Just the fact that we were going to have our first child, the fact that I was in contention at the PGA, I don't know if it really played a factor or not. I hope it didn't. It probably spurred me on more than anything, and I played well because of this other thing, this other great thing that was going to happen. Knowing Phil, I don't think it will interrupt his concentration or bother him at all tomorrow. It looks like he's extremely focused, the times I've seen him on TV, and it looks like he's on a mission a little bit. Amy being pregnant probably relaxes him a little bit and turns some of the focus away from the U.S. Open onto the pregnancy."

Like Mickelson, Stricker was prepared to pull out of a major to be with his wife at the delivery.

"I didn't have a beeper but I had a private plane waiting," Stricker said. "Nicki later told me she wouldn't have called, but knowing Phil and Amy, I've got to believe they have a pact that she would call and he would go."

Tied with Woods for third place was Tim Herron, or "Lumpy" as he was known on Tour for his sack-of-potatoes build.

Herron came from a family golf heritage. Lee, his grandfather, and Carson, his father, both won Minnesota state golfing titles and played in the 1934 and 1963 U.S. Opens, respectively. At age 29, Lumpy already had won three events during his four years on the PGA Tour. But his 70 in the dire third-round conditions had to rank high among his family's greatest golfing feats.

Memorable inside Herron's third-round scrapbook were his feats on 15 and 16.

Facing an eighty-foot shot from just off the fifteenth green, Heron grabbed his putter.

"I told my caddy I've been putting it pretty well off the green," Heron said. "So I putted it up there, and I got it up there stiff."

The ball stopped six inches away from the cup, allowing him to save par.

Heron then escaped trouble on 16 by hooking a 6-iron through the trees on his second shot and salvaged a two-putt par save.

Herron smiled and waved to the crowd throughout the round. Afterward he sounded reluctant to accept the fact he was in contention.

"You know U.S. Open probably isn't my style of golf, because I don't drive it real straight, but this week I'm driving it good, and the last six months I've driven it really good," Herron said. "I missed one fairway today and missed it by a huge margin where I had an actual shot. I played well and I have the greens down, lagging the ball very well. And I hope for a good day home."

Billy Mayfair stood alone in fifth at 213 and Jeff Maggert was in sixth at 214 to round out the group with the best chances of upsetting Stewart's final round.

Stewart was the only player in the field under par, at one-under 209. Weather conditions coupled with the toughness of Pinehurst No. 2 made the prospect of the winner finishing over par a distinct possibility. Not since 1978, when Andy North finished one-over at Cherry Hills, had an Open champion finished over par.

Woods spotted several dots on the greens signifying hole locations for the final day and smiled.

"Oh, Lordy, they're going to be tough," Woods said. "Some are in corners, some are near slopes. The pin at 13 is on a slope. If they cut the hole right, the pin will tilt a little."

Amy Mickelson had other worries. Sometime Saturday night she began to experience contractions. She went to the hospital where she begged for time. Doctors administered a drug in hopes of delaying labor.

"I didn't know about it," Mickelson said. "Turns out, on Thursday the doctor checked her again and said, 'Oh my goodness, if I'd have seen this [before Phil left for the Open] I wouldn't have had

Phil go.' Amy didn't tell me that either. She ended up staying on her back, keeping her legs elevated, and not really doing much at all for the next few days.

"Saturday night she started having some contractions. She had had contractions multiple times throughout her pregnancy and we had to go to the hospital and get some medication to stop them from causing a premature birth. But this wouldn't have been premature. She was able to get the contractions to stop Saturday night and so she never called me and let me know. She spent about three hours there."

Phil Mickelson's baby was closer to being born than he knew. The chances of Lefty becoming a father on Father's Day were greatly enhanced.

Tracey Stewart had walked the course to watch her husband play the first two rounds of the Open, but due to the size of Saturday's crowd she opted out of following him.

"I told him I would watch on TV because it was too hard to see him," Tracey said. "He understood and I told him I'd meet him afterward."

Because Stewart led the tournament NBC cameras captured most of his swings on the back nine. Tracey watched with interest and concern.

"He continued to play well, but he was having trouble with his putting," Tracey said. "I kept seeing him on TV wanting to watch the ball go into the hole.

"I'm not a golfer, but I'd watched him play for twenty years. I knew a lot about his game. He was moving his head. Watching that on TV made me want to scream when he missed a putt."

Payne had needed thirty-one putts during Saturday's round.

At the conclusion of the third round Tracey made her way to the press tent.

"Since he was leading I knew that's where he'd be," Tracey said.

"He was already answering questions when I got there, so I just slipped into the back of the tent and waited."

Payne finished with the media then walked over to Tracey.

"I want to go hit balls," he said.

Stewart remembered his prolonged session with the media after the third round at Olympic, which had cost him the opportunity to practice at the previous year's Open.

"You need to practice some putting, too," Tracey said. "You were really moving your head today. You're wanting to watch it go in."

"Really?" Payne said.

Tracey nodded and they headed to "Maniac Hill," Pinehurst No. 2's driving range. Dusk approached and the air turned cool. Stewart hit shot after shot while Tracey and Mike Hicks watched. Tom Meeks spotted Stewart practicing and walked toward him.

"He sees me and tells Mike Hicks, 'Fill in some of these divots up real quick, there's Tom Meeks and I want him to see me practicing some shots out of these sand-filled divots.'" Meeks laughed. "Kind of having some fun with me."

After hitting balls for more than an hour, Stewart headed toward the putting green ready to implement Tracey's simple advice: Hold your head still and see the club hit the ball. Keeping his head stationary, Stewart began putting with his eyes closed.

"He started making everything, you could see he felt confident," Tracey said.

The putting tip served as the perfect elixir for combating the mind games Stewart would endure while trying to sleep holding the U.S. Open lead after 54 holes. Having a family also helped Stewart relax. He called Aaron, who told him about a friend who had gotten a new skateboard, but he couldn't call Chelsea, who was attending a basketball camp.

"We cooked dinner like we did every night and low-keyed it," Tracey said.

Payne answered phone calls then watched the Stanley Cup hockey finals. Among those Stewart talked to were J. B. Collingsworth, Stewart's pastor at the First Baptist Church in Orlando, who gave him a verse and told him he wanted him to think of the verse when he went to the course Sunday. The verse read, "I've set the Lord continually before me, He is at my right hand and I will not be shaken."

Collingsworth then told Payne, "I believe with all my heart that God's going to let you win this tomorrow. And I want you to know that he will be at your right hand and I know you will not be shaken."

Payne and Tracey stayed up late so he would sleep late the following morning.

"Because the tee times at the U.S. Open are late we'd watch TV until midnight or later because he didn't want to go to bed too early and get up too early, then have all that time to kill until 2 o'clock when he teed off," Tracey said. "So the plan was to stay up late, get up around 9, have breakfast, take a shower, and get there about two hours ahead of time."

Idle time could easily have led to anxiety about how the day might transpire. Flashbacks from the past could be good or bad.

There was the Open he'd won eight years earlier and the one that had gotten away the year before. Which outcome would Sunday bring?

CHAPTER THIRTEEN

A SUNDAY FOR THE AGES

JUST BEFORE LEAVING his home in Mebane to make the sixty-three-mile drive to Pinehurst, Mike Hicks kissed his wife at the door and told her, "If we make four birdies today we'll win."

While Hicks weaved through the back roads, Stewart experienced a range of emotions prior to the final round of the U.S. Open on Father's Day.

The plan to sleep late worked perfectly. Tracey and Payne ate their breakfast of mangos and muffins, then Payne set up the ironing board and ironed while watching the early coverage of the Open and talking on his cell phone.

"He was just trying to look and see what the other guys were doing out on the course, where the pin placements were and all that," Tracey said. "Because they played so late and they started the coverage so early, you could see what everyone was doing."

Everything looked normal when Tracey left the room to take a shower. When she returned she found Payne's eyes brimming with tears.

"What's wrong?" Tracey said.

"They showed a thing about my father on TV," Payne said.

Since it was Father's Day, NBC's U.S. Open coverage had a segment about the father-son relationship shared between Bill and Payne Stewart. Memories of his father rushed over him.

Payne had gravitated to golf naturally through the influence of his father.

William Louis Stewart grew up in Springfield, Missouri, where he played football, basketball, and golf in high school before attending Southwest Missouri State Teacher's College in Springfield. A gifted athlete, Bill continued to play three sports in college, lettering in football, basketball, and golf, but neither the gridiron nor the hardwood could make his heart pitter-patter like being on the links. Golf owned Bill Stewart's soul.

"He could have been a pro," Bee Payne-Stewart said of her husband, explaining that when she became pregnant with the couple's first child, Susan, Bill thought more about establishing a steady income. Professional golf simply didn't pay enough in the post World War II years.

Bill got his golf fix by competing in amateur events. The Missouri state amateur titles he won served as a testament to his golfing skills.

The couple's second child, Lora, was born six years after Susan. Both Stewart girls enjoyed accompanying their father to the golf course, they just didn't get the bug.

On January 30, 1957, the couple had their third child, William Payne Stewart, and schooling the boy became Bill Stewart's higher calling in golf. Payne Stewart was born to be a golfer and took to the sport early in his childhood.

Bill and Bee began taking their 3-year-old son to the Hickory Hills Country Club in Springfield.

"He'd be out there with us when we walked the course," Bee said. "He'd have his club and ball with him and he'd hit it then chase it down the fairway. He had a lot of energy and just loved the game."

At age 4 Bill began to give Payne lessons.

"His father insisted that he practice, practice, practice," Bee said.

Most weeks Bill's job called for him to hop into his car on Monday and drive all over Missouri and parts of Kansas, Illinois, and Iowa making sales calls until Thursday. Bee usually received a reminder before he left.

"When [Bill] traveled, he'd tell me be sure and take Payne out to practice," Bee said. "After [Bill] died I told everybody he taught me how to be a widow because he'd be gone all week then on weekends he'd be at the golf course."

If Payne wasn't taking lessons from his father he was caddying for him, a practice he began at age 6. While carrying his father's bag, the impressionable son had the opportunity to observe his father's soft hands and competitiveness on the golf course. The son absorbed the father's golfing wisdom like a sponge.

"My dad told me you feel a shot," Payne said in a 1987 *Sports Illustrated* article. "You feel the line of a putt. You don't try to manufacture it."

Bill's influence led to Payne's unorthodox putting stroke that saw him lift the heel of the putter and strike the ball with the toe of the face.

Though golf held a lofty plateau in the Stewart household, Bill and Bee worked to make their kids well rounded. They regularly attended a Methodist church in Springfield and Bill had a sense of fun; he could dance.

"Bill was a marvelous dancer," Bee said. "All the ladies always wanted to dance with him."

Bill taught all of the kids how to dance by waltzing around the living room with them standing on the tops of his feet.

Bill and Payne "were very close and demonstrative," Bee said. "Of course the whole family is. We've never held back our affection for each other. We've always shown it and the girls are the same way.

"Payne was a great teaser and his father was the same way. I guess Payne came by it naturally. And he did inherit his athletic talent, because he was so talented in golf and sports. He had his father's talent. You can attribute that to his father's training."

Stewart's first win on the PGA Tour came in 1982 when he captured the Quad Cities Open, a win he would always single out as the one he relished most for the simple reason his father had been there to watch. Was Bill happy about seeing Payne win his first victory?

"Oh hell yeah," Bee said. "Bill stood down there when they introduced [Payne as the winner after the tournament] and just cried."

Toward the end of Bill's life Payne informed him during a quiet moment that Tracey and he were expecting their first child. Tears formed in Bill's eyes prior to the father offering the son some sage advice on becoming a parent: "Don't buy expensive baby furniture. It just wears out." Bill's remark tickled Payne, who often shared the anecdote with friends.

Watching the NBC segment, Payne remembered that anecdote along with all the laughter and love they'd shared.

"I just stood there and bawled in front of the television and thought about my father," Stewart said.

He composed himself, then dressed in navy blue plus fours with a matching tam; white knee socks and white golf shoes; and a red-and-blue-striped shirt. Bad weather prompted him to throw on a blue rain jacket.

Tracey drove him to the clubhouse and dropped him off, telling her husband she loved him and offering him encouragement.

"Believe in your heart that you can do it," Tracey said.

"I've got a big heart, Love," Payne said.

Payne grinned at their little joke. Years earlier an EKG revealed an anomaly in his heart that enlarged it and would one day make a pacemaker necessary. Payne used the diagnosis to poke fun at favorite sports writer clichés such as he had a "big heart" or "a lot of heart."

Tracey returned to the condominium to root down in front of the TV and watch Payne compete for the prize he held so dear.

While Stewart was experiencing a rush of emotions about his father, Phil Mickelson talked to his wife on the phone and was told everything was fine.

"She played a good poker face," Mickelson said.

Lefty's sense of anticipation about becoming a father for the first time had now been joined by the anticipation of winning a major for the first time. The drama would continue yet another day: Could Mickelson possibly do both? What if that beeper went off sometime on the front nine after he'd taken the lead? Would he follow through with his promise and rush off the course to fly to Arizona to watch the birth of his daughter on Father's Day?

Anticipation hung like clouds in the air above Pinehurst No. 2. Would this be the day a special U.S. Open unfolded, where a player distinguished himself for generations to come with his accomplishments? America would tune in to watch the truest form of reality TV.

Had a visitor been plunked down in the middle of the Village of Pinehurst, he might have ventured to guess he'd landed on the other side of the Atlantic Ocean at the British Open instead of the normally steamy U.S. Open. The weather felt better suited for St. Andrews than North Carolina in June. Temperatures fell to the mid-

60s, or about 20 degrees below normal, and a steady drizzle quietly soaked the course, making a noise that sounded like bacon frying when the drops pitter-pattered off the canopy of pine trees.

Pinehurst No. 2 remained a test of survival. Chris Perry, who completed the tournament at seventeen-over in a tie for forty-second place, turned playful upon reaching the eighteenth green.

"I thought it would be kind of funny to throw up the surrender flag and just crawl to the green on my knees," he said after performing the gesture.

Darren Clarke shot 71 to finish eleventh and make him the top European in a year when the European players had such high hopes. Colin Montgomerie shot 72 for a fifteenth-place finish.

"It looks awful on paper, but this really is a tough course," Montgomerie said. "Anyone in sixteenth or seventeenth place has done well. . . . I am leaving in a good mood, flying home tonight feeling very happy. I played very well. Some of the good shots were penalized, and bad shots very much penalized. Lady luck plays a huge role here."

Cool temperatures and rain could not soothe John Daly's temper. In fact a fire hose on full throttle likely would have failed to control the steam under his collar.

Daly began the day at sixteen-over and made par on the first four holes like he'd taken his medicine and planned to work hard toward a respectable finish. Then he bogeyed 5 and added a triple on 6, putting him at four-over for the day when he stepped to the No. 8 tee. His drive found the fairway, but his approach shot went through the back of the green and he chose to putt up the bank to the green. With little hesitation, Daly pulled back his putter and followed through, sending the ball up the hill. Unlike the Little Engine That Could, Daly's ball could not get over the hill. A change of direction followed, reversing the ball back to Daly's feet where he once again attempted the shot only to have the ball return to him again. Only this time he didn't wait for the ball to return to a stop. Instead he met the ball halfway up the bank and whacked it with his putter to send the ball rocketing off the front of the green. Daly received a two-shot penalty for playing a moving ball. He finished off the hole with a three-putt to record an 11.

"I told myself and my caddie that if the ball dares to come back down the hill, I'm going to do what Kirk Triplett did last year—take my two shots so I just don't go stupid," Daly said.

Doug Ferguson believed the Daly episode had been inevitable.

"After they'd been dealing with the turtlebacked dome greens and the little things like that, I just felt like by the end of the week you were going to see Daly's patience at nothing," Ferguson said. "He would have been about two or three months from ending his sobriety at that point."

Daly shot 83 to finish last in the field at twenty-nine over 309. Upon completion of his round, Mount Daly erupted.

"All credit to whoever wins, but I don't consider the U.S. Open a major anymore," Daly said. "The USGA tries to embarrass the players. From now on, my majors are the British Open, the USPGA, the Masters, and the Tour Championship."

Daly added he didn't know if he wanted to "waste" his time going to the Open at Pebble Beach in 2000 because "I don't want to see the USGA spoil that course as well."

Daly's feelings aside, the leaderboard showed that the USGA had done its job. Stewart, who was the only player to start the final round under par, was a former PGA and U.S. Open champion; Mickelson had the most wins on the U.S. Tour without winning a major; and according to world rankings, David Duval, Vijay Singh, and Tiger Woods were three of the top four players in the world.

"You looked at that leaderboard and you had them all right

there," Hicks said. "Duval, Tiger, Mickelson, Vijay, they're all right there. I knew that if we just hung in there anything could happen."

Larry Guest sat with Stewart in the locker room prior to Stewart's warm-up for Sunday's round.

"Phil Mickelson was in there and they talked about Phil's situation," Guest said. "Payne joked about, you know, 'I hope your wife calls today.' He was obviously just playing around. Then they had more of a serious discussion. Payne complimented him for his attitude. I remember him telling Phil something to the effect, 'I wish I'd have had my life in perspective at the same age.'"

Stewart seemed loose and calm.

"We were on the practice tee, which we always do, especially on a weekend like the U.S. Open," Gary Koch said. "We, meaning me and the other announcers, always try to go to the practice tee and just kind of hang out there. Some guys talk to you and some guys don't. We respect that. They're in their office and we certainly don't want to bother them in any form or fashion. But obviously if they want to talk we can gain little tidbits of information that might be of interest to the viewers. And when we were talking to Payne, he was in as good a mood, just relaxed and jovial, as you could possibly be in that situation. And to me it was a big difference from when I'd seen him before in similar situations.

"I don't know whether it was how much he grew mentally or he just seemed a lot more at peace with himself. There was a calmness about Payne Stewart that week at Pinehurst that was about as eerie as the weather."

Stewart began to hit balls before abruptly stopping.

"He said something to Mike Hicks about his sleeves bothering him when he swung," Koch said. "Then the next thing you know, he's saying to Hicks, 'You got that knife in there?' He pulls a knife out and just starts cutting the sleeves off. It looked kind of ragged and Payne never looked ragged."

The unseasonably cool weather made for a borderline call whether to wear a jacket.

"It was just cool enough to wear something like that," Hicks said. "But it was too warm to wear a full jacket. And the sleeves on this thing went down to just below his elbow, so they were a little too long. He cut them off once and they weren't short enough. He hit a few balls and they were bugging him. So he went back and got some scissors and cut them off again. What a weird day at the end of June in North Carolina, sixty-eight degrees and overcast."

Dr. Richard Coop remembered visiting Stewart on the range prior to him teeing off.

"I was on the range and I usually go over and try to get one idea [on a golfer's] mind before they go to the first tee," Coop said. "And it was amazing when I went up to Payne, he finished my sentence. I knew then that the best thing for me was to get out of the way. Just let him go. The one thought was, 'Just give yourself a chance.' By that I meant put your game out there, give it a chance to win. Don't try something bigger and better than you've been doing. Give your game a chance to play on the course. And he knew what I was going to say. It was almost eerie. I looked in his eyes and I said to myself, 'Let me out of here, he's where he needs to be.'"

Stewart did not mention seeing the NBC segment on the relationship between him and his father.

"He didn't talk to me about that," Coop said. "I'm not sure he could have. Payne was a very emotional person. I think he would have cried again and I don't think he wanted to do that. And I didn't want him to get emotional. I didn't bring it up.

"Looking back, I don't know what I would have done if he'd have brought it up. I don't think it would have lasted long. He just might have said something like, 'Did you see that thing about my dad?' Because he talked a lot about his dad."

Stewart's father wasn't at Pinehurst, but a man who had once been a father figure appeared on the range in the form of his old coach, Harvie Ward, who lived in the Village of Pinehurst.

"I had seen Payne during the tournament but hadn't been able to speak to him," Ward said. "And my wife said to me the last day, 'You've got to go over and talk to Payne. You can't let him come here and you not go over and say hello.' So I got up and went over there and he was hitting practice balls, getting ready. When I walked up he hit a big old pull hook. And as I walked up to him I said, 'I never taught you to hit that shot.' He turned around and laughed. Mike Hicks started laughing, so he came over and hugged me, asked how I was doing, some small talk. At this time I realized he seemed to have gotten things together."

Ward's visit could have been a distraction, but wasn't according to Hicks, who said, "Payne enjoyed seeing him." Hicks added: "The years had passed and time heals all wounds."

Shortly before Stewart teed off, Paul Jett's maintenance crew was just beginning to mow 18, roughly six hours later than the time when they normally mowed.

"Instead of mowing all the greens in two and a half hours we mowed the first seven holes then we stopped and let play catch up to us," Jett said. "Then we mowed two or three more and let the first group catch up to us."

They continued to mow No. 2 in said fashion until they finished, mowing 18, the final hole that needed mowing, just as the first group of the day stood on the No. 18 tee.

"The reason being we wanted to maintain the green speed throughout the day," Jett said. "On Saturday the eighteenth green probably was mowed by 8:30 or 9 o'clock and sat there all day. So 18 and the other greens were definitely faster on Sunday."

Duval, who didn't make a birdie on Saturday, teed off Sunday trailing by three shots and needing to make something happen. He did. First he landed his approach shot a foot from the hole at 2. The gimme birdie moved him to one-over for the tournament. Then he ran in a thirty-foot birdie on 3 to move to even-par. Every player and fan at Pinehurst knew anything could happen where the No. 1 player in the world was concerned.

"When I reached even, I felt like I was sitting on the winning score and all I had to do was make pars the rest of the way," Duval said.

Woods teed off in the next to last group with Tim Herron. Woods's aura coupled with the fact he'd kept his composure and remained in contention had perpetuated the belief that Sunday's round would be yet another coronation for golf's prodigy. Every timid contender's worst nightmare occurred when Woods birdied 1.

Stewart and Mickelson heard the roar.

Stewart didn't seem flustered; however, he did experience a rare moment of indecision, which was out of character for the mode in which Stewart had operated throughout the tournament.

"I didn't pull a club for him except for a lay-up shot for him on the tenth hole one of the days," Hicks said. "I'd give him the [yardage] number and he'd occasionally ask what the shot was playing. You'd get the number it was playing and boom, he'd pull the club. He was in tune to what was happening."

Hicks watched Stewart on the first tee wrestle in his mind with whether he should deviate from his plan.

"The hole was into the wind and it was raining and we had hit 3-wood all week," Hicks said. "But he was up there on the tee debating on whether to hit driver. He had his hand on the driver. Mickelson already had his driver out and he was swinging it. Payne didn't say anything to me, but if he had, I was going to say, 'Stick to the game plan.' And I could tell that he was thinking and thinking. He pulled out his 3-wood and stuck to his game plan and hit a beautiful 3-wood down there."

Other than Stewart's sand wedge, which was the closest thing he had in his bag to what might be considered a "pet" club, Stewart loved hitting his 3-wood.

"Payne's 3-wood was hot," Hicks said. "He could hit that thing probably two-fifty, two-sixty, he would draw it. It was hot. That's why he hit 3-wood off that first hole. He wasn't that far behind Mickelson and Mickelson hit a good drive and was down there pretty good. Into the wind, cool and raining like that. We hit 7-iron into that green on Sunday; 3-wood, 7-iron, that was pretty big."

When Stewart struck his approach shot he sent a spray of water dancing into the cool air. When the ball landed he had a fifteen-foot putt for birdie. He sank the putt to go off and running with a two-shot lead at two-under.

Chuck Cook left Pinehurst Saturday night to be with his kids in Austin, Texas, on Father's Day, a practice he'd always followed. But Sunday afternoon his focus remained at Pinehurst No. 2; he sat glued to the TV watching the tournament.

"Payne dropping one on top of [Woods] was kind of like, 'back in your face,' " Cook said.

Woods gave back his birdie when he bogeyed 3 to move back to one-over then he dropped in his second birdie of the day on 4 to go back to even. But prosperity just didn't seem to suit Woods and he bogeyed 5 to go back to one-over. He shot an even-par 35 on the front to remain at one-over at the turn.

Herron started the day two shots off the lead and quickly realized how playing in one of the two final groups of a U.S. Open could bring about some distractions he normally didn't encounter.

"One thing I learned is that I'm going to have to get used to all the disturbances there are," Herron said. "You have to time your shots because the gallery is moving around and yelling, and you have to be ready for that."

Herron had worse problems than crowd control beginning on the par-3 sixth hole when his tee shot landed in a greenside bunker. Herron blasted out and the ball rolled back to him.

"I hit a poor bunker shot," Herron said. "That's usually a strength of my game, but it wasn't the last two days."

Herron's redo lie didn't help his cause.

"I had no stance for a shot," he said.

He walked off the No. 6 green saddled with a double-bogey 5 and couldn't stop his tailspin before making bogeys on 7 and 8. In a matter of three holes Herron had turned an even-par round into four-over and six shots out of the lead.

"I didn't feel any more nervous than usual," Herron said. "I even fell asleep about 10 [Saturday night]. I was going to sit up and watch the hockey game, but I just dozed off. Then I had to figure out what to do from nine in the morning until I played [at 3 P.M. Eastern time]. If I had been nervous, it would have shown in my putting. My putting was pretty good. . . . I felt comfortable. But I didn't feel comfortable with my swing."

Stewart and Mickelson's pairing began to resemble an exclusive duel for the title from the outset of the day.

Stewart bogeyed 2, but the manner in which the bogey happened felt like Christmas. He underplayed his 3-iron approach and the ball flew to the right of the green, leaving him a chip shot from a difficult area.

"Payne had continued to aim at the middle of the white areas we'd marked out on every hole no matter where the pin was," Cook said. "He hit the ball in one blue area the whole week and that was on the second hole on Sunday."

Blue indicated danger in Stewart's yardage book.

"We both knew walking up there we were in a bad spot," Hicks said. "At that point you don't want to give one away, but if you just give one away that's okay. Just don't give two away, which is the key in that tournament. Don't make doubles or others. You're going to make bogeys."

Stewart mulled over his options with a serious expression on his face. A moment later he chipped from the difficult location but didn't put enough steam on the shot and the ball failed to make it to the green. Stewart had not made a score higher than bogey all week, but when the ball began to roll backward a big number seemed a distinct possibility. Stewart's fortunes hung on every revolution of the ball like a crapshooter's on a roll of the dice. A double or triple bogey could have sunk his chances right there.

Somehow Stewart's ball grabbed the side of the hill and stopped. He watched in disbelief at the result, nervously sweeping the club back and forth along the grass before approaching his ball where it sat in the gift lie.

"He caught a real break," Hicks said. "I think the ball hung there because of the moisture we were having at the time. If the greens had been dry that ball would have rolled back to his feet. There was so much moisture out there because of the mist and the little bit of rain we had. He was lucky to make bogey there."

Stewart followed his adventure on 2 by sticking a 9-iron shot two feet from the pin at 3. A feat even more outstanding considering the fact Tom Meeks called the pin placements at 3 and 9 his "zingers" for the Sunday round."

"They were very good attention-getters," Meeks said.

Stewart sank his second birdie of the day to move to two-under, pushing his lead over Mickelson back to two shots.

Stewart acknowledged the crowd's roar in understated fashion after sinking his birdie. Coop remembered marveling at Stewart's composure.

"I have a video I use in all my golf talks now," Coop said. "You watch him [at Pinehurst] and he never got too high and never got too low. If he made a birdie he acknowledged the crowd, but never really got high and did anything wild. And when he made a bogey he didn't get too low either. Throughout the tournament he maintained such an even keel from an emotional point."

Stewart was jazzed after the birdie, as attested by Steve Grandoff, a videographer shooting the U.S. Open for Sky Sports, who happened to be in the restroom facility between 3 and 4 shortly after Stewart finished playing 3. Due to the damp conditions, his equipment malfunctioned, prompting his partner and him to try and dry it out inside the restroom. Suddenly Stewart burst through the door.

"Something wrong?" Stewart said.

Grandoff explained their problem and Stewart smiled at them.

"Boys, you better get that thing working, I'm about to win this thing," Stewart said.

Grandoff smiled remembering the anecdote.

"You believed him when he said it," he said.

Playing conditions continued to add an odd element to the competition, particularly on the greens.

"I can tell you this," Hicks said. "While we were getting that heavy mist the greens were a little slower. When the ball was rolling you could see it spitting up moisture. They weren't as fast as they could have been if they were dry. They were still fast, obviously.

After a putt you could actually see the line of the ball, that's how much moisture was on the greens. It wasn't a hard rain. It was almost like dew just settling on the top. It wasn't soaking into the green."

Stewart hit into another divot on 4, but dealt with it and made par. Mickelson remained steady by making pars on the first six holes to keep Stewart from running away and hiding.

Stewart had a forty-foot birdie putt on 7 that broke from left to right and nearly fell before bouncing off the right edge. He made the par putt coming back to remain at two-under. Mickelson countered by sinking a right-to-left breaking birdie putt from twenty-five feet to move to one-under, one shot behind Stewart.

Stewart looked calm and he felt good while making his fashion statement with cutoff sleeves.

"It was misty earlier in the day, chilly," Hicks said. "It stopped raining around the eighth hole and the mist subsided. We took the umbrella down and didn't break it out the rest of the day. But it stayed overcast and it was cool. I think Payne had such a good feel going that he didn't want to take off [his makeshift vest]. Because it got warm enough to where he really didn't need it. But he had such a good rhythm and feel going with it on that he played the whole day with it on. It wasn't like he was overly warm in it. He certainly could have taken it off and been quite comfortable. But I think he had such a good feel for his swing with it on that he didn't want to take it off."

Stewart's saves continued to mount, enlightening Mickelson to the fact he'd be harder to get rid of than bubble gum on the bottom of his shoes. When Stewart hit his tee shot into the trap at 9, he popped the ball out with a shot that appeared to lack the necessary energy to get the ball anywhere near the cup. But the veteran who had spent so much time doing his pretournament homework on the greens knew he only had to get his ball over a ridge and the ball would filter toward the hole. Stewart's ball finished six feet away and he sank his par putt.

Mickelson and Stewart each shot 34 on the front nine.

"I thought I played a beautiful front nine, except for the [tee] shot on 9, but that was a great par," Stewart said.

Up ahead, Duval fought to follow his strategy of making pars, which was sound. Problems came when he tried to implement the strategy. He remained at even par after five holes before the par train he hoped to ride came to a screeching halt. First came failed up-and-downs on 6 and 8 that resulted in bogeys. Then his tee shot found a greenside bunker at the par-3, 179-yard ninth. If Duval had any weakness it could be found in the sand. He hit what he believed to be a good shot out of the trap only to watch the ball roll off the green. Duval then did some of his best work of the day by sinking a seven-foot snake of a putt to dodge a triple.

Having dug himself into a hole with his front-nine 37, Duval had no choice but to attack on the back. Aggressiveness is risky at any U.S. Open, a point driven home to Duval in the form of three additional bogeys en route to his second consecutive 75. Despite leading the field with greens hit in regulation at 65 percent, the No. 1 ranked player in the world finished at seven-over for the tournament.

On the periphery of contention sat Singh. The more he continued to hammer away at par, the closer he edged toward becoming a threat. He made seven straight pars to start his day then birdied 8 to move to one-over. When he added a birdie at 10 Singh officially had put himself in the hunt at even-par.

Woods made par on 10 before hitting his approach to 11 within ten feet of the hole. Facing a birdie putt that would have put him back at even-par, Woods drew back his putter to begin an adventure.

"I pushed the first one," he said of the putt that finished two feet from the hole. Then he missed the gimme coming back when the ball hit the cup and made a right turn.

"I pushed the first one and then overhit it," Woods said. "Then I pulled the second one coming back, hit a bad putt, it was inside left and I just basically yanked it. That was a putt I should have made. It's unfortunate that I didn't. But if you look at my entire week, I made a lot of putts to save myself. A lot of putts from fifteen feet and in just for pars, and without those I wouldn't have been in the position I was coming down the stretch."

Woods left 11 at two-over.

Herron and Woods received a slow-play warning on No. 8. Accordingly they once again were "put on the clock."

Woods expressed his displeasure at the USGA's action.

"I disagree with being on the clock when you're in the last few groups of a major championship," Woods said. ". . . With the greens as severe as they are, if they're flat, fine, put us on the clock. But if they're severe, it takes time to figure out the slopes. I understand the pace-of-play rule, but there are exceptions to it. And by looking at these greens, I think that's a pretty good exception."

Woods stopped to talk to a rules official when he walked off the tee on 13.

"The guys behind us should be on the clock," Woods said, citing Stewart and Mickelson's pace. "They're a hole behind. We're a half a hole behind and we're already on the clock."

"They've been on the clock," the official said, noting Stewart and Mickelson had been put on the clock shortly after Woods and Herron had.

Being on the clock didn't bother Mickelson. He had been put on the clock every day of the tournament and had his own method for managing such a warning.

"Typically what happens is there's a big delay and we wait and wait, and then those groups take off and then there's a gap and we're timed," Mickelson said. ". . . So when that happens you just take the precaution."

Mickelson's caddie began running up to Mickelson's ball so he could calculate the yardages because the clock didn't start until a player reached his ball.

"And what's funny is that when I get on the clock I have to walk slower," Mickelson said. "Because if I walk quickly up to the ball the timer starts quicker. . . . So I just walk slower now."

Stewart took a one shot lead to the final nine holes, kicking off a memorable back-nine battle for the championship beginning on the imposing tenth hole, the longest No. 2 had to offer.

"When you're standing up on the tee there you know if you don't hit the fairway you're probably going to make a 6," Hicks said. "You're not going to be able to hit it far enough to knock it on the green in three. So the tee shot is very important. If you hit the fairway then the hole becomes a playable hole.

"Of course the tee shot is the most important shot in all Opens. You've got to hit the fairway. If you hit the fairway you walk off the tee and you think, 'We should make a par here.' That's the whole thing with the U.S. Open, you've got to hit the fairway off the tee."

Stewart's drive split the fairway and his second shot successfully dodged the bunker guarding the left side of the fairway to leave him with a sand wedge to the pin.

"But then I played a bad shot on my third shot, spun it back," Stewart said.

Stewart's third-shot landed way short of the pin and the ball rolled back off the green and into heavy grass above the bunker.

"He just didn't hit his wedge hard enough," Hicks said. "You had to hit it absolutely perfect to get it to that hole. He didn't hit it hard enough and it didn't get up."

Mickelson didn't fair much better when his shot went left into a greenside bunker.

Stewart was away and hit first, assuming an awkward stance in the bunker so he could hit his ball sitting in the rough. The result wasn't pretty. Stewart's fourth shot left the rough with little conviction, making a veiled attempt to climb the ridge before rolling backward to leave him with a fifty-foot putt for par.

Seizing his opportunity, Mickelson used his fourth shot to put the ball two feet from the hole. Mickelson made par, Stewart two-putted for bogey, and the twosome was tied for the lead at one-under with eight holes to play.

"That was a letdown [at 10]," Hicks said. "Looking at that hole you're thinking par for sure, maybe bogey; Payne made 6."

Both players made par at 11 before Stewart hit his drive on 12 into the rough.

"That rough was nasty, it was wet and it just wasn't—it was nasty," Stewart said. "So I wasn't thinking about Phil or Tiger or David or anybody. I was thinking about getting the job done and doing what I had to do to give myself a chance."

Less experienced players might have felt time was running out with just seven holes remaining and tried to make something happen. Stewart showed maturity by chipping out from the rough then hitting a pitching wedge to fifteen feet and two-putting for a bogey.

Mickelson made par to remain one-under and take the lead.

Stewart had no reaction. Few words were exchanged between Stewart and Hicks other than Stewart's yardage requests. They had fallen into the harmony of silence.

"Payne was in tune to what was going on," Hicks said. "He didn't get up, he didn't get down."

Hicks broke the silence by telling Stewart, "There's a long way to go in this golf tournament."

On the short-par-4 thirteenth, Stewart used a 3-wood on the tee, then hit a 9-iron to fifteen feet from the pin and sank the putt for his third birdie of the day to pull back into a tie for the lead.

"I came right back with a birdie on 13," Stewart said. "And there it was. I just wasn't going to hand the trophy over to him."

Mickelson didn't expect Stewart to go away.

Looking at Stewart's history "Every time whether he's won the tournament or not, when he's faltered slightly, he's come immediately back with a birdie," Mickelson said. "And after he bogeyed 12, I knew that, because the pin was susceptible on 13, I knew he was going to make birdie there."

Stewart and Mickelson's duel continued to take center stage, but the cheers from just ahead served as a reminder to everyone that Woods and Singh were still kicking and doing what needed to be done to stay in contention.

"Obviously you can't help but hear the roar," Hicks said. "It's a gut-wrenching thing. I've got the best seat in the house watching all this stuff go down and you just look at the board and see who's playing good, who's got it going. What hole they're on. I don't know whether Payne was watching the board or not, but I sure was."

The scoreboard told the story. Singh had run together four consecutive pars after his birdie at 10 to stay at even par. Woods looked even more formidable going down the stretch. He'd followed his bogey at 11 with pars at 12 and 13.

"I saw the leaderboard change and I knew that Payne and Phil were going to make mistakes on the back nine because they were pulling the clock," Woods said. "We were pulling the clock as well. . . . And I figured if you rush a U.S. Open, you're going to make a mistake. And they made a couple of bogeys in that same stretch when it was on the clock. I just tried to post an even par, basically, and I thought if it didn't win, it would get into a playoff."

"Tiger Mania" intensified on 14 when Woods hit his approach and it stopped twenty feet from the cup. When Woods sank the birdie putt he dropped to one knee and pumped his fist while the crowd roared their approval. The possibility of seeing a memorable charge by Woods energized the gallery. The birdie moved Woods to within two shots of the lead.

"We heard the roar," Mickelson said. "He was still a couple of shots behind us, but we knew he was making a move."

Stewart and Mickelson each made par at 14 and didn't lose any ground after Woods made par at 15, as did Singh playing in the group ahead of him.

Singh had patiently remained behind the leaders at even par until he decided to gamble at 16. After hitting his drive into the left rough Singh tried a fairway wood, hoping to get home in regulation. He pulled the shot, sending a low ball screaming into the rough short of the green. Singh needed to hit his wedge tight if he hoped to escape with a par. Instead his ball flew well past the cup. He left 16 with a bogey and the accompanying feeling he'd gambled away any chance he had of catching the leaders.

Woods experienced a better outcome at 16.

At one-over, Woods knew he needed to make a move if he wanted to make things interesting. And in Tiger-like fashion he did just that, hitting a low iron shot that finished twelve feet right of the hole. He then sank the putt for birdie, one of only three made on 16 during the final round. Once again a roar rang down the fairway telling Stewart and Mickelson all they needed to know: Tiger Woods had turned up the heat.

Stewart and Mickelson arrived at the par-3 fifteenth each waiting for the other to blink in this test of wills.

Most of the trouble at 15 sat on the well-bunkered right side. A small green with sloping edges kept anything but a perfect shot from sticking.

Stewart's 4-iron missed the green to the left before a 7-iron chip shot left him an eight-footer for par.

Mickelson faced a forty-foot birdie putt knowing that a 2 could slam the door on Stewart. Showing the heart of a champion, he refused to lag for his par, opting to charge the cup instead. From the outset of the right-to-left breaking putt's journey it appeared Mickelson would be rewarded for his boldness. At the last second the putt rolled over the right edge of the cup and sprang left. He settled for par.

Stewart then missed the eight-footer for par.

"I thought I made that putt," Stewart said. "When I looked up I couldn't believe it didn't dive in the hole."

Stewart's mouth mimed a "whew!" and he wiped his thumb across the front of his putter. He felt robbed by the miss.

"Coming off the green Payne told me it was the best putt he'd hit all week," Hicks said. "And he missed it. That put Mickelson back up.

"I don't think he was disgusted or anything that he missed. He was just surprised. He'd been hitting it where he wanted to all week and the ball had been going in. So when he hit it where he wanted to and it didn't go in he was surprised."

Mickelson stood at one-under and Stewart at even par.

"With three holes to go I felt like I was in control of the tournament," Mickelson said. "Because I was leading and it's a very difficult course to make birdies on. All I needed was pars. I felt one-under would be good enough to win or make a playoff at worst."

Woods and Stewart trailed Mickelson by one shot.

Stationed at NBC's tower on 16, Koch observed the drama unfolding on the final holes.

"The holes [16] at the time was the longest par-4 they'd ever played in a U.S. Open," Koch said. "Since that time they've played a couple longer than that. But I remember the last day with it kind of wet and drizzly and cool. Guys couldn't hit the green. We had the computer in our tower and I want to say less than 6 percent of the guys were hitting the green in regulation, which is unheard of on a par-4."

With bunkers lining the left side, a faded tee shot worked best at 16. The green sat on a rise with two bunkers front and right. To reach the green in two it required a shot that carried the green.

After hitting an average drive, Stewart selected a 2-iron for his approach shot and his ball nipped a tree along the left side.

"Payne ended up short, like thirty or forty yards from the green in two," Koch said. "He tried to hit some kind of long iron and it didn't go the way he expected it to. Then he hit a fairly ordinary pitch shot, it must have gone twenty feet past the hole."

Mickelson's positive karma received a boost from Stewart's shot.

"When he bladed his chip shot past, I didn't really consider him the number-one threat," Mickelson said. "I thought Tiger up in the group in front of me was the number-one threat."

Hicks shrugged his shoulders when asked what kind of shot Stewart had tried to hit on his third shot.

"The pitch, I don't know what he was trying to do there," Hicks said. "Fly it back there, I don't know. It was an awful shot."

Turns out Stewart's brain had taken a holiday.

"For some reason I felt like I needed to chip that ball in and I hit a very poor chip, and I shouldn't have thought that way," Stewart said. "I should have just—it felt like I needed to do it. And as it went twenty-five feet past the hole, I said, 'You didn't need to do that.'"

The hole was cut over the front right portion of the green.

"Mickelson hit a fairly long iron in and it looked to be a real good shot and it just missed the green by a small margin," Koch said. "Then he hit a poor pitch shot, I thought, for the conditions. It was a pretty straightforward little shot. He left it six or seven feet short."

To this day Mickelson laments his pitch shot at 16.

"I had a very easy chip I thought to get up and down on 16, and it's one of the two shots in my career I'd like to redo," Mickelson said. "And I hit a poor chip to ten feet." (Note: Mickelson said the other shot he would like to have back if given the chance would be his first putt at 16 on the final day of the 2001 PGA Championship. He ran his birdie putt eight feet past the hole and made a bogey before losing to David Toms by one shot.)

Stewart stared at a treacherous twenty-five-foot downhill putt. If he erred even slightly, the end result could have been devastating. He examined his putt and decided on the line he wanted to take.

"I don't know what to say," Stewart said. "I just went through my routine that I'd been doing all day long with my putting and I made my stroke, kept my head down, and when I looked up it was dropping into the hole."

Stewart had a miraculous par.

"It was a double breaker, too," Koch said. "It went left and then back to the right. I mean, it was just boom! Right into the hole."

Mickelson judged the pace of Stewart's putt and thought Stewart had put too much steam on it.

"When his putt reached the hole, it was going so fast that I think it would have gone off the green to at least the edge, fifteen or twenty feet by, because it was downhill and the ball wouldn't have stopped at the clip it was going," Mickelson said. "But it ended up hitting the back of the hole, popping up, and going in. And that's when I realized, 'If I don't make this putt, we're tied.' I thought I was going to have a two-shot lead on him with two to go."

Mickelson pulled his putt to record his only bogey of the round to drop back into a tie with Stewart.

"The tendency for me this whole week was to pull my putts a little," Mickelson said. "And that's what happened on that one. I read it as a double breaker, and I just pulled it a little too far right to get all the break back to the left."

Mickelson's shoulders slumped.

"When Mickelson missed you could just see how deflated he was when he walked off the green," Koch said.

Mickelson said he was disappointed that his first bogey had come at such an inopportune time.

"But I felt like I still had a very good chance," Mickelson said.

Doug Ferguson had thought the outcome of the tournament had been decided.

"When Phil and Payne were coming up to 16, you've got Phil eight-to-ten feet away and Payne's way back there," Ferguson said. "So I'm typing my Phil Mickelson wins U.S. Open story. That turned around and it was staggering."

Ahead at 17 Woods needed to make something happen and chose to employ a "soft 7" in an attempt to hit the ball 170 yards and carry the right bunker. He didn't make it. His ball landed in the sand, putting him in a situation where he knew he needed to get up and down to remain in contention. He blasted to within five feet; Woods would later say the par putt he faced was eight feet. If he sank the putt he would remain at even-par.

"Unfortunately I just hit it too hard," Woods said. "The line I chose, I chose inside left, and if you look at it, it hit the inside left of the hole and lipped out. But at that pace you had to go left center, and unfortunately I hit it too hard."

The scoreboard at 17 told Stewart and Mickelson of Woods's fate.

"I think by the time we finished 16, we kind of knew it was a two-horse race unless Phil or Payne totally collapsed by making a double or whatever," Hicks said.

The situation called for daring. Could either golfer muster the courage to attempt a shot that would give them an opportunity to take the lead with a birdie? The situation also called for caution. The U.S. Open's arms were wide open to welcome either player smart enough not to blow their portion of the lead.

Stewart arrived at 17 brimming with confidence. All week he'd enjoyed a feeling similar to what he'd experienced at the seventeenth hole at Hazeltine in 1991. "Every time I hit a shot, it was right at the pin [at Hazeltine]," Stewart said.

At No. 2 Stewart had enjoyed success during the first three rounds, making par each day after hitting quality tee shots directly at the pin.

Hicks believed certain players just enjoyed a comfort level at certain holes.

"Some holes don't fit some guys' eyes and some holes do," Hicks said. "From that standpoint, there were certain holes that fit his eyes. Seventeen was one of those holes."

In addition, the hole perfectly suited Stewart's ability.

"Sunday's shot at 17 favored a right-to-left player like Payne because the pin was back left," Hicks said.

Standing over the ball, Stewart tapped the ground several times with his 6-iron, allowing a moment for those watching to marvel at his ability to execute a golf swing during such a pressure-filled situation. Stewart eased the club back and followed through with the rhythm of a metronome.

"He hit a nice draw in there," Hicks said. "It was a beautiful shot."

Stewart watched his ball land, prompting him to briefly stop chewing his gum. His opened mouth remained frozen in awe at his shot when it eased to within four feet from the flagstick.

"Well, really it was that shot where he knocked it close where the realization that he could beat me entered my mind, because until then I felt like I was in control, making pars, and that I was playing well," Mickelson said. "And as soon as he knocked that ball to within four feet, I realized that par might not be good enough."

Mickelson didn't waver.

"Phil steps up to the tee and hits a spectacular shot as well, particularly considering the situation," said Koch, who turned his attention to 17 since Stewart and Mickelson were the final group. "At that point it still looked very much up in the air. You had no idea about what was going to happen."

Mickelson's 7-iron shot finished eight feet from the hole, prompting his characteristic excuse-me smile that displayed his dimples and made him look embarrassed by his success.

"He putted first and I expected him to make it," said Stewart, who squatted like a catcher behind home plate, nervously picking at his fingers while he waited for Mickelson to putt.

Mickelson read the putt and felt like it had a tendency to go left early and right at the end.

"I tried to play it straight and I just pulled it just a little bit and it didn't take the break going left, and then it just missed too far to the right," Mickelson said. "I didn't get it out far enough on the left side of the hole. I needed to have it about left center, halfway there."

Hicks didn't remember any reaction from Mickelson.

"You know I wasn't really paying attention to him," Hicks said. "We were just trying to take care of what we were doing. I really didn't pay any attention to what Phil was doing. Obviously, you're watching when he's putting, trying to make that putt for par on 16, and you're watching that putt. But you've got to take your hat off to Phil, to hit the shot he hit at 17 after Payne had stuck it in there. We hit a 6-iron to within about four feet and then Phil hits a 7-iron to within six feet. Phil stepped up to the plate when he had to there and hit a very good shot to 17. But there again, he just didn't make the putt."

Mickelson settled for par.

Stewart's stone face remained expressionless. He circled the pristine seventeenth green that had been trampled for four days but didn't show so much as a cleat mark. Four feet separated him from taking a one-shot lead heading into the final hole into the U.S. Open. Stewart eyed the putt he determined he needed to play on the left edge of the hole, then pulled the trigger.

The putt tiptoed toward the hole and dropped into the center of the hole.

"And I did it again, and I made another one," Stewart said of his fourth birdie of the day. Would Hicks's declaration to his wife prove to be prophetic?

Stewart handed his putter to Hicks, hitched his pants, and walked toward the eighteenth tee, chomping his gum in staccato fashion. The birdie gave him the lead with one hole to go.

Hoping to have a chance for a playoff, Woods faced a twenty-five-foot birdie putt on 18.

The putt was "straight up the hill left-to-right, broke about two feet, and wasn't that hard of a putt," Woods said. "It was just a putt that I figured I could make."

He didn't, dropping to a knee and staring at the ground as if he'd been lanced in the stomach by the putter that had betrayed him. Still in agony over his miss, Woods stood and pinched the bridge of his nose with his thumb and forefinger like the miss had brought on a sinus headache.

"Tiger struggled on the greens pretty much the whole week," Koch said. "He missed a number of short putts. That was still at a time when his philosophy on short putts was to just jam everything into the hole. I think if you watch him putt, especially now in major championships, his philosophy has changed a little bit. He tries to die the ball a little bit into the hole instead of being so aggressive all the time on the short putts. I do remember him missing a lot of short putts over the course of the four days."

Watching on TV, Tracey Stewart saw her husband's birdie putt at 17 drop, then headed for the course to watch the finish.

Of the approximately thirty thousand in attendance, all were pressed together in a semicircle around the eighteenth green and standing ten deep along the fairways where possible. Wearing raincoats and holding umbrellas, those who remained had fought the elements to watch until the end. An electric feeling had buzzed around the grounds all day in anticipation of something special happening. Such an occurrence seemed preordained given all the story lines converging at the eighteenth hole of Pinehurst No. 2. Could the wily veteran hold off the youngster from attaining his first major and redeem himself a year after Olympic? Or would the youngster simply rise to the occasion and create a memory golf fans would remember for generations to come? One hundred and fifty-six golfers had begun the week filled with hopes of becoming U.S. Open champion before experiencing Darwinesque golf where only the strong survived. Now, after seventy-one holes, just one hole remained to settle the championship between the last men standing, Stewart and Mickelson.

Stewart moved to the eighteenth tee holding a one-shot lead. Both players had finished Saturday's round with birdies. Mickelson had to have a birdie or hope Stewart couldn't make par. Would Stewart take a par at this point? You bet.

No. 18 had a long, deep bunker down the right side. If a player's tee shot went into this bunker he rarely left the hole with anything less than bogey. What appeared to be a greenside bunker at the front right portion of the green could be deceiving since it was further from the green than it looked. The optical illusion could lure players into not hitting enough club on their approach shots. A swale in the middle of the green served to protect back pin locations like the back-right location on Sunday.

The 446-yard par-4 ranked as the sixth toughest for the tournament with a 4.324 scoring average. Only twenty-eight birdies had been made over the course of the week as compared to ninety-four bogeys.

Knowing when to play it safe is critical to the success of any PGA Tour professional. Given the control and distance he had with his 3-wood some might have deemed the prudent move to be leaving the driver in the bag. Such a consideration never entered Stewart and Hicks's minds.

"Eighteen, that's a driver hole all the way," Hicks said. "The hole is straight uphill. If he hits 3-wood there you've got a long way to get home. You don't want a real long iron going into that green."

Both men knew that missing the green and finishing in one of the forbidden areas could have meant a big number. And Stewart had managed to get into the position he now found himself in by avoiding big numbers. He had not made a score higher than bogey in his previous seventy-one holes.

Stewart stood on the eighteenth tee viewing the surreal scene in cool weather under gray-tinted skies. Dr. Trey Holland told *Golf World* magazine: "I remember thinking a time or two that it felt like *Golf in the Kingdom*." Holland referenced the Michael Murphy novel that had become a golf classic.

Was Stewart really holding the lead in the U.S. Open with one hole remaining or was he dreaming? Stewart pulled out his driver and took a smooth swing that sent his drive over the fairway trap on the right. He couldn't see where his ball had settled, but had a pretty good idea when he saw a marshal walk to his ball and stick a yellow flag in the rough. He turned to Hicks.

"That's in the rough," Stewart said.

"Yeah, I think it is," Hicks said.

How many demons could one man's mind be expected to battle? Stewart's demons were far more sinister than any sense of déjà vu. Could he possibly let golf's most prestigious prize slip from his grasp two years in a row? A huge test of character remained for the knickered one.

Stewart had blown a four-shot lead on the final day of the 1998 U.S. Open to lose by one shot to Lee Janzen. His last opportunity to force an 18-hole playoff had gone out the window when he missed a birdie putt on the final hole. Now clinging to a one-shot lead over Mickelson, whose drive had split the fairway, Stewart needed to escape trouble on the seventy-second hole of the 1999 Open to avoid a similar fate. Nobody could have faulted the poor guy for coming unglued. Weekend golfers get rubber knees standing over a three-footer to win a two-dollar Nassau—and this was the U.S. Open. And he was forty-two, long past the age when the nerves of most Tour players had begun to alter their ability to execute.

"Payne drove the ball right where we had decided to aim, which was right on the cut, right on the edge of the bunker on the right because the rough on the right was real sparse compared to the rough on the left," Cook said. "So he was going to play right down that right edge. And he hit it probably in the only spot over there where the grass was real heavy on that side. He thought he had driven it into the fairway."

Stewart had followed the prescribed route, he just "didn't catch the ball solid enough" according to Hicks.

"That probably cost him three or four yards," Hicks said. "He hit a driver. If he'd have hit it really solid on that line his ball would have been in the fairway. He just missed it enough to where it didn't carry a little part of the rough. It was the worst lie he had all week. I mean there was no way he could get the ball to the green."

Koch watched the events on 18 unfold and saw a different Payne Stewart than the one he'd watched the previous year at Olympic.

"When he hit his drive on the final hole it was over the hill, you couldn't really see whether it was in the fairway or not," Koch said. "You got up there and the ball missed the fairway by about two feet. But there was absolutely no reaction from him whatsoever. There was no shrugging of the shoulders, no head dropping, no 'Geez, how did I miss the fairway?' None of that. You could tell all he did in his mind was plan out. 'Okay, I'm going to have to pitch the ball into the fairway. How far am I going to have to go to be able to play a good third shot into the green?' And to me, that whole scenario just showed the difference in Payne Stewart from the year before."

When Stewart reached his ball he found the kind of lie he expected.

"So I dealt with it," Stewart said. "The only option I had was 'give yourself a chance to get it up and down with your wedge game.' And my wedge game was pretty decent all week."

Stewart and Hicks examined his lie in the wet Bermuda rough that sat two hundred eleven yards from the pin.

"What do we have short of those traps over there?" Stewart asked.

Hicks gave Stewart the yardage.

"There was a bunker short of the green on the right," Hicks said.

"That was the last place he wanted to be. He didn't want to have a long bunker shot. He would have been dead. There's no way he could have made par from there. He was playing percentage golf, which is what you have to do in a U.S. Open. You've got to play percentages. I mean, what were the percentages of getting to the green from that lie? Maybe Phil would have tried to hit a 7-iron onto the green from there, who knows. But you have to play percentage golf. You hit it into the rough. You get it back into play. You don't make the mistake of hitting it into trouble twice."

Mickelson watched from the fairway.

"I knew from his lie that he was going to have to lay up," Mickelson said. "It didn't mean that he was going to make 5, he was going to have a good chance at 4, it just meant there was no way he was going to make birdie."

Hicks handed Stewart a 9-iron and Stewart hacked it back to the fairway just short of the trap, approximately seventy yards away.

"I had no chance to even think about the green, so I took my medicine, and put the ball out there where I at least could give myself a chance to get the ball up and down," Stewart said, noting he'd opted for a similar tack throughout the week. "When I was in a bad position I didn't compound the situation by making two mistakes in a row."

Mickelson readied for his second shot. His beeper hadn't sounded and now the likelihood of staying at Pinehurst another day looked inevitable and inviting.

"I knew that if I could make a birdie that that would at least be enough to tie," Mickelson said. "And I wanted to at least give myself a chance at birdie and if not, I felt like 4 still had a good chance at a playoff."

Mickelson's expression turned pained after hitting his second shot. He mouthed "Oh no" immediately after the ball left his club.

But the shot wasn't hit as poorly as he feared. His ball landed safely on the green, leaving him with a twenty-two-foot birdie putt.

"I was going right of the pin and had I hit it the right distance, had I hit it back to the pin, it would have landed right of the green and kicked down the slope," Mickelson said.

Pondering how best to get up and down, Stewart's gum chewing turned his jaws into a clenched fist. First and foremost, he needed to land his next shot on the green.

"I figured out, 'Okay, you want to be underneath the hole putting back up at it,' " Stewart said.

Stewart and Hicks surveyed the situation.

"We knew Phil had hit a decent shot," Hicks said. "I knew it wasn't stiff by any means and he had a tough putt. And I walked up close to the green and got the yardage and came back. It wasn't a great yardage. It wasn't a full sixty-degree wedge, it was in between. It was a tough shot. Plus, you did not want to hit the ball over the green."

Tracey arrived at the eighteenth green before her husband's third shot.

"There were so many people there I couldn't see anything," Tracey said. "Then I saw Phil walking toward the green; I couldn't see Payne."

Tracey did see a USGA official standing next to her.

" "Where's Payne?" Tracey asked.

"He's out on the fairway," the official said.

Tracey felt a pang of anxiety and thought, "Here we go again."

"I didn't want a playoff," she said.

Since 1993 when Lee Janzen won his first U.S. Open, no third-round leader had managed to win an Open without the benefit of a playoff.

Tracey wasn't the only one watching and feeling a wave of anxiety. In the media tent, reporters scrambled to extend hotel stays and change flight reservations. Pinehurst was not an easy destination to reach, making any such alterations a difficult proposition.

While the media would suffer a great imposition if a playoff occurred, the USGA would not.

"An eighteen-hole playoff as long as it's in effect will always be controversial because it's very tough on the operations of the tournament," Fred Ridley said. "There's really no impact on what [the USGA does] because when we do the hole locations we do it for five days. So we already have them for Monday. There's really nothing we have to prepare for once the tie happens."

Stewart selected the 60-degree wedge and took an easy pass. The ball set out on a straight line toward the pin before stopping short and leaving him a fifteen-foot uphill putt to save par.

"I would have liked it to have been a little closer," Stewart said.

Stewart would have liked a closer shot, but Hicks thought the shot had been a work of genius.

"There again, there's course management," Hicks said. "He gave himself a putt at it. He gave himself a chance. That's what you do in those tournaments. You give yourself a chance. Instead of trying to hit the ball to within a foot, he gave himself a chance."

And Stewart had eliminated the all-too-real possibility of hitting a shot that could creep over the ridge at the back of the green and roll into trouble.

Stewart walked to the green accompanied by the cheers of an appreciative gallery and looking nothing like the Tour's pretty boy. The cut-off sleeves of his vest showed frayed edges and his white stockings were spotted with mud and grass like a prized Thoroughbred's legs on a rainy day at Churchill Downs.

One man's faith in himself could be felt by the gallery in Payne Stewart's comeback story of a man who had found tranquility in his life and had reached back to find the courage to climb a mountain he'd failed to climb only twelve months earlier. He hadn't let his disappointment defeat him. Could Payne Stewart finish off his quest to climb back to the top of the golf world if only for a day?

"What an atmosphere," Hicks said. "I remember the stands were packed, there were people everywhere. But you're so caught up in what you're doing that you don't really notice anything. You couldn't smell the roses because you didn't have them. I mean, Payne could have lost that tournament right on that green. Mickelson makes and we miss, it's over. There were no roses to smell."

Stewart reminded himself about Tracey's advice from the previous night: *Keep your head still.* Thinking about Mickelson's upcoming birdie putt would not have been a positive thought. If the left-hander sank, Stewart would have to make par to tie. If they both missed, an eighteen-hole playoff awaited the following day.

"At that point you're hoping Phil doesn't make his putt, at least I was," Hicks said. "And it's like, 'It's all come down to this. Here we are after four days and it's down to this.'"

Mickelson's arms hung low, greeting the grip of his short-shafted putter so he could make his familiar easy stroke. The ball broke right to left, rolling toward the cup. A slam dunk would make Stewart's fifteen-footer look like fifty. Lefty could silence all of his critics if the ball just dropped. How many times had he been asked about his failing to win any majors? And to win his first major with a birdie putt, could there be a better gift for Amy and their baby?

Mickelson missed.

"When Phil missed, I'm thinking here it is, he's got a chance to win," Hicks said. "But I didn't think he would make it. I'll be honest with you. I did not think he would make it. I thought we would be back the next day. I mean how many fifteen-footers are you going to make to win the U.S. Open? Uphill, dewy, it's just impossible. I mean really, to think about it, there aren't many guys who are going to make that putt, including Tiger."

Stewart had studied Mickelson's putt and began to calculate the path of his putt.

". . . After watching Phil's putt break hard up there right to left, I practiced there before during the practice rounds, I knew my putt was going to go up and was going to go right," Stewart said. "Even though the mound wanted to influence that, I just knew in my mind that it was going to go to the right a little bit and so I stood there and read it. And I said this is just an inside left putt, just believe that."

Woods watched and understood some of the thoughts that rattled around in the minds of players in Stewart's situation.

"You've got to put everything aside and focus on your task and somehow control your emotions inside, and your adrenaline level and whatever your conscious mind may be thinking," Woods said. "Whatever it is, you've got to fight that inside. I think that's one of the challenges that we as players face in major championships, trying to handle the mental side of the game."

Pinehurst found a silence normally reserved for funerals of beloved dignitaries when Stewart moved toward his ball and went through the same routine he'd used throughout Sunday's round. He took his position to the side of the ball, made two practice strokes with his eyes closed to feel the distance, then he aimed his putter on the line he saw. A sea of cameras faced him, waiting to click the instant he putted.

"You've always wanted to putt to win the U.S. Open," Stewart told himself. "Well, you've got it right here."

Now the fate of the tournament shifted to Stewart and his flat stick: Sink the fifteen-footer and all the bad memories from the year before would be erased.

Mickelson watched Stewart and thought, "If it goes in, I'm going home tonight and I'm going to see Amy. And if it doesn't go in, then I've got to stick around for another day and just hope that the baby doesn't come."

The left-hander had a feeling about what Stewart would do.

"I thought there was a good chance he would make it," Mickelson said. "His putt was straight uphill and he could be aggressive with it."

At no time in the storied history of the U.S. Open had a player sunk a putt of any significant length on the final hole to win the celebrated tournament. The tension could be felt in the pro-Stewart gallery that wanted to see him accomplish what he could not accomplish the previous year. Somehow he managed to look calm, but the nerves inside his gut churned when he drew back the putter.

"I said, 'Hold your head still' and I made the stroke," Stewart said.

The ball rolled up the hill and broke slightly to the right. The gallery followed the ball's path as it made its ascent up the slope. They'd watched Stewart grind for four days; if justice could be served on a golf course Stewart deserved to win this title.

Janzen, who finished at eighteen-over for forty-sixth place, watched Stewart putt as he had the year before at Olympic.

"As similar as the situations looked, it was a different kind of pressure," Janzen said. "At Olympic, if he missed it, it was like he'd blown a lead to lose the U.S. Open. And the putt he had at Olympic had about a six- or seven-foot break. I think the putt at Pinehurst was a lot easier. I was ready for him to make the one at Olympic, but I knew his chances weren't real good. I was convinced he'd make that one at Pinehurst."

Cook remembered the pretournament scouting of the course Stewart and he had done.

"In the two days that we practiced, we were trying to look for where the pins would be," Cook said. "And that putt on 18 went the opposite way from the way it looked like it would go. We must have hit a hundred putts from the same spot to where that pin was. And it looks like it's got to go left. It looks like it's going to break six inches to the left and it breaks four inches to the right. It was an unusual deal, but his preparation that week paid off. We had guessed at the right place. It was the obvious place. The pin was right back of the neck [of the green]. That was an A pin for sure, so we practiced that. It was amazing, every day we practiced that putt and Payne said, 'I can't believe that putt breaks right.' And for him to have that putt and to trust it and remember it, that was just mind-boggling to me. I'm watching the TV and I'm saying, 'Oh man, trust it Payne, trust it.'"

Adhering to his wife's advice, Stewart did not move his head to track his putt until the ball had traveled some distance.

"When I looked up, it was about two feet from the hole and it was breaking right in the center and I couldn't believe it," Stewart said.

"The ball fell into the middle of the hole igniting a roar that echoed like the Hallelujah Chorus throughout the hallowed church of golf, Pinehurst No. 2.

"I couldn't believe my eyes," Stewart said.

Mickelson's face assumed a bemused expression.

Stewart punched his fist into the air, striking a cranelike pose while he screamed in joy, his noise sending out a plume of frosty breath into the chilly air. Stewart then turned to receive Hicks, who he picked up in a bear hug—he'd just won the U.S. Open.

Stewart and Hicks whiffed in their attempt to connect on a high five.

"You beauty! You beauty!" Stewart said.

"Yeah, you are something," Hicks said. "You're unbelievable."

People often pick up the oddest things at such moments, which held true with Hicks while in Stewart's grasp.

"The biggest thing that I felt at that moment was I really didn't know how strong he was until he lifted me off the ground," Hicks said. "I couldn't believe how solid he was."

Hicks still has a hard time describing the emotions and the feelings he experienced that day.

"Payne kept calling me beauty, that was one of our nicknames for each other," Hicks said. "I've been blessed over the years just being able to be there and watching it that close. God sure has blessed me with a lot of good memories. And that was one of the greatest moments in golf history. I don't think anybody would argue the point that that was one of the most exciting U.S. Opens ever televised. It was the most special thing that's happened to me other than the birth of my children and the day I got married. It was incredible. It's something that will always be with me. I don't have to relive it. I see it all the time."

Mickelson moved toward Stewart to offer congratulations; Stewart grabbed the face of the man he'd just defeated. If anybody could have empathy for the second-place finisher at a U.S. Open, it would be Stewart.

"Good luck with the baby," Stewart said. "There's nothing like being a father."

Mickelson took the gesture as sincere.

"The most memorable thing [from the tournament] was on the eighteenth green when he reiterated the same things he'd told me before the round," Mickelson said. "He'd just made a putt to win the U.S. Open and instead of relishing in his victory he comes over to me and tells me being a father is the greatest thing I could imagine and how happy he was for Amy and me. And I just thought that was really cool."

Stewart broke from Mickelson and moved to the hole where he retrieved his ball and offered an unrestrained "yelp!" to the crowd before kissing the ball.

Tracey fought the crowd to get close to her husband.

"People were screaming and shouting so loud that I was right next to him but he didn't see me," Tracey said. "I was calling but he couldn't hear me. Then he finally turned around and he hugged me."

"I did it, I kept my head down," Payne whispered into her ear. "All day, all day, I did it. I kept my head down."

"I'm so proud of you, I know you did," Tracey replied through her tears.

The final tally told the tale of the ledger. Stewart had hit just seven greens in regulation to Mickelson's eleven, and he'd ranked fiftieth out of sixty-eight in driving distance (255.3 yards) but Sunday he'd needed just twenty-four putts to Mickelson's twenty-nine.

"You guys watched it," Stewart said. "I putted my little derrière off today."

Hicks noted that "keep your head still" is a cliché, but it remains unchallenged for its truth when it comes to putting.

"If you move you're apt to mishit it, push it, pull it, whatever your tendency," Hicks said. "He really stayed in that last putt nicely."

Paul Jett watched the putt and remembered the late mowing schedule that day.

"We mowed six hours later than normal," Jett said with a smile. "You just wonder if that allowed Stewart's putt to roll just one more revolution."

Tom Meeks went to the scoring area after Stewart's heroics.

"Just as I got there, Payne's coming out and his wife is waiting for him," Meeks said. "Before he goes over to her, he sees me and he grabs me and takes me in through some swinging doors that go into a little hallway toward the men's locker room. He goes inside these swinging doors and he actually embraces me and says, 'You set up one hell of a golf course.' I'll never forget that. It's the highest compliment you can get."

Having worked with Stewart to keep him mentally tough, Coop drew great satisfaction watching Stewart handle adversity to conquer 18.

"It just gives you chills," Coop said. "Considering all he'd gone through the year before. It was just fantastic to see. He didn't even flinch and he made every intelligent decision. Not to try and hit anything more out of the rough than he hit, he just took his medicine. The easiest thing to do there is try and be a hero and knock it on the green somehow. He was very deliberate. He had thought he had hit it in the fairway. You can't see over the bunker. I know that when he got there and saw that he wasn't in the fairway, that had to really shake him. And that's where I think you can get emotional decisions being made, but he didn't. He had a very intellectual decision just to wedge it up there. I think that's where Mike [Hicks] being with him helped a lot. Mike just encouraged him to get into a position where he could get his wedge shot up there. He'd been hitting good wedge shots all day. He putted well all day. He let his putter work for him. Going back to when we talked about the Cs on your scorecard for challenges, that was the biggest C. That was huge."

Coop reached Stewart shortly after he sank the putt.

"I told him, 'You can't doubt yourself now, you've done too much now. You can't deny this one. You can't say you didn't earn this one,'" Coop said. "That was a great, great win. And he handled it so well with Mickelson, too, I thought. He was empathetic to him and understanding about being a father. A big part of Payne's life was being a father. That was important to him."

Stewart spoke of his faith first after winning.

"All I wanted to do was give myself a chance," he said. "And I've got to give thanks to the Lord for giving me the ability to believe in myself. Without that peace that I have in my heart, I wouldn't be sitting here in front of you now."

Stewart had played with peace in his heart and resolution in his mind.

"Last year after the Open I kept hearing from people, 'What a great effort you gave it,'" Stewart said. "Well, I didn't want to hear that today. That motivated me like you can't believe."

Stewart had grown considerably as a man since his Open victory in 1991 and planned to handle the spoils of winning differently than he had the first go around. He wasn't going to drop everything to chase the money like he had after the '91 U.S. Open.

"I think I'm a lot more prepared to deal with everything that goes along with holding on to this trophy for a year," Stewart said. "I don't plan on changing my schedules. I plan on doing the same things that I've been doing that got me in position to win today, which is working out and spending a lot of time at home.

"I have so much fun being at home, being a father, getting up in the morning, making breakfast, taking my kids to school, going to high school athletics, that's what my life is right now," Stewart said. "And I'm not going to do what I did in '91, along that line."

Nick Price, who finished in a tie for twenty-third place, admired Stewart's victory.

"As a player you've got to deal with [what happened in '98 at Olympic]," Price said. "But here he was. He'd been on the Tour for so many years. You have to ask yourself how many more opportunities are going to come your way. Having gone through a pretty down time Payne showed a lot of courage, a lot of balls, really."

David Whitley, who had been one of Stewart's harshest critics in print following the loss at Olympic, felt happy with the outcome of the tournament.

"You don't ever feel good when you have to criticize someone," Whitley said. "I really enjoyed being able to write that Payne had come through at crunch time. Nobody could criticize him anymore."

A longtime rule of sports journalism is "No cheering in the press box." An exception to the rule came in the aftermath of Stewart's final putt.

"Yes, some of the cheering was because we didn't have to come back on Monday," Ferguson said. "But I also think there was some cheering when that putt went in because we'd just seen one of the greatest finishes ever seen in a U.S. Open and everybody was glad about that."

Shortly after being awarded the championship trophy, NBC's Dan Hicks interviewed him in front of the crowd for a national television audience at which time he looked over at the gracious Mickelson and spoke.

"You'll win yours," Stewart said. "I know Amy's at home and I'd like to express to Phil and Amy that being parents is a special thing and I'm glad he made the commitment, whether he got the beeper today or not, he was going to be there with his wife and that's very special. I was with my wife for both of my children. There's nothing like being parents. Phil's going to have his opportunity again. As for me, I might be on the short list."

Stewart gushed about fatherhood and told the media about seeing the NBC segment on his relationship with his father earlier in the day.

"I probably got a lot of strength from that," Stewart said.

He'd just won his second U.S. Open, but the victory still didn't hold a candle to his first win on Tour, the 1982 Quad City Classic, the tournament he held dearest.

"That will never change," Stewart said. "Because my dad was there to see it."

Once the hoopla died down, Tracey flew home to Orlando while Payne loaded into a van with Hicks and they headed toward Hick's home in Mebane. Stewart had committed to play in an exhibition at Hicks's home course and despite winning the Open and all the opportunities and demands created, Stewart honored his commitment.

Mickelson left for home immediately after the tournament and Amy told him of her weekend.

"It was a bit of a gamble on her part," Mickelson said. "Because had she delivered Amanda without me being there, without calling me and giving me a chance to be there, I think it would have been something that would have been very hard for me to forgive her for, to miss out on that."

Fortunately, Amy had not delivered and the Mickelson's went to bed Sunday night believing the birth of their daughter was still a week away.

"We woke up Monday morning at nine o'clock and her water had broke," Mickelson said. "So we went to the doctor, the hospital, and so forth. The reason why I think that's important is because had there been a playoff, had Payne not made that putt, I wouldn't have been able to play."

Stewart and Hicks left Pinehurst at 10 o'clock that night and began the drive. Ahead in Mebane a celebration awaited them.

"You have to go through Siler City to get to my house," Hicks said. "Remember Siler City in *The Andy Griffith Show*? We actually stopped in Siler City and got some beverages for the ride home."

Hicks's next-door neighbor was a state trooper. He had walked in Stewart's group on Sunday and escorted them home Sunday night, taking the wheel for the celebrating pair.

"We stopped in this little convenience store and Payne's wearing this wild T-shirt and a pair of jeans," Hicks said. "He puts a twelve-pack of Bud Light on the counter and the girl had no idea who he was. He'd just won the U.S. Open and she didn't have a clue."

The mood inside the van remained festive. Stewart returned Cook's call during the ride.

"Well, I guess you're drinking champagne," Cook said.

"No, actually I'm in the back of Hicksy's van drinking a twelve-pack of Bud Light," Stewart said.

"I can't believe you remembered that putt broke right," Cook said.

"I hit that putt so many times, how could I forget," Stewart said.

Most of Hicks's neighbors greeted them when their van arrived.

"We had the trophy, we had beverages out of the trophy, I think we went to bed around four-thirty," Hicks said. "I got Payne up at about nine the next morning. He showered, ironed his outfit, and we left by nine-thirty. When we got to the club it was just like any other day. Payne takes the trophy and sets it up in the pro shop there at the club."

Hicks laughed recalling how Stewart putted on the first two holes with his eyes closed and sank both putts.

"He literally had his eyes closed the first two holes of this exhibition," Hicks said. "Kind of like Michael Jordan shooting free throws with his eyes closed. And let me tell you he was really chirping. He made that one and said, 'That's four one-putts in a row.' Then he made the second and he said, 'That's five one-putts in a row' going back to 16 the day before.

"But he was feeling good about himself and he should have been. He had just accomplished a goal that at his age was hard to accomplish. And he'd done it in such dramatic fashion. It was just such a special way to do it, so he was feeling good about himself. It was a great day."

CHAPTER FOURTEEN

TOO YOUNG TO GO

HAVING DISTINGUISHED HIMSELF with the lasting memory of his career, Payne Stewart appeared to be touched by the angels.

In addition to the winner's purse he'd won of $625,000, Stewart secured a spot on the 1999 U.S. Ryder Cup team. In the press conference after the Open, Stewart told the media how much that meant to him.

"Three-hundred points will put me up to 917—thank you very much—and I will be on the team," Stewart said with exuberance in his voice. "I'm on the Ryder Cup team now. I have contended all year long that the Ryder Cup is what is motivating me."

Stewart's life seemed to glow. He had happiness in every area, his marriage, his family, and his profession. Using his newfound putting system, he'd finished the season second on the Tour at 1.726 putts per hole, behind Brad Faxon's average of 1.723, and he did his part for the United States team that won the Ryder Cup. His life seemed blessed and he had much to live for in that life.

Then Payne Stewart was gone in an instant.

Stewart—along with golf-course architect Bruce Borland and Stewart's agents, Robert Fraley and Van Ardan—boarded a twin-engine Learjet in Orlando at 9 A.M. on a Monday morning headed for Dallas. Stewart was scheduled to scout a site in suburban Dallas that might have been used for his fledgling golf-course-design business, then head for Houston for the Tour Championship. He never reached his destination.

Stewart's private jet left Orlando at 9:19. Nine minutes later, the tower radioed that the plane had been cleared to go to 39,000 feet. Shortly thereafter, air-traffic controllers noticed the plane had climbed well above its assigned altitude, thus beginning a bizarre and tragic day. Controllers tried to get an explanation for the plane's mysterious climb, but their calls went unanswered. At that point, the Federal Aviation Administration enlisted the help of the air force. Several F-16s were dispatched to check on the errant jet, which also missed the left turn it was scheduled to make toward Texas and continued heading north.

One of the F-16 pilots noticed the cockpit windows were obscured by what appeared to be a light coat of frost. Tracey Stewart heard the news about what had happened and tried to call her husband on his cell phone but received no answer.

At 1:24 P.M., the plane fell to earth at 600 mph and disappeared from the radar, crashing in a grassy field in northeast South Dakota. All aboard were dead.

Planes that fly above 12,000 feet are pressurized, because the air at altitudes above that is too thin to breathe. If a plane loses pressure, those aboard could slowly lose consciousness or, if an aircraft broke a door or window seal, perish in seconds from lack of oxygen.

Once reaching a cruising altitude, pilots often switch on the autopilot. If they pass out, the plane could continue until it ran out of fuel. The plane in which Stewart traveled apparently had been set on autopilot, which enabled a cruise covering 1,400 miles across half a dozen states. Everyone aboard was believed to have been dead long before the plane ran out of fuel and augered into the ground. A lack of oxygen from a loss of cabin pressure apparently was the cause of the deaths.

Among the items surviving the crash were two devotional books Payne Stewart had been reading and the W.W.J.D. bracelet, which did not have a scratch.

The golf world mourned the loss of a man who had evolved into one of the most popular players on Tour.

Tracey Stewart spoke of her late husband at his funeral.

"You are the light of my life and my tower of strength and you will be in my heart forever," she said. "After eighteen years of marriage, you are still the most beautiful man I've ever seen. Not because of the way you looked on the outside anymore. But because of what was on the inside."

Dr. Richard Coop had been playing telephone tag with Stewart for days until Stewart called him the night before the accident and they talked for almost a half an hour.

"I'd never seen him as happy on every part of his life," Coop said. "His family was good, his kids were doing great in school and in athletics. We were going to go up to my hometown in Kentucky where he was going to design a golf course in a couple of weeks. He was excited about designing. He was going to do a new clothing line with an upscale clothing company. He was hitting the ball well again. We were kind of making plans for a sort of spring training for the next year in January. Then it happened. You just wonder if that wasn't preordained somehow. Basically he was telling me it was all right that he was gone. That's always stuck in my mind. I've never been able to decide whether it was a high being or what, but that was scary. It was reassuring and I think it helped Tracey a lot to know he was that happy when he went out."

Many tributes were paid to Stewart in the days following his death, but it was Bob Estes who offered a remembrance of Stewart and his greatest victory when he hit his putter off the tee for his first shot of the Tour Championship. Estes's shot traveled approximately fifteen feet, the length of Stewart's winning putt in the '99 Open. After hitting the bizarre shot, Estes turned and said softly, "The first shot's for Payne."

EPILOGUE

SINCE FALLING SHORT at the 1999 Open, Tiger Woods has accelerated his pace to overtake Jack Nicklaus's all-time majors record of eighteen. The golfing prodigy is the favorite for virtually every tournament in which he plays.

Mike Hicks denies stories that he was supposed to be accompanying Stewart on the ill-fated flight. As planned, he'd returned to Mebane from Orlando a day before the accident because his flight reservations from Greensboro to Houston had been made months earlier. Hicks now caddies for Lee Janzen and holds the belief that Payne Stewart's fate had been God's plan.

"He knew he was taking him from us in a couple of months," Hicks said. "He gave Payne the opportunity to profess his faith and he did a lot of good. Payne brought a lot of people to the Lord. God's got a plan for everything and he definitely used Payne to witness to a lot of people. And he gave Payne an opportunity at the

Open to profess his faith on national television. Then he captivated the whole world the way that plane went down.

"He was such a unique person with the way he lived his life, especially the past couple of years. He was a much better person to be around than much earlier in his career when I was working for him. He was real cocky and arrogant. But he had become more of a people person and was more receptive and generous and thoughtful to people's feelings than he was earlier in his career."

Phil Mickelson's wife, Amy, delivered their first child, a daughter, Amanda, the day after the final round of the '99 Open. Following Stewart's accident Mickelson began to view his defeat somewhat philosophically.

"I never thought I'd say this, but I'm glad Payne won that now," Mickelson said. "It was a very difficult loss to accept for a long time, but I expect to have a lot of opportunities [to win a U.S. Open]. That was his last one. It makes losing that tournament a little easier now."

Almost five years after coming up short against Stewart at Pinehurst, Mickelson won his first major by sinking an eighteen-foot putt on the final hole to capture the 2004 Masters.

David Duval, who lost the much-hyped "Showdown at Sherwood" later in the summer of 1999, managed to break through and win his first major by claiming the 2001 British Open. He has since struggled with his game.

Ron Philo continues to personify the soul of the U.S. Open. Though he has not qualified for another since qualifying for the '99 Open, he has continued to try. Why? Because he's a golfer and that's what golfers do. It's the golf championship for the United States.

Stewart's story has touched many, including the people in his hometown of Springfield, Missouri, where they dedicated a statue of him. Bee Payne-Stewart said she was pleased with "the expression on his face, and the fact that it's so huge, because he was a huge person."

Lora Thomas, the late golfer's sister, spread some ashes around the statue's base and approximately six hundred people gathered on the east lawn of the Missouri Sports Hall of Fame for the unveiling of the $175,000 memorial.

In May of 2001, the PGA announced Stewart had been voted into the World Golf Hall of Fame. Stewart and Greg Norman were voted in through the PGA Tour Ballot.

Stewart finished his career with eleven PGA Tour victories. The Payne Stewart Award was established by the Tour in 2000, honoring the PGA golfer who exhibits professionalism, commitment to charity, golf tradition, and personal presentation.

A statue of Stewart in victory pose looks out on the No. 18 green at Pinehurst No. 2 approximately fifty yards from where Stewart's historic putt took place. The inscription reads:

On June 20, 1999 Payne Stewart holed a dramatic 15-foot putt on the 18th hole of Pinehurst No. 2 to capture the United States Open Championship. It was truly one moment in time.

Stewart's family traveled to Pinehurst for the dedication ceremony for the statue and Aaron Stewart, who is the spitting image of his late father, recreated his father's deed by sinking the same putt.

Every Sunday the pin placement on the 18th hole of Pinehurst No. 2 is located where Stewart's putt dropped. And the flag for Sunday's pin is different than any other day of the week to commemorate Stewart's victory. Written on the flag are the words, "One Moment in Time."

John Brendle expressed the feelings shared by many who feel the void from losing Payne Stewart way before his time.

"There's not a day that goes by that I don't think about Payne Stewart," Brendle said. "I miss his friendship. He was my best friend.

And he did so much for me as far as just the people I met. My life slowed down after Payne died."

While the circumstances of Stewart's death were bizarre, the lasting memory of Stewart supersedes all the fashion statements the charismatic golfer made wearing his plus fours and tam. Painted in every golf fan's mind is a picture of a grinder, a competitor who reached inside for all the heart he had to claim the 1999 U.S. Open, the greatest U.S. Open ever played.